LITERATURE AND ENVIRONMENT
ESSAYS IN READING AND SOCIAL STUDIES

LITERATURE AND ENVIRONMENT

ESSAYS IN READING AND SOCIAL STUDIES

Edited by
FRED INGLIS

With a Foreword by
DENYS THOMPSON

1971
CHATTO & WINDUS
LONDON

Published by
Chatto & Windus (Educational) Ltd
42 William IV Street
London W.C.2

*

Clarke, Irwin and Company Ltd.
Toronto

ISBN 0 7011 1763 X

© Arthur Capey 1969, 1971. © Terence Barnes 1966, 1971. © Fred Inglis 1968, 1971.
© Seymour Betsky, Alan Budd, Ioan Davies, Andor Gomme, Fred Inglis, David McLellan, Raymond Williams 1971

© Fred Inglis and
Chatto & Windus (Educational) Ltd 1971

All rights reserved. No part of this publication may be reproduced, stored in a retrieval system, or transmitted, in any form, or by any means, electronic, mechanical, photocopying, recording or otherwise, without the prior permission of Chatto & Windus Ltd.

Printed in Great Britain by
Cox and Wyman Ltd.
London, Fakenham and Reading

Contents

Acknowledgements	*page* 6
Foreword *Denys Thompson*	7
The Contributors	11
Introduction *Fred Inglis*	13

A Map of the Literature

1 The Post-War English Novel *Arthur Capey*	15
2 Post-War Drama *Terence Barnes*	41
3 Contemporary English and American Poetry *Fred Inglis*	61

A Case-Study in Literature and Culture

4 The Contemporary American Novel *Seymour Betsky*	92

The Lines Redrawn

5 An Introduction to Reading in Culture and Society *Raymond Williams*	125

Essential Connections

6 Sociology and Culture *Ioan Davies*	141
7 Political Theory *David McLellan*	170
8 Economics *Alan Budd*	185
9 Work and the Intellectual *Fred Inglis*	211

Postscript

10 Home Thought from Home: Landscape and Society *Andor Gomme*	242

Note

Earlier versions of chapters 1, 2 and 3 have appeared in *The Use of English*; parts of chapter 6 in *The Listener* and parts of chapter 9 in *The University of Denver Quarterly*. Part of the bibliography of chapter 5 is reproduced by courtesy of The College of Librarianship, University of Wales.

Acknowledgements

The publishers and the editor make grateful acknowledgement to the following for permission to use copyright material.

J. V. Cunningham and The Swallow Press Inc, Chicago, for lines from 'To What Strangers, What Welcome' (copyright © 1964). Edward Dorn and the Fulcrum Press for 'Mourning Letter, March 29, 1963' from *Geography* (copyright © Edward Dorn 1964, 1965, 1966, 1967, 1968 and Edward Dorn and William Morrow and Company Inc for an extract from *The Shoshoneans* (copyright © 1966 by Edward Dorn and Leroy Lucas). F. T. Prince and Rupert Hart-Davis Ltd for lines from 'Gregory Nazianzen' from *Doors of Stone*. The Macmillan Company, New York for lines from Edwin Arlington Robinson's 'Merlin' from *Collected Poems* (copyright © 1917 by Edwin Arlington Robinson, renewed 1945 by Ruth Nivison). Alan Stephens and The Swallow Press Inc, Chicago, for lines from 'The Vanishing Act (Syllabics for T. G.)' from *The Sum* (copyright © 1958). Wallace Stevens, Faber and Faber Ltd and Alfred A. Knopf for 'The House was Quiet and the World was Calm' from *Collected Poems* (copyright 1960) and lines from 'Reality is an Activity of the Most August Imagination' from *Opus Posthumous* (copyright 1960). Charles Tomlinson and The Oxford University Press for 'At Barstow' from *American Scenes and Other Poems*. MacGibbon and Kee Ltd, New Directions Publishing Corporation and Laurence Pollinger Ltd for lines from William Carlos Williams' 'By the Road to the Contagious Hospital' from *Collected Earlier Poems* (copyright © 1938 by William Carlos Williams). Yvor Winters, Routledge and Kegan Paul Ltd and New Directions Publishing Corporation for 'The Marriage' from *The Giant Weapon* (copyright © 1943 New Directions Publishing Corporation).

Foreword
DENYS THOMPSON

EDUCATION has been compulsory, universal and free in this country for nearly a century. Why this should be so, and what the character of the education given ought to be, was glimpsed by Matthew Arnold, in his first year as an H.M.I., when he wrote of the schools: '. . . their effects on the children are so immense, and their future effects in civilizing the next generation of the lower classes, who, as things are going, will have most of the political power of the country in their hands, may be so important'. And by 'civilizing' he meant nothing patronizing or restricted, but the result of a full liberal education. The barbarian aristocracy he regarded as past praying for; the middle classes he hoped would be educable enough to transmit their 'civilization' to the masses. The main means would be literature, especially poetry–'the future of poetry is immense, because in poetry . . . our race will find an ever surer and surer stay'. Accordingly he expended energy and spirit, and risked the loss of his post, in fighting the utilitarian, narrowly vocational notion of education that was for many years the official policy he was supposed to implement. He saw clearly that in a mass society with a new consciousness the old would not do, and that it was no longer possible for the young in an industrialized country to absorb an education of a sort from their environment. There could be no more Cobbetts, to say as he did of the countryside where he had played with his brothers:

This was the spot where I was receiving my education . . . and I am perfectly satisfied that if I had not received such an education, or something very much like it; that, if I had been brought up a milksop, I should at this day be as great a fool, as inefficient a mortal, as any of those frivolous idiots that are turned out from Winchester or Westminster School or from any of those dens of dunces called Colleges and Universities.

Instead, education must be developed in scale; its quality must be improved; its character must be humane.

As the first products of a more or less compulsory schooling emerged, Northcliffe came on the scene and deliberately cashed in on the ration of mechanical literacy doled out by the state, so that the minimum, intended solely to be of service to employers, became also a medium for exploitation by the gutter press. Not that one should attribute too much to a particular megalomaniac, for Northcliffe was merely thrown up by the social, psychological and industrial conditions of the day; had he died in infancy, another of the type would have appeared. It is interesting all the same to speculate what might have happened if the attempt had been made to supply a good popular newspaper. As it was, ignorance, prejudice and fear were capitalized, and we had the jingoism of the 90s and the flag-waving and atrocity-mongering of 1914–1918. Since then more drugs to divert attention have been provided by the well-organized entertainment industry, and in our precarious affluence we have the whole gamut of the colour-supplement life (cf. p. 213), desperately and obediently consuming all we can from tobacco to processed food and holidays.

In all this education has lost its way, and the irrigating stream envisaged by Arnold peters out in a sandy delta. Some powerful currents persist, not only in universities but also in schools of every kind, where thanks to the blessed freedom enjoyed by teachers in England to a degree elsewhere unparalleled it is still possible for good work to be done. But there is no unifying conception, only the guerilla skirmishes described by the Editor on p. 233. Thus at university level we have specialisms, with teachers combining only when their pay is involved; and the lack of a purposeful general education is evident in the hopeless atseaness of many architects, planners and designers, with the results so sharply presented by Andor Gomme. (Not that these particular people are any worse than other products of expensive education . . .) Correspondingly in the secondary schools at least there is a fragmented curriculum of gobbets for examined regurgitation. All along the line there is lack of attention to ends. What Ronald Blythe noted in talking with an intelligent day-release student has a wide application:

. . . Books? The question brings the inevitable embarrassment. The village people of all ages seem frightened at the mere mention of books. Why isn't this book-fear dispersed at an early time? Why should it exist at all? A seventeen-year-old wrought-iron worker from the village, a good craftsman and an apparently lively youngster, said, 'Yes, I have read books. I read Enid Blyton when I was at school.' The normality of reading scarcely exists. To nearly every person interviewed, it was a strange thing to have read a book. The book is a kind of frontier across which few seem to have the nerve to pass . . .

Terry is grateful for the extraordinary amount of tangential information Mr Austin has been able to throw off upon such subjects as natural history, politics, current affairs – even art. To an outsider, many of the students appear famished, starving for something more than the curriculum provides, and there seems to be a unique opportunity to accomplish on the young adult scale something comparable to what Sybil Marshall achieved in the condemned Cambridgeshire playground . . .

However, education is still the point at which men of good will can exert themselves with more chance of accomplishment that that to be found in most occupations, still a field in which specialisms can be more profitable for being pursued with cognisance of other disciplines, and their relationships. Such a consciousness will enable specialist practitioners to feel more clearly the contribution they can make to purposes outside their own compartment. Education must independently and surely evolve its own aims; a mere relationship of subservience to media-conditioned goals is unacceptable. Society's present aims do not command assent, as formulated by bankrupt political parties, unirrigated by a healthy tradition or a living church, despite an occasional Paul Oestricher (cf. p. 175). The conventional wisdom, once decocted by the media, has about as much nutritional value as convenience food. It is in education that the analyses of specialisms can be seen to reach a consistent diagnosis and to point in one direction. In the words of the Editor, 'the complex, mighty life of a national education is the source of a nation's moral and intellectual energy and this will in a secularized world be true long after the disappearance of conventional nationhood'.

This book is a move towards understanding between specialisms and the sensing of a common concern. In this it is uncommonly effective, perhaps at this date uniquely so. On the one hand it is evident in the first five essays that the literary critic makes full use of eclectic borrowings from other specialisms; it is not 'literary'. (Some of the best literary criticism never is; one just hears, as in the writing of D. W. Harding, an unstrained voice that seems to offer no more than the application of common sense.) Their findings commend themselves often on apparently non-literary grounds. On the other hand one can see how literature constantly leads outward; the good writer like Wordsworth's poet is always 'a man speaking to men'. The light of literary criticism can be brought to bear even on 'a highly developed subject' (p. 209), to measure its human relevance, trace its implications for the rest of us, and insist on underlying issues. To make the connections, in short. Thus in these pages Andor Gomme points to what is involved by a continued increase in the British birthrate and suggests that the whole of England has as large a population as it can comfortably take. Population increase with its concomitants is only one phenomenon on which the bearings of their own interests are being forcefully presented by specialists; Noam Chomsky is one, I. A. Richards (in recent books not yet published here) another. Physically no doubt there is space for many more millions, if they survive self-poisoning and conflict between the well-fed and the under-fed, but life for them will have to be in unprecedented conditions, which will be about as human as the being of a modern hen is galline. This is the sort of prospect that lies before us if we accept 'the hard-mouthed cant of the social sciences' that claim to be 'value-free' (p. 223).

Muck-raking is not the method of this book, but a good deal of cant is disposed as it goes about its main purpose. That is, to give us an idea of the connections to be made and the work to be done if we are to avert the present threats of world revolution or Russian-American monopoly. 'The human alternative,' as the Editor puts it on p. 218, 'is to get clear of capitalism, and so to organize (as is perfectly possible) modern technology that economic life serves human need, and then with the new techniques offered by electronics, communication systems, atomic energy and minute but intensive heavy industry plant it will be at least imaginable to live in small, free, and self-subsistent communities'.

The Contributors

Terence Barnes is Head of the English Department at Bishop Wordsworth's School, Salisbury, and was an early and frequent contributor to the famous Cambridge periodical *Scrutiny*. He contributed the essay on modern drama 'Shaw and the London Theatre' to *The Penguin Guide to English Literature, Vol. 7: The Modern Age*, and has recently published *English Verse: Voice and Movement from Wyatt to Yeats* (Cambridge) and *Poetry Appreciation* (Faber).

Seymour Betsky is Professor of American Literature at the University of Utrecht. He took his two post-graduate degrees at Harvard, and subsequently came to work in Cambridge, England, before returning to the U.S.A. to teach in Montana, New York University and Wellesley College. He went to Utrecht as Fulbright Professor and stayed there, since when he has been a main force in the development of an international programme investigating the relations between the forms of literature, its culture, and its society. He has published literary-critical and literary-sociological articles in numerous periodicals, notably *Scrutiny, Sewanee Review, The Universities Quarterly, Poetry (Chicago)* and *Victorian Studies*, as well as contributing the essay on Thackeray and Trollope in *The Penguin Guide 6: Dickens to Hardy*.

Alan Budd is Lecturer in Economics at the University of Southampton and Ford Scholar and Visiting Professor at the Carnegie-Mellon University, Pittsburgh, for 1969. He took his first degree at L.S.E. as an evening student and later as a Leverhulme scholar, and took his Ph.D. in the study of economic decision-making at Churchill College, Cambridge.

Arthur Capey is Senior Lecturer in English Literature at St Hild's College of Education, Durham. He read English at Cambridge, taught for eleven years in a number of Secondary schools and, since 1964, has worked in Colleges of Education. He is a regular contributor to *The Use of English*.

Ioan Davies is Senior Lecturer in Sociology at the University of Essex. He has contributed to many journals, notably *The British*

Journal of Sociology and has been consultant sociologist to the government. He is the author of numerous articles and books, is a regular contributor to *New Society*, and his most recent publication is *The Management of Knowledge* (1970).

Andor Gomme is Senior Lecturer in English at the University of Keele. He read English and Moral Sciences at Cambridge and took his Ph.D. there. He has taught at Keele since his year as Visiting Professor at the University of Montana, 1962–63. He is regularly architectural reviewer in the *TLS*, and a recent publication is his very large-scale study *Architecture of Glasgow* (Lund Humphries).

Fred Inglis is Lecturer in English and Education at the University of Sheffield. He read English at Cambridge and took his second degree in education at Southampton. He taught English in schools and at Southampton College of Education before taking up his present post. His most recent publications include *The Elizabethan Poets* (Evans), *An Essential Discipline* (Methuen) and *The Englishness of English Teaching* (Longmans).

David McLellan is Lecturer in Politics and Government in the University of Kent at Canterbury. He obtained a D.Phil. at Oxford and has been Visiting Professor at the State University College, Geneseo, New York. He is author of *Karl Marx: The Early Texts* (Oxford), *The Young Hegelians and Karl Marx* and *Marx Before Marxism*. He is engaged at the moment on the definitive biography of Marx.

Raymond Williams is Reader in Drama at the University of Cambridge, where he took his degree. He served in the Guards during the war, and worked in the Oxford Extra-Mural Department from his demobilization until going to Cambridge in 1961. During this time he edited *Politics and Letters* and published his classic study *Culture and Society 1780–1950* (Chatto & Windus). Since then he has pushed on his inquiry into the relations between art and literature of all kinds, mass communications, and politics. He has published two novels, *Border Country* (Chatto & Windus) and *Second Generation* (Chatto & Windus), as well as *The Long Revolution* (Chatto & Windus), *Communications* (Penguin), *Modern Tragedy* (Chatto & Windus) and *The English Novel from Dickens to Lawrence* (Chatto & Windus). He is about to publish a study of the town and the country in literature.

Introduction

THIS book began as a review for interested students and teachers of all disciplines and persuasions who wanted to find their way through the bewildering and densely populated territory of postwar literature in England and the U.S.A. Given such variety and conflict of opinion about the literature, it was necessary to offer a series of preferences, of judgements which suggested this writer rather than that for attention. It follows that in giving reasons for such preferences a critic (i.e. a reader) commits himself to some systematic account of the map or chart of things as he sees them. To describe an ongoing or a past literature one must, for lucidity and honesty, declare one's bearings, one's point of reference. In doing this, one is constructing, however provisionally, a critical diagnosis of a point in history. Any diagnosis of the health of a literature must lead back to the society which produced it, to exploring the difficult, nervous, and uncertain tensions between culture and society. And such inquiry leads in its turn outwards until one crosses the boundaries of the first kind of social analysis and finds oneself needing another, with other contours and bearings. The study of literature is one means to discover the expressive centre, the significant meanings of a society's life. But it is merely acquisitive to claim the supreme function for any one discipline. There are essential relationships between the conventional disciplines of sixth form and further education study. The varying perspectives—literary criticism, sociology, politics, economics, aesthetics, history, philosophy, psychology—compose a structure of interlocking parts, and no honest or intelligent work can go forward which ignores either its own necessary connections or its temporary and malleable nature.

This collection of essays starts out from the study of literature in its three familiar forms: novels, plays, poems. It goes on in Chapter 4 to study the relations between a particular literary form, the novel, and a particular culture, modern U.S.A. The fifth, pivotal chapter takes up the same theme. It outlines the tensions between a culture and its society and goes on to show how any inquiry into their nature will take in for new purposes several of the adjacent disciplines, but that the inquiry will only have meaning in so far as it remains securely rooted in actual living. Chapters 5, 6, and 7 offer introductory guides to three of these neighbouring disciplines. To some extent the three must seem arbitrarily chosen. Why not history? Why not, crucially, modern analytic philosophy? But every discipline has its necessary place in the structure, and no book could adequately introduce them all. Sociology, politics, and economics compose a trio whose interests are particularly close and whose techniques and assumptions are still comparatively new and therefore unfamiliar to those raised on conventional 'A' level diets, as well as extensively misvalued by neighbours in departments of humanities. These three fields of interest bear heavily upon any student who hopes to understand and work towards a living culture. The concluding essay in Chapter 9 proposes a generalized version of intellectual reponsibility for anyone who takes seriously the disciplines discussed in the book and its prevalent tendency, and it concludes by trying to exemplify in quotation the *kind* of moral effort required on the part of an intelligent man in order to be alive in his society and to know what matters in his human contacts. The postscript indicates what may be thought of as the most urgently needed of such efforts in our country now.

No doubt a student must learn his way through a particular form of study. Yet there is a swelling dissatisfaction with fragmentary theories of knowledge which is to be found in modern primary school methods, in Colleges of Education curricular studies, and in new University courses. The drive to restore lost connections bears witness to a deep need for the integration of knowledge, to a sense of desolation in the intense privacies of our specialisms. In some cases the drive for integration leads to hopeless contradiction; elsewhere, the specialists gaze nostalgically after a lost age of knowledge in unity; mostly, we all get on within the demarcations passed on by history and by accident. Yet the commerce across old frontiers is increasing. The great lesson of social anthropology is that there are many pictures of the world and they confirm, ramify and complement one another in manifold ways. When one culture meets another there is a shock. This book aims to make the inevitable experience of such shocks one which braces and revives.

I

The Post-War English Novel

ARTHUR CAPEY

A COMPREHENSIVE survey of English fiction from 1945 to the present is beyond the scope of this essay. What is attempted is an analysis of certain representative books and authors, and the definition of a suitable introductory reading list. The time available for 'general reading' is limited, and the principles of selection which place *Middlemarch, Anna Karenina* and *The Rainbow* among the essential texts inevitably exclude all but a very little of our recent fiction. The reasons for reading modern novels are different. They may not be established classics, few may even warrant a second acquaintance; but because they belong to our own time the reading and discussion of them can bring into focus contemporary values and attitudes. The following notes are offered as a contribution towards the collaborative reading of fiction in sixth forms and liberal arts courses, and in higher education.

I

It is a sound educational principle to begin where one's students are, and that place is often Ian Fleming. The attractions of James Bond—the individuality of his missions, his magnetic charm for the universal female of the ski-slopes, advertising and the secretary's chair, the comfortable superiority of his car, his diet and his muscles—are the modern equivalent of the attractions of Richard Hannay, though being modern they are rather more gratifying and disturbing. In *Dr No* Bond comes face to face with a naked girl, who on seeing him covers her nose; thus is her primitive innocence, Eve's before the Fall, intimated. Fleming, of course, is concerned to cover her (crooked) nose so that we may enjoy an unobstructed view of her loins, and when she later shows all the signs of a sophisticated tart in pressing Bond to join her in her sleeping-bag we are not to register surprise but merely to enjoy that too; innocence has its limitations for the purveyor of cheap thrills. Elsewhere in the Bond cycle the hero's genitals are beaten with rods until he faints; subsequent medical examination reveals 'nothing organically wrong', and James duly protests his indestructible manhood in his customary style; the sex and the violence are here identified as closely as in any of the incidents Hoggart anatomizes in *The Uses of Literacy*. Marriage, for Bond, represents a death more final than any beating can induce, and when he does marry and motors dreamily along with his true love, the large fast car of his malicious enemy steals up behind them and 'misdirects' the bullets into the girl's neck. The heartbroken Bond is thus free to accept a further assignment from M.

Two other writers who enjoy a considerable vogue are Nevil Shute and H. E. Bates. Shute was described in 1961[1] as 'the most characteristic post-war best seller'–characteristic in that 'his heroes are the people who get things done, ordinary people obsessed by some vision'. 'The last section of *A Town Like Alice*, in which the heroine introduces shoe-manufacture into a remote Australian farming settlement, is a sort of parable of private enterprise, with strong political overtones.' Mr Bates in *The Darling Buds of May* goes extravagantly beyond Shute's doctrine: road tax, inland revenue, marriage, restraint as well as 'the restraints', are cavalierly disposed of; the reader is expected to applaud the antics of a raucous, frivolous crew and to join in the 'uproarious' fun. Bates is vulgar not only in the usual sense of the word but in the sense exemplified by the common people in Crosland's poem *The Eagle*: 'O my! aint 'e a' 'orrible bird!' they cry, seeking assurance from each other that only one response is possible to the 'poor, downcast, draggled lord of the air'. And 'vulgar' in this secondary sense is not too strong to apply to the work of Nevil Shute, which with its 'commonplace "congratulation-system" of heroism and sentiment'[2] requires from the reader a simple, accommodating gesture: 'Here is a good yarn; put your feet up and enjoy it.'

The relevant point is not, however, whether light evening reading is permissible for students who have been pursuing serious academic interests all day, but whether the light reading is genuinely the unambiguous relaxation it purports to be.

THE POST-WAR ENGLISH NOVEL 17

Besides a story that 'rattles along', each of the writers specified offers propaganda on behalf of a way of life or an attitude towards life that asks merely for the reader's uncritical, self-indulgent endorsement. Whatever their inequalities in range of interest and material, all three are writing their 'light' fictions for purposes more personal than perhaps they are aware, and their influence needs to be resisted.

A submerged propagandist intention may be observed not only in much 'holiday reading' but in novels apparently addressed to a serious public. C. P. Snow presents us in *The Masters* and *The Affair* with a peculiarly confused example. He seems to want to draw our attention to 'the real Cambridge', by which we are to understand the Fellows' Garden, the Senior Tutor's rooms at dusk, the Master's Lodge; and to invite our respect for a way of life that is beyond our reach.[3] Yet at the same time he offers to reveal the unsavoury secrets of 'the club', the sorriness that underlies the grandest things. The one purpose interferes with the other. Long before the end of *The Affair* it has become certain that the fellow-travelling don, unjustly dismissed for supposedly cooking his research-thesis, will be reinstated. But equally we are asked to agree that the young man is unsuited to the couth Combination Room, that his communist views and his rude wife would be out of place there. The dilemma is solved by the four just men—senior Fellows, if you please—in a comfortably cynical manner: the red don is reinstated, but there will be no renewal or extension of his fellowship when it expires next month.

The 'affair' invites serious treatment, but Snow will only hint a fault and hesitate dislike. The red don's crime proves to have been no more than a communist's uncouthness; the young man, unlike the younger Lewis Eliot in *The Masters*, has not deferentially listened and waited his turn, but has spoken out, and so must go. Eliot, who in *The Affair* is no longer a Fellow but one who 'keeps in touch with the College' from his London address, apparently endorses the decision; he is at any rate not disposed to make an issue of it. He is an establishment figure—cautious, committed only as far as his communications allow, content to achieve a tidy compromise. And from Lewis Eliot the author cannot stand aside even a little; he is so wedded to this recurrent representative of clean hands and stability in the corridors of power that he cannot see the latent possibilities in his material for ironic and detached art.

2

If 'propagandist' is too strict a term to describe the confused intentions of Snow's work, it applies precisely to the later novels of Evelyn Waugh. The 'social satirist' of the pre-war decade, the author of *Decline and Fall* and *Scoop*, became after 1945 less concerned to write astringent comedy and less prepared to conceal his religious beliefs; and Waugh's religious beliefs, as expressed in *Brideshead Revisited* and the trilogy *Sword of Honour*, take the form of propaganda for Roman Catholicism. At the death-bed scene in *Brideshead* we are ostensibly invited to choose our own interpretation of the dying man's moving finger – does it express his annoyance at the sensation of oil on his forehead, or is he trying at last to make the sign of the cross? But Waugh is no real liberal here: those who believe must assume the best, those who do not are unqualified to judge. The propagandist is at work outside the proper realm of the novel, that of psychological analysis; he allows himself the luxury of an assertion, to dispute the validity of which leaves the reader uncomfortably at odds with the author.

Sword of Honour shows the propagandist at his most cavalier. Crouchback, last in line of a noble recusant family (so close to the heart of England as to have a chapel and vaults within the walls of a Dorset parish church), is isolated from his fellow officers in 1940 not only by his age, his incompetence and his proneness to accidents, but by his religion. Waugh proposes to redress the bias by having Crouchback attempt to seduce his former wife with the pitiable justification that she is still, in the eyes of the church, his wife; by showing Uncle Peregrine, who admits to having slept with a woman on two occasions without enjoying the experience (this is the sort of negative touch we get in the pre-war *Vile Bodies*), as rather too certain of his place in the catholic scheme of things; by showing the wife, who ultimately rejoins her broken-legged husband from motives of convenience, as finding in the catholic faith a further convenience. But Waugh's critical manner is transparent, even at such moments as these. The catholic coterie which meets at the club or at Uncle Peregrine's assumes, without the author's dissent, that the world is a catholic world. And when Crouchback's father, shortly before his death, delivers the authoritative advice – 'Quantitative judgements don't apply' – we are expected to take it as carrying the imprimatur of the novelist himself. The implications of the dictum for young Crouchback become, as the mists clear, 'Take back your wife, do the only completely unselfish thing you've ever had the opportunity to do.' Virginia is subsequently conveniently killed by a flying bomb, and Crouchback lives happily ever after with a thoroughly nice young girl.

Crouchback is potentially the unhero whom everyone ridicules, the doormat for a whole range of unpleasant or idiotic characters to wipe their feet on; and his adventures in the Highlands, Crete and Yugoslavia show Waugh the entertainer at his most skilful. But the comedy is impregnated with the quirks and prejudices of its author. A crusade against the Bolsheviks would have been preferable to Crouchback; the problem of Finland was a 'betrayal'. Yugoslav freedom fighters, legendary during the war, are now shown up as bogus, neither believing in freedom nor taking their share of the fighting. The problem in London is where to get a decent meal. We are left with a series of amusing anecdotes about the various incredible people thrown up by the war; the war itself does not begin to make itself felt except as an uncomfortable nuisance. Waugh's brilliance is fundamentally frivolous.

There is nothing frivolous in the novelist commonly set beside him. Graham Greene, even in his 'entertainments', addresses himself seriously to the nature of man and the pathos of human existence. His settings, too, are closer to the real world of war and war's alarms, of suffering humanity, of whole societies rather than coteries. If Greene's world is also a catholic world, it encompasses more of the world to justify the assumption; and the problems set – to the priest in *The Power and the Glory* or to Scobie in *The Heart of the Matter* – are more searching. Greene at his best can show something of the grandeur underlying the sorriest things.

The pervading atmosphere of the novels, however, is one of impersonal disgust. This from *The Quiet American* is characteristic:

After dinner I sat and waited for Pyle in my room over the rue Catinat: he had said, 'I'll be with you at latest by ten,' and when midnight had struck I couldn't stay quiet any longer and went down into the street. A lot of old women in black trousers squatted on the landing: it was February and I suppose too hot for them in bed. One trishaw driver pedalled slowly by towards the river-front and I could see lamps burning where they had disembarked the new American planes. There was no sign of Pyle anywhere in the long street.

The casual, impassive tone flatly refuses to respond to the scene: 'I suppose [it was] too hot for them in bed'; and the emptiness of the street acts as a metaphor for the emptiness of the speaker's emotions, the disenchanted manner of the cynic who

turned to go indoors when I saw a girl waiting in the next doorway. I couldn't see her face. only the white silk trousers and the long flowered robe, but I knew her for all that. She had so often waited for me to come home at just this place and hour.

'Phuong,' I said–which means Phoenix, but nothing nowadays is fabulous and nothing rises from its ashes.

The explicitly anti-Laurentian assertion comes as no surprise, such is Greene's power to evoke sterility and despair. Sex is invariably presented as distasteful, unwholesome or furtive.

There was never any question in those days of who wanted whom – we were together in desire. Henry had his tray, sitting up against two pillows in his green woollen dressing-gown, and in the room below, on the hard wood floor, with a single cushion for support and the door ajar, we made love . . .

And then the stair squeaked. For the moment neither of us moved. The sandwiches were stacked uneaten on the table, the glasses had not been filled. She said in a whisper, 'He went downstairs.' She sat in a chair and I put a plate in her lap and a glass beside her. (*The End of the Affair*)

Graham Greene is of course an unusually gifted writer. The full account from which this passage is abstracted is perfectly controlled. The furtiveness of the occasion is made to depend ironically on 'the door ajar', and the uncomfortable posture of the lovers is seen to contrast with the two-pillowed luxury enjoyed by the cuckolded husband. Even the sandwiches and glasses acquire a nerveless numbness from the squeaking stair, and the original pretence of a buffet lunch to cover the scheme for adultery attracts to itself a deeper hollowness when the man puts 'a plate in her lap and a glass beside her'. On this occasion, for the first time in ten years, the woman has been satisfied; and we are made to feel the inadequacy as well as the circumscribed triumph of the union.

No one could suppose that Mr Greene likes the degradation he writes so compellingly about. But the positive values against which we can measure the degradation are not to be found in his books; we have to supply them from our knowledge of other literature and life. The alternatives to Mr Brown, the disillusioned figure of *The Comedians*, are a pair of deluded vegetarians, a man who lives in a fantasy world which finally destroys him, and a dedicated communist. The only alternative to the cynical Fowler in *The Quiet American* is the ridiculously idealistic Pyle. That these are not the only real alternatives is the basis of the criticism; that Fowler should be presented as the ordinary man with the ordinary attitudes ('Ordinary life goes on . . . that has saved many a man's reason') suggests that the artistic imagination has become imprisoned by the material it focuses on.

A similar criticism applies to *Animal Farm*. Orwell shows warmth and pity for the lesser animals' predicament, before and after the revolution; much of the satire is acutely and enduringly relevant. Humanity is seen from the start as brutal, drunken and slothful, and therefore less than human. The irony, that it is the animals who show the real human virtues of industry, literacy and order, is however ultimately a destructive irony—not because these virtues are lacking in Jones and his men, but because the virtues are increasingly distorted by the most intelligent of the animals, the quasi-human pigs. Intelligence itself is denigrated by its ascription to the pigs alone, who use it finally to identify themselves with the human beings they at first displaced for reasons we could feel were perfectly acceptable. Whether this irony is foreseen by Orwell—it is certainly not understood by the watching animals, beside whom we are invited to place ourselves–seems doubtful. Orwell, on the side of the down-trodden, cannot really see any further than them.

3

The world of a Henry Green novel makes a refreshing contrast with those of Graham Greene and Waugh. A limited number of people, each given limited scope as a character, a restricted setting, and a brief space of time–these constitute the formula on which Mr Green's fictions are based. But when you have read one of his books you have not read them all; you are merely equipped to state the formula. *Concluding* describes a day in the life of a residential training college for women some years hence; in a small cottage within the grounds lives Mr Rock, who has done the State some service and is now retired, with his granddaughter, his pig, his goose and his cat. The various connections between the 'great Place' (like 'State', 'Rules' and 'our Work', its standing requires the capital) and the humble cot form the substance of the book's conscious yet unobtrusive art.

Mr Rock feels that his position is precarious, that the sufficiency of his primitive countryman's way of life is threatened variously by his age, the hostility of the formidable spinster-Principals ('I must have that cottage, Baker,' declares Edge), and the unfortunate liaison between his granddaughter and one of the male lecturers. State cottages–there are no others–are scarce, the conditions attached to their tenancy are strict, and Mr Rock understands how privileged even he is in being allowed one for life. Nor is he economically and socially as self-sufficient as his habit of stowing away all letters unopened implies. If he chops his own wood and carries his own buckets, he yet depends on the college for his pig-swill and his breakfast; his cat spends a lot of time at the college; and the students who visit him and his pig, and beg him to dance with them at the founder's day ball, inevitably draw him from the security of his privacy.

To Edge and Baker Mr Rock constitutes a disturbing influence. Their carefully Regulated life in the service of the State is agitated by his enigmatic presence–exercising his pig in the grounds, calling his goose home, undermining their

THE POST-WAR ENGLISH NOVEL 23

Authority by talking with the girls. The Principals feel no more secure than Rock. Their day begins with the disappearance of two girls, only one of whom is eventually found ('in our pyjamas'); and although they depart as usual for Town to sit on committees they are soon observed returning, no committees having met. An authoritative circular, enjoining all colleges to consider how best to implement the Decision to add pig-farming to the curriculum, has to be concealed from Miss Edge, who is subject to irrational fears lest the body of the missing girl is hidden beneath the floral display for the ball. And Miss Baker, meeting Rock on her walk, is nervously confounded by his manner.

Mr Rock, we might say, is on the side of life, while the Principals are against it: 'Everyone was frozen in the high summer of the State.' The movement and music of the starlings ('I'm glad I had that once more,' says Mr Rock) contrasts with the compulsive movement of the students to the canned music at the ball, and it is Mr Rock who responds to the relaxed physical charm of Moira and who is sensitive to the motives for Mary's disappearance. And yet the evocation of the dance is positive; we are aware of the vitality and poise of the dancers, the genuineness of their delight in the occasion. These girls have known nothing of life except under the State, and yet they associate easily with Mr Rock; the sterility of their ecstatic behaviour as they dance with each other is not enough to inhibit an equally genuine response to life (which for some of them, it is rumoured, means visiting Adams the gardener in his hut). The 'little red State tourer, which hummed up the main drive at twenty miles an hour', is a remarkably vital metaphor for institutional regularity and hierarchy: 'A cloud of white dust attended it, was always at a respectful distance, following behind.' The effect is not unlike the final movement of *The Dunciad*. Miss Edge is 'drunk' with cigarette-smoke when she obliquely proposes marriage to Mr Rock, but the fire is only a small one and is easily stamped out; and we feel the resumption of her spinsterly norm as a positive act. Even at the end, when his straying animals have returned and a contented Mr Rock falls asleep (while over at the Place Mary is still missing and her recovered friend is barred from society), the sufficiency and preferability of Mr Rock's world are not unequivocally presented: his granddaughter has gone to rejoin her lover; there is no 'conclusion'.

Metaphor, image and symbol are not for Mr Green, as they are for Iris Murdoch in *The Sandcastle*, intellectually separable from the authentic life of the book, nor are they the sort of marginal artistry that Sillitoe attempts in having Arthur Seaton trip over a root. The living and the literary are in harmony and give substance to each other; the whole is unusually intelligent, pregnant and controlled. If *Concluding* lacks the depth and scale of *Dr Zhivago* or *By Love Possessed*, it is at any rate one of the finest novels to appear in this country since *Mr Weston's Good Wine*.

Joyce Cary has been criticized for inviting us to choose 'between those who are fundamentally hypocrites and those who are fundamentally outside accepted codes and conventions'.[4] But this 'flaw' in his work is rather the kind detectable by logical reasoning from a summary statement of the case, than the kind that sticks in the gullet as we read. The case is this: Mister Johnson the African clerk in the service of the Nigerian colonial administration, Sara the skilful housekeeper and confidence-trickster, Gulley Jimson the painter of distinction, are so vital and exuberant, and withal so innocent, that 'our sympathies flow inevitably towards [them] . . . because they manifestly are the ones who stand for life', and necessarily away from 'the forces of convention and respectability'. Put thus, the case suggests that Cary has so simplified the issues as to compel the reader to commit himself to black or white, knowing that he is to elect for white.

The process of reading the novels, however, is not so simple. Cary's critical distance from his unconventional characters is maintained to the same degree as Mr Green's from Rock, though more ambitiously and so more remarkably. The illusions of grandeur in Mister Johnson are presented with simultaneous sympathy and detachment. The vitality and naïvety of the man affect us inwardly, so that we long to help him; and yet what he *is* we are aware of objectively. When he speaks with pride of his shoes, his wife or his relations with Rudbeck the European officer in the area, we respond to his buoyancy while blushing with shame for him; and yet our pity for his predicament is continually qualified by exasperation with one who is a fool in a world too sophisticated for him. Ultimately when he kills a man he asks Rudbeck the last favour of death by shooting rather than the statutory hanging; and although there is, as Arnold Kettle notes,[5] an element of 'paternalism' in Rudbeck's attitude at this point, Cary keeps his sympathetic distance from both priest and victim—Johnson dies sure of his illusions and as content with his 'day' as Mr Rock. The whole is a triumph of objective art.

Gulley Jimson in *The Horse's Mouth* does not command the same kind of sympathy—perhaps because he gets rather more from his fellow characters. He likes to pretend that he is self-sufficient under his leaking roof and his newspaper sheets, but never refuses the occasional drink or meal. As a social being he is impossible to live with—Coker puts a pillow down the middle of the bed when she sleeps with him (a fine touch this, for there is no question of conventional immorality)—and impossible to help. He steals paint because he wants to paint, or snuff boxes because he needs to clear a space on the table to practise his art. The exasperating nature of the man is set, not against hypocrites, but against social beings who want to help him and whom he continually frustrates. We feel not only the vitality of the artist but also his fleeting and tenuous grasp on any reality outside himself, however much it is concerning itself with *his* reality. The criticism of Jimson is inseparable from the praise. In the following scene, while Coker tries to extract money from his former patron, Jimson is (or pretends to be) more interested in a painting of Sara now in Hickson's possession:

'Well, what about it?' Coker asked. And she turned to me again. But I dodged round and took another walk down the room. 'Don't go walking like that, Mr Jimson,' she said to me, 'come here and show your boots.' But I was taking a long eye at Sara's left shoulder. The one holding the towel. It got the right light from the top corner of the room. Showed the modelling. . . .

Coker and Hickson were getting confidential. And Hickson was saying, 'I don't think you understand the whole position, Miss Coker.'

I moved off to the other side of the room. And took Sara from the new angle. And called up Coker's arm for comparison. Yes, I thought, the Coker forearm is a marvel. But the upper arm's much too tight. Too anatomical. . . .

'Mr Jimson,' said Coker, quite loud, too loud for her manners. But I was reflecting deeply on matters of real importance. . . .

Besides Cary and Henry Green, L. P. Hartley seems no more than a workmanlike craftsman. His irony is not the product of imaginative intelligence, but a matter of application from the novelist's vantage-point. In *The Brickfield* boy meets girl, and is discouraged from openly developing the relationship by the gloomy, withdrawn household from which the girl is periodically released. There are various sinister suggestions about the reasons for her parents' withdrawal and close watch on their child, but it transpires that nothing sinister is intended. In due course the girl suspects that she is pregnant and drowns herself in despair; thus real gloom ironically displaces the imaginary. The final irony, when the girl is found not to have been pregnant after all, is a crude imposition upon the narrative.

The Go-Between is a more remarkable book. A fatherless child is invited to spend the summer holidays with his best friend's rich family, where he becomes a reliable messenger between the affianced daughter of the house and the 'Laurentian' workingman to whom she is not engaged. There are fine things in this novel – Hartley catches precisely the speech and glances of the adults uneasy yet controlled in the presence of the children, the bewildered yet co-operative behaviour of Leo the young go-between – but hardly enough to substantiate the claim that he is in 'the tradition represented by Henry James'.[6] Hartley is not sufficiently in control of his material. The principal experience which Leo, looking back, sees as the blight upon his life is the premature witnessing of the sexual act between the girl and her lover in the wood-shed. Yet the man has been represented as vital and powerful, and in preferring him to her fiancé the girl (we have been led to suppose) is preferring life to a conventionally suitable marriage. The stigma attached to her is attached also to Leo, who is made by the mother to feel a guilty party to the sordid affair; he is thus twice blighted, and we are left uncertain whether the responsibility for his traumatic vision in the wood-shed should be laid at the door of sex, or of the way of life in the household that necessitated the secrecy of the messages.

4

Lucky Jim, which on its appearance in 1954 was felt to express the frustration of young intellectuals faced by authority and privilege, today seems not nearly so topical–perhaps because the modern Jim is more explicitly a member of a movement. Amis's Jim is a junior lecturer at a provincial university, and has various grievances–against his starchy superior, Professor Welch, against Mrs Welch, at whose house-parties Jim feels ill-at-ease, against the aridity of official historical studies, and so on. We are expected to sympathize with Jim, to feel his irritation towards girls who will or will not sleep with him, to share his enslavement to the smoking habit, to be as gauche as he is in house-party manners, to prefer beer to polite cocktails and when drunk to burn our hostess's sheets. For Jim is an ordinary chap, totally lacking the social graces, which are presented for our ridicule and contempt. Raymond O'Malley has described the novel as 'a boorish attack on established decencies'[7]; but the radical criticism is that Jim is merely gauche, merely a boozer and smoker. In place of his professor's Merry England he offers not the substance of *English Wayfaring Life* but incoherent and farcical nonsense. Ultimately he escapes from the university (a significant anti-academic gesture) through the good offices of a business man who recognizes his ability–an irony that seems to have escaped the author, who is so identified with Jim as to indulge in the dream of the jackpot. Later Jims, in *I Like It Here* and *Take a Girl Like You,* continue to stick their tongues out at society but are not so conspicuously rewarded for doing so: when Jenny Bunn, training-college teacher from a nice home, is finally bereft of her maidenhead, the incident occurs in no romantic or even personal setting but in an alcoholic haze of routine insensitivity. Amis is incomparably cleverer than his immediate predecessor in the genre, John Wain, but the destructive intention behind his work has grown more comprehensive, and less entertaining, over the years.

Iris Murdoch's first novel, *Under the Net,* resembles *Lucky Jim* sufficiently to be discussed beside it. Jake Donague, intellectual, translator and philosopher, is an ineffectual young man, incapable of pursuing a rational course and happy to submit with equal elasticity to the pressure of external facts and obscure inward promptings: he is adrift in a world which is more or less indifferent to his parasitic presence. Miss Murdoch's treatment of this material is curiously brilliant. She ranges easily between the extremes of Wodehousian comedy—as when Jake steals a film-star dog, or breaks into hospital to 'rescue' a patient—and the questionably serious presentation of people and motives. But neither 'comic' nor 'serious' adequately describes the effect Miss Murdoch achieves. The theft of the dog is not only funny; we are invited to wonder whether it indicates something more important than mere watchers on the shore can allow. When Jake rescues Hugo, from whom he has earlier filched ideas for a philosophic treatise, we are led to suppose that he is not simply sticking his tongue out at the ward sister, that his purpose belongs to a 'higher realm' than the merely physical context of the hospital. Iris Murdoch is extremely clever. Her artistry is to weave the improbable and the fantastic into the normal world, so that we cannot be sure, moment by moment, just what level of reality is being presented. We are in constant danger of being hoodwinked.

Jake, turned out of his lodgings by one girl, goes in search of the other; there is a faint chance that she may take him in.

I looked at the house with suspicious curiosity, and it seemed to be looking back at me. It was a brooding self-absorbed sort of house, fronted by a small ragged garden and a wall shoulder high. . . . Finally, with a slow crescendo in the region of the heart I pushed open the gate, which was a little rusty, and walked up to the house. The windows gleamed bleakly, like eyes behind dark glasses. . . . The door opened quietly and I stepped on tiptoe into the hall. An oppressive silence surged out of the place like a cloud. I closed the door and shut out all the little noises of the river front. Now there was nothing but the silence. . . . I moved to the nearest door and opened it wide. Then I got a shock that stiffened me from head to toe.

I was looking straight into seven or eight pairs of staring eyes. . . . I stepped back hastily, and the door swung to again with a faint click which was the first sound I had heard since I entered the house.

The objective reality of the house, with its rusty gate, its door and its proximity to the river, is modified by the 'suspicious curiosity' of Jake, onlooker and intruder. It thus acquires the character Jake expects it to show—indifferent to him and 'self-absorbed' as Anna is likely to be; not only indifferent to him, however, but to the whole world beyond itself, as the 'ragged garden' and the wall and the excluding silence within variously testify, and which the strange activities of the masked faces (for so the 'staring eyes' prove to be) help to substantiate. But there is also the element of menace here—the house 'seemed to be looking back at me . . .', 'the windows gleamed bleakly', the silence is 'oppressive' and total. At first Iris Murdoch seems to be inviting us to play the game of shuddering at Bleak House; Jake's palpitating heart and stifled movements, and the literary reference to *The Listeners*, all suggest that the author is mocking 'thick-coming fancies' and seem to prepare us for the discovery that Jake's imagination has been playing him tricks. But Miss Murdoch is really tricking us: she holds back the revelation of the actors and Anna until she has made the reader's heart miss a beat. Only then is the whole fabric of the fantasy allowed to disintegrate under the cool rational tones of the 'explanation': Jake is forced back to reality—Anna, pursuing her own illusions, won't have him.

This passage is representative. The brilliance is of the surface only, an elaborate game. In waving away the fantasy Miss Murdoch proposes nothing in its place but a different form and degree of unreality; she can crumple the cardboard 'walls of Rome' (to use the metaphor she provides herself later in the book), but no real walls of Rome exist for her. The impulse behind her work is, despite the fascination of her 'games', negative and destructive. What begins in *The Bell* as a sympathetic account of a nunnery and its neighbouring lay community collapses, by way of mock thrills and discoveries, into a pronounced sneer; religious and lay alike are humiliated, the monastery shuts its doors and the lay people disperse. Mr Kettle's judgement on *Point Counter Point* is not altogether inapposite to the work of Iris Murdoch: 'It is no good trying to say what is wrong . . . in terms of construction, style, characterization and the technical weapons of literary analysis because what is wrong is wrong at the very heart. There is no respect for life in this novel and without such fundamental respect, words curdle and art cannot come into being.'⁸

It is the lack of 'such fundamental respect' that should lead us to question the status of *Lord of the Flies* as a modern classic (and set-book for the middle school). Perhaps we are so inured to negation and destruction in contemporary literature that we can believe there is evidence of positive, wholesome life in Ralph and Piggy, and 'psychologically valid' gangsterism in Jack. The author himself implies, through Ralph on the last page, that paradise has been lost:

> For a moment he had a fleeting picture of the strange glamour that had once invested the beaches. . . . 'We were together then . . .'

But there has in fact been no paradise, pictorial or human, to lose. Even the order that Ralph and Piggy attempt to impose on the stranded collection of schoolboys is represented as a juvenile game, 'intellectual' and futile; and the only real power shown is the rhythm of the primitive destructive dance. Ralph at the end laments 'the fall through the air of the true, wise friend called Piggy'–of whom these are actually the first kind words written. Both individually and collectively the boys are subject throughout to the author's contempt and disgust; and we are finally shown a muted Jack, 'a semicircle of little boys . . . standing on the beach making no noise at all', and Ralph 'squirming a little, conscious of his filthy appearance' to a smart naval officer who observes that 'the kid needed a bath, a haircut, a nose-wipe and a good deal of ointment'. The language invites us to despise them all, as much for dropping their primitive pretences, their 'fun and games', as for letting themselves get out of hand. Nor has adult civilization, Golding implies, anything to give these children but subjection to itself, its 'revolver' and its 'sub-machine-gun'. The dead parachutist (the 'lord' of the flies) is a symbol of the ready and total collapse into barbarism even of the adult restraints–the same restraints that are so readily and cynically reasserted at the close. Mr Golding in fact offers only an alternative to *Coral Island*, in the rejection of which–its outlook and values–he has nothing positive to say.⁹ Here is no growing point for our fiction, merely an illustration of its current disease. Cary's *Charley is my Darling* and Barstow's *Joby*, which have attracted nothing like the same attention, effectively place the celebrated brilliance of *Lord of the Flies*.

5

Joe Lampton in *Room at the Top* is a lucky Jim with his feet on the ground. His similar working-class grammar school background leads him not to the university, the advantages of which he recognizes in the manner of C. P. Snow, but to a safe and salaried post in the superior neighbouring town hall. Joe is good at his job and liked by the girls. His twin aims, to be rich himself and to marry the most beautiful girl in the town, are finally achieved when he learns that Susan has gone to London for her wedding-dress. The price this junior Epicure Mammon has to pay is, however, considerable: his dream is not exposed to ridicule, but curdles in its fulfilment; he is to be married to a girl he does not love. But the morality of *Room at the Top* is not so compelling as the summary of its 'message' may suggest. Joe is subject to certain social and personal restraints, but none of these is sufficient critically to expose him. The whole society of Warley is geared to helping along the path of material ambition the young man who has entered it for that purpose alone, and when Joe 'kills' Alice (Susan's rival for his affections) 'nobody blames [him]'. Mr Braine thus stigmatizes the society, and presents Joe as the one person sensitive enough to stand apart from it:

'Nobody blames you, love. Nobody blames you.'
I pulled myself away from her abruptly. 'Oh my God,' I said, 'that's the trouble.'

There are earlier signs of Joe's capacity for self-criticism. 'I felt guilty,' he admits, sitting beside Susan at the pictures. 'I was manœuvring for position all the time, noting the effect of each word; and it seemed to devalue everything I said.' But Joe's flashes of insight are not generally trustworthy: 'I didn't, at the age of fifteen, share my father's pride, because the hypothetical car which he'd so highmindedly rejected was all too real to me.' Neither does he, we protest, share it now; the values by which his father lived are irrelevant to Joe, despite his statement of his parents' goodness, his sentimental journey to the bombsite that had been their home, and his occasional excursions to Aunt Emily's house in Dufton. His opinion of Dufton is explicitly anti-life and arrogant, its town hall clerks 'zombies', its people 'dead' and 'dreary'. Even when Joe feels 'choked with [his] own selfishness' he thinks not of Dufton but of Warley Moor: 'there was nothing in my heart to match the lovely sweep of the moor and the sense of infinite space behind it and a million extra stars above'. And Warley Moor's value, in the context, is sentimental.

The positive alternative Mr Braine offers to Joe's progress *should* have been Dufton but in fact is the uninhibited sexuality he enjoys with a married woman. However preferable this to the methodical seduction of Susan, it is just as selfish and rather more socially chaotic—though neither Joe nor the author sees it in these terms. Mr Braine is concerned less to present moral alternatives than to force Joe into self-awareness—an awareness so sickening that he turns in hate upon the world which has permitted him to believe in himself so uncritically: 'I saw quite clearly that there were no dreams and no mercy left in the world, nothing but a storm of violence.' *Room at the Top*'s power, ultimately, is to sicken the reader, to induce in him a sense of futility and aridity. *Life at the Top* takes up the story ten years later, but is unconvincing: there was nothing to resurrect from the ashes of the earlier novel.

In *Saturday Night and Sunday Morning* the *Daily Telegraph* found 'a novel of today with a freshness and raw fury that makes *Room at the Top* look like a vicarage tea-party'. The comparison is not inept. People at t'top in Warley claim familiarity with the leading clergy, and in *Life at the Top* they actually attend church. The church in Sillitoe's Nottingham is not even a background presence, and there is in Arthur Seaton's futile progress none of the ambition or the education of Joe Lampton. Whether Mr Sillitoe intends to present Arthur's life as futile is questionable. It is certainly allowed its attractions: working skilfully for five days, drinking deep and distributing largesse at the weekend, enjoying the pleasures of a married woman's bed without the responsibilities—this is 'a good life'. Arthur Seaton is agin the government, the bosses and all social restraints; his philosophy is explicitly selfish. As a Lucky Jim of the working classes he can envisage no hand extended to help him along, nor does he ask for one. When he meets opposition he is defiant and happy:

> He would be seeing Brenda tomorrow night. He lit a cigarette and whistled a tune as he walked. The thought made him feel good.
> Too deeply engrossed in it, and straying too close to the side of the lane, he tripped over a tree-root. A dozen curses raced from between his lips as he righted himself. Then he laughed, and walked on.

How does Mr Sillitoe stand in relation to the insensitive brute of his creation? Mrs Bull the gossip, Jack the spineless husband, Robboe the wages clerk who 'respects hard work', the cousins who lie and cheat, the swaddies who beat him up – these are the ordinary people of Arthur Seaton's world and (one is led to suppose) of Mr Sillitoe's. Like his hero, the author worked in a Nottingham cycle factory, and the authentic vitality of the world described clearly derives from personal observation. Mr Sillitoe's own life has not, however, ended in a cycle factory, with the prospect of earning less as year succeeds to year, eventually being hooked into marriage and sitting in front of a television set. The differences between author and character could have provided the moral perspective in which to view the character's motives and actions. But the creation of an insensitive brute has constrained the author's imagination. His own attitude to Mrs Bull, Jack and Robboe is so close to Arthur's that there is no room for the required detachment to find expression. Indeed, the only detachment shown is Arthur's own, when towards the end he is saving up for marriage, spending his days fishing and philosophizing: 'And trouble for me it'll be,' he says, 'fighting every day until I die' – but 'The float bobbed more violently than before and, with a grin on his face, he began to wind in the reel.'

This Sporting Life also draws for its material on the industrial squalor of the north and for its theme on the young man who leads an 'heroic' existence. What distinguishes David Storey from his compeers is his recognition that it *is* merely an existence, that the 'life' of a footballer is nasty, brutish and short; that the setting of the ground, the interest (both personal and financial) of the club directors, the character of the town's support, are similarly ugly and transitory. Mr Storey is bemused neither by the scene of his novel nor by the motives and activities of his hero. Arthur Machin, despite his comparable self-interest and brutality, is neither a Lampton nor a Seaton; the pitiable figure of Johnson, the supporter who hangs around Arthur, helps us to keep our proper distance. Whereas Braine and Sillitoe seem often to be sucked in by the 'reality' they present, we can trust Storey to keep his moral feet, as it were.

The achievement is the more remarkable for the subjective form the novel takes. It is Arthur's tale and outlook that are presented, and yet Storey manages with the minimum of comment to establish for our contemplation the nature of the case. The implicit judgement on Arthur and his environment may be illustrated by the description of his first game for the club. Arthur 'seems to inflate' as he runs on to the field into the 'blinding light' of the great occasion; to the roar of the crowd and 'The Entrance of the Gladiators' the players move 'importantly' and ceremonially into position. The deflation is registered thus:

> It took me most of the first half to realize I was being starved of the ball by my own side. It was the hooker, Taff Gower, who was organizing it, I decided,

and so is rather more deflating than Arthur, preening himself on his detective qualities, is aware. The egoist does not inquire into Gower's motives, he simply sees 'an early end to [his] ambitions'.

> As we folded down for the next scrum his face was farther forward than mine. 'Why're you keeping the ball from me?' I asked him. His head was upside down, waiting for the ball to come in, but he was grinning, fairly politely. I could see the back of his throat. When he spat I couldn't move my head . . .
> I waited three scrums to make him feel relaxed and also to get the best opportunity. I kept my right arm loose. His face was upside down, his eyes straining, loose in their sockets, to catch a glimpse of the ball as it came in. I watched it leave the scrum-half's hands and his head buckled under the forwards' heaving. I swung my right fist into the middle of his face. He cried out loud. I hit him

again and saw the red pulp of his nose and lips as my hand came away.

Calculated brutality is thus answered in kind. But Arthur is less concerned to repay an insult than to find 'the best opportunity' of establishing himself, of reviving his gladiatorial ego. He chooses the hooker's most 'professional' moment to assert his own professional rights, and stands quite detached from the bloody scene he has caused, from the referee's 'violent mimes of justice' as he sends the opposing hooker off, from the crowd 'throbbing with rage'. Storey shows a different sort of detachment: he keeps the crowd, the pugilists, the referee and the innocent hooker in perspective, and does so while apparently looking through Arthur's eyes. Arthur may enjoy the 'real drama', but Storey plainly hates it. And when the trainer congratulates Arthur at half-time with 'You'll do just fine at this club' we realize that Storey hates not only the physical brutality and the injustice but the individualism which distorts the word 'club': 'Get this, lad,' declares the trainer, 'I'm on my own side.' So is Arthur, the reinflation of whose ego subsequently involves ignoring a call to pass the ball, unfair handing-off a tackle, and 'a soaring of [his] guts' as he touches down between the posts. Arthur the gladiator, 'keeping [his] eye on the delight of the crowd', is unaware of the irony:

> Everything was luminous, sparkling. The houses beyond the stadium turrets, the silhouetted trees at Sandwood, the ice-blue sky, the mass of people–they were all there intent on seeing me.

In the course of the book the transitoriness of such gladiatorial fame gets increasing attention. Already we have the hooker, battered and toothless, 'working out his last days in the game with the "A" team'. Later we have the departure of the leading directors of the club, not with a bang but a whimper. And the centre of interest by the end has shifted to the question of retirement and provision for the future. The pervasive atmosphere is one of squalor and insecurity, in individual lives and personal relationships as well as in setting; and yet when Arthur lies with his landlady and then watches her trudge into the garden to hang out the washing, when he takes the kids out for a good time in his fast car, when his club director's wife attempts to seduce him, or whenever the whining Johnson appears at his elbow—on all such occasions we are aware of the writer's pity, never of his complicity.

The fourth novelist in this group is Stan Barstow, who has a more affectionate attitude towards the West Riding than Mr Storey and is more personally committed to it. Indeed, failure to distance himself is responsible for the indulgent clichés of *Ask Me Tomorrow* and *Watchers on the Shore*. Yet he achieves in *A Kind of Loving* a certain moral and artistic poise. Vic admires Ingrid because she is different from the tarts in the stripmagazines, because she approximates to his idea of a woman to marry for life. In associating with her, however, he finds her incapable of thought and serious reading; she is in fact a prisoner of her respectable upbringing. But Vic desires her physically and despite dissatisfaction with the affair cannot bring himself to cut loose irrevocably. The impasse is decided by the girl's pregnancy, and a marriage is hastily arranged.

The marriage gets off to a bad start. Vic finds living under his mother-in-law's roof increasingly intolerable, and he runs away. But our sympathy with Vic does not permit us to luxuriate in his attitude to marriage with the mother-dominated girl. His sister takes a dissentient line. The secondary problem is eventually solved by the couple moving into a separate flat; but the basic one—how to live with that girl—remains. The book is thoroughly wholesome, its chief faults—the stiff-jointed presentment of the perfect marriage between Vic's sister and an English teacher, and the unmitigated hostility towards the mother-in-law—marginal matters.

6

In *The L-Shaped Room*, which examines a related contemporary problem but in a more familiar setting, change and decay are established early.

> My room was five flights up in one of those gone-to-seed houses in Fulham, all dark-brown wallpaper inside and peeling paint outside. On every second landing was a chipped sink with one tap and an old ink-written notice which said 'Don't leave the tap Driping'. The

landing lights were the sort that go out before you can reach the next one. There were a couple of prostitutes in the basement...

In the adjoining room is a kindly black man, in another a young Jewish writer. Jane herself, pregnant from a single unfortunate occasion and turned out by a Victorian father, has come to a house where no questions are asked. In that house, peopled by social outcasts, grow love and goodness: Jane sleeps with the Jew, and the black man makes a cradle for the baby; ultimately she is reconciled to her father, and her faithful friends turn up at the christening.

The L-Shaped Room is interesting more for what it might have been and for what the author appears to think it is than for what it actually is. Miss Banks's assault on racial prejudice, parental inhumanity and 'pre-Wolfenden' hypocrisy is made strident by the stance of the heroine. In mentioning the prostitutes along with the paint and the taps Miss Banks is inviting us not to be shocked at their 'open' presence; after all, Jane, an inexperienced girl from a nice home, is not shocked. This emancipated attitude brings author and heroine so close together that the reader feels he is being pressed into responding likewise. 'Wonder why he changed his name – and then changed it back again?' muses Terry, the original seducer, of Toby the Jew. 'I thought,' and here Miss Banks and Jane speak with one voice, '*He changed it because of people who feel like you, and he changed it back because* – but there was no sure answer to that yet. Until I saw him, it was nothing but a hopeful symptom.'

The encounter between Terry and the Jew is insecurely managed. As 'Cohen' savages the insulting Englishman we register each blow as one for the cause, and yet Jane herself remains apart from the fight. The Jew is mystified by the failure of Terry to hit back, but the reader sees the beating as a self-induced punishment, as what Terry has sought in vain from the wronged girl: 'Don't you want to – to hurt me in some way – punish me for all you've done through?' – 'No ... I feel different now. More peaceful about it.' Unfortunately we are prepared for the beating, for seeing it as just retribution, by Terry's reaction to the gentle, all-forgiving girl:

A look of gratitude and relief flattened out his face for a moment.

His mouth relaxed open and he stared into my eyes. 'You mean it,' he said at last. 'Thank God, you really mean it.'

The language here is not that of the all-forgiving girl but of the author whose intense dislike of Terry insists on someone punching that highly unattractive face. Jane and Miss Banks are entangled: Jane can make a 'light' reply to the heavy sighs and self-recriminatory words of her seducer, but Miss Banks through the agency of Jane sends him to look for the Jew rather as the schoolmaster tells the boy to fetch the stick. Thus we are not only asked to view the punishment as a racialist's deserts or as self-purifying flagellation, but feel uncomfortably that it is Miss 'Jane' Banks's revenge upon his too obvious relief.

The confusion of Miss Banks's purposes is reflected also in the ungainly shape of the book. But when all objections have been urged it should be stressed that *The L-Shaped Room* does present constructive and hopeful moral views. Edna O'Brien's progress, on the other hand, has been steadily downhill. The notion of life in her books is of something coarse and sexually obsessed: a little girl is expelled from her convent school for an obscene sketch of the chaplain with the mother superior; an adolescent girl lives in sin with an older man in a country house; a divorced woman sits on a park bench with her legs apart; an older divorced woman begins her wicked month with a 'satisfying' union, goes south in search of further erotic experiences, and returns with an 'infection'. There seem to be good reasons why Eugene, patron, lover and husband, should eventually tire of the cheap and nasty girl he has befriended; but Eugene himself provides no standard by which we may judge the behaviour he denounces – he is a cruel and cynical man. Miss O'Brien, in exposing the aridity of sexual obsession, has no redemptive challenge to offer her soiled heroines; her vision of human relationships in the modern world is quite without hope.

'Narrowness and pessimism' were the main characteristics of modern English fiction noted by Arnold Kettle in 1953;[10] there is no reason now to alter his diagnosis. The habit of doing dirt on life is so widely established that concepts of 'reality', 'experience' and 'truth' have themselves become infected. The uncritical, 'autobiographical' posture so commonly adopted makes Mr Inglis's strictures on *All the King's Men*[11] – that

Warren tries a too 'limited method and manner', that too often he 'means us to take the speaker at his own valuation'–as commonly applicable. Even where signs of health can be detected the range is too restricted to release an important influence: one can discriminate between *Concluding* and Muriel Spark's *Girls of Slender Means* or distinguish *This Sporting Life* from the general run of 'working-class novels'–but the vitality and variety of *Dr Zhivago* or *By Love Possessed* and the critical proportion maintained are qualities absent from post-war English fiction.

NOTES

[1] P. N. Furbank, 'The Twentieth Century Best-Seller', in *The Modern Age*, ed. Boris Ford (Penguin), p. 433.

[2] P. N. Furbank, op. cit., p. 434.

[3] cf. William Cooper's *The Ever-interesting Topic*, in which the masters at 'a great public school' dress for dinner, eat in 'the Combination Room', drink the best claret, and never seem to take a lesson. But they do secure the dismissal of two headmasters and hobnob with governors.

[4] Gilbert Phelps, 'The Novel Today' in *The Modern Age*, p. 484.

[5] Arnold Kettle, *An Introduction to the English Novel*, Vol. ii (Hutchinson), p. 195, revised edition.

[6] Gilbert Phelps, op, cit., p. 481.

[7] Raymond O'Malley, 'One More Irrelevance', in *The Use of English*, XV 4, p. 7

[8] Arnold Kettle, op. cit., p. 178.

[9] In one of his later novels, *The Inheritors*, he does create an authentic paradise threatened by forces too great for it–but the innocence at stake is that of Neanderthal man, and human beings are the spoilers.

[10] Arnold Kettle, op. cit., p. 206.

[11] Fred Inglis, *An Essential Discipline* (Methuen), p. 203.

READING LIST

C. P. Snow: *The Affair* (Macmillan). *The Masters* (Macmillan). *Corridors of Power* (Macmillan).

Evelyn Waugh: *Men at Arms* (Chapman and Hall). *Officers and Gentlemen* (Chapman and Hall). *Unconditional Surrender* (Chapman and Hall).

Graham Greene: *The Power and the Glory* (Heinemann). *The Heart of the Matter* (Heinemann). *The Comedians* (The Bodley Head).

Joyce Cary: *Mister Johnson* (Michael Joseph). *The Horse's Mouth* (Michael Joseph). *Charley is my Darling* (Michael Joseph).

Henry Green: *Doting* (Chatto and Windus). *Living* (Chatto and Windus). *Concluding* (Chatto and Windus).

L. P. Hartley: *The Go-Between* (Hamish Hamilton). *The Shrimp and the Anemone* (Faber and Faber). *The Brickfield* (Hamish Hamilton).

Kingsley Amis: *Lucky Jim* (Macmillan). *Take a Girl like You* (Gollancz). *One Fat Englishman* (Gollancz).

Iris Murdoch: *Under the Net* (Chatto and Windus). *The Bell* (Chatto and Windus). *The Italian Girl* (Chatto and Windus).

William Golding: *Lord of the Flies* (Faber and Faber). *The Inheritors* (Faber and Faber). *The Pyramid* (Faber and Faber).

Muriel Spark: *The Ballad of Peckham Rye* (Macmillan). *The Prime of Miss Jean Brodie* (Macmillan). *Girls of Slender Means* (Macmillan).

John Braine: *Room at the Top* (Eyre and Spottiswoode). *Life at the Top* (Eyre and Spottiswoode).

Alan Sillitoe: *Saturday Night and Sunday Morning* (W. H. Allen). *The Loneliness of the Long Distance Runner* (W. H. Allen).

David Storey: *This Sporting Life* (Longmans). *Flight into Camden* (Longmans) *Radcliffe* (Longmans).

Stan Barstow: *A Kind of Loving* (Michael Joseph). *Joby* (Michael Joseph).

Lynne Reid Banks: *The L-Shaped Room* (Chatto and Windus). *An End to Running* (Chatto and Windus).

Edna O'Brien: *Girl with Green Eyes* (Cape). *August is a Wicked Month* (Cape).

2

Post-War Drama

TERENCE BARNES

THE theatre-goer who wants to sample the new, the drama-group in search of contemporary stimulus, the teacher, at whatever level, who feels he needs to base some of his work in English on reading or acting plays, and who wants to escape from Shakespeare and come nearer his own time than Shaw, can all find much recent work in print. Publishers and educationists seem eager to push the *avant-garde* into the lecture hall and the classroom; from the boards of the theatre to the Boards of examining bodies *il n'y a qu'un pas*, and this is something, I think, that we should all applaud. But at the same time we must recognize, in a good deal of the frenetic chat that goes on about the modern theatre, the sort of public relations job that is now done on modern art in general. O monstrous, but one halfpennyworth of criticism to this intolerable deal of advertisement! Value in a play, it seems to be assumed, varies directly in proportion to its oddity, its capacity to shock, its dependence on tricks of production, in short to its distance from everything we traditionally associate with drama. Yet there is interesting work being done; some of the shocks are salutary, and some of the changes in technique are functional rather than fashionable. We know the old forms must be broken and we realize that convention may become a constriction; but we must also realize that the row we hear going on about the modern theatre has been going on a long time—indeed since Ibsen—and that few contemporary commentators have much of value to add to it. One popular argument seems to go like this: because Ibsen and Chekhov were booed by the conventionally minded and suppressed by the censor, therefore the work of Mr X, which has had the same treatment today, must be as good as.... The argument, alas, is false.

In a way the whole concern today of those dramatists who

try to do more than shuffle well-worn clichés of situation and feeling into patterns that Aunt Edna can be persuaded to think new and surprising (*Separate Tables* and *The Prime of Miss Jean Brodie*) is to make the fable they devise and the characters they animate stand as emblems of general truths about society and people, about public and human relationships. They want, in short, to fire our imaginations, and most of them seem to feel that bourgeois realism won't any longer do. Bolt turns from *The Cherry Tree* to *A Man For All Seasons*, Osborne from *Look Back in Anger* to *Luther*, Peter Shaeffer from *Five Finger Exercise* to *The Royal Hunt of the Sun*. Invoking the past is, we recognize, a standard Romantic and post-Romantic procedure–even Mr Rattigan has done a play about Alexander the Great, and his *Ross* is an attempt to find a 'hero' in more recent history. In the past there appear to be patterns, guide-lines, significant relationships of broad bands of power which the diffuse, bloodless, shifting, unfocused life and politics of the modern world fail to supply. When Princes ruled, the King was a valid symbol; his life and death touched all imaginations: 'Attention must be paid.' So, in comedy, the solid bourgeois household, with its extended kinship and its servants, admirably served Molière's needs. The last modern dramatist able to call on such social support was Chekhov, whose characters, in their remote country houses, where a decaying tradition is unsettled by returning exiles, sapped by futile bureaucracy, overturned by the thrusting forces of the new, are sustained only by a stoical unhelpful duty, towards art, or the forests, or the fields. Another relationship, that of master and servant, which has scaffolded so much traditional comedy will no longer work; it has expired, not with a bang but a titter, in Jeeves.

For all this, our contemporaries feel, the suburban drawing-room is no useful substitute and so they seek their symbols in history, in nonsense, or 'among the unfenced regions of society' in clochards and caretakers. I assume that the 'Art of the Theatre', in so far as there is such a thing, is interpretative; the writer is the creator, and if his writings, his words, are 'sovereign' enough for us to want to get to know them better outside the theatre, then what he has written is literature and must be judged as such. What we have to ask ourselves is whether the rhetoric the author has constructed works on our imagination, and whether we are convinced by the characters who speak the rhetoric. It is not very fashionable to talk about 'characters' but all the great plays we go back to are full of men and women we remember. This is not the only reason for their permanence, their classic status, and may in many cases not be the most important one; yet it is something they all have in common, and it is one reason why the drama, like the novel but unlike poetry, will travel. Pushkin must, to those who have no Russian, remain remote. Not so Turgenev or Chekhov. Much we may no doubt miss in translation; but enough comes through to make us feel them to be part of our European heritage because we feel we know the worlds they present, and we feel so because we recognize the beings who inhabit those worlds. Much modern drama, seeking to break the bourgeois bonds, comes to resemble, so full is it of bloodless types, the Morality play, and we all know the text-books tell us (truly enough) that the Elizabethans improved on the Morality because they substituted people for types. Moreover the Morality was based on a tradition-sanctified universally accepted scheme of values and beliefs, which today we lack.

And so such plays as Wesker's *Trilogy*, based on values to which the author is deeply and sincerely committed appear to many to be 'propaganda'—the word has become pejorative precisely because there is no longer one faith to propagate—and therefore limited; and this is true whether we sympathize with his views or not. Yet we must also consider that they do follow a line of thought, and this gives them a certain toughness. They are at any rate about *something*. Amid the flat wastes that surround us any eminence, however small, is a relief, and we are grateful for it.

We can roughly divide new drama into three classes: the chronicle morality play—*Galileo, A Man for All Seasons, Luther*; the post-Shavian rhetorical naturalistic play with a message—*Look Back in Anger*, the Wesker *Trilogy*; the exploitation, grim or gay but always unsettling, of the irrational—*The Caretaker, One Way Pendulum, Next Time I'll Sing to You*.

I must confess that I tend to find the first class boring. The moral schema too often obtrudes, and I recoil instinctively from the play 'that makes you think'. But this doesn't mean that such plays are valueless, or lacking in interest for many types of student. The simplicity—naïvety if you will—of their themes, the clear antitheses of their problems, are easily grasped and invite discussion and argument. They contain, after all, goodies and baddies. From the struggle of sheriff and rustler to that between proletarian and capitalist is not a great leap, and it might be claimed that the Marxist myth is slightly more relevant than the western one.

A Man for All Seasons is respectable enough to be a set book. It is serious and intelligent. To me it seems dull, but I have seen an impressive school production which was much enjoyed by the cast—the people who really matter on these occasions.

Here is part of the scene between More and Norfolk, when the latter pleads with him in the name of friendship to give in to the King.

NORFOLK: . . . listen to what I have to say. You're behaving like a fool. You're behaving like a crank. You're not behaving like a gentleman—All right that means nothing to you: but what about your friends?

MORE: What about them?

NORFOLK: Goddammit, you're dangerous to know!

MORE: Then don't know me.

NORFOLK: There's something further . . . You must have realized by now there's a . . . policy with regards to you. [*More nods.*] The King is using me in it.

MORE: That's clever. That's Cromwell . . . You're between the upper and the nether millstones then.

NORFOLK: I am!

MORE: Howard, you must cease to know me.

NORFOLK: I do know you! I wish I didn't but I do!

MORE: I mean as a friend.

NORFOLK: You *are* my friend!

MORE: I can't relieve you of your obedience to the King, Howard. You must relieve yourself of our friendship. No one's safe now, and you have a son.

NORFOLK: You might as well advise a man to change the colour of his hair! I'm fond of you, and there it is! You're fond of me, and there it is!

MORE: What's to be done then?

NORFOLK [*with deep appeal*]: Give in.

MORE [*gently*]: I can't give in, Howard–[*smile*] you might as well advise a man to change the colour of his eyes. I can't. Our friendship's more mutable than *that*.

NORFOLK: Oh, that's immutable, is it? The one fixed point in a world of changing friendships is that Thomas More will not give in!

MORE [*urgent to explain*]: To me it *has* to be, for that's myself! Affection goes as deep in me as you I think, but only God is love right through, Howard; and *that's* my *self*.

Perhaps this quotation will show why I feel the play to be serious. Its problems are, through the optic glass of history, clearly focused, and these problems, of conscience, integrity, friendship and state power are patently relevant to our world. I think it dull because its language, though clear, is neutral and rhythmically dead. But I think many groups would enjoy the play, and when they discuss its themes they won't be wasting their time.

Bolt's play is safely pushed back in time. The Wesker *Trilogy* deals with the contemporary world, spanning two generations. Fascism, the Spanish war, communism, strikes, political commitment, poverty, ignorance, the retreat from mass production to craftsmanship and its failure, all jostle together in its scenes. Wesker seems to me worth attention because of his concern for people and values; he *is* 'talking about Jerusalem'. 'If you don't care,' says Ronnie, his somewhat unsubstantial protagonist, 'you die.'

Here is part of the last scene in *Chicken Soup with Barley*. The disillusioned Ronnie is arguing with his mother:

RONNIE: What has happened to all the comrades, Sarah? I even blush when I use that word. Comrade! Why do I blush! Why do I feel ashamed to use words like democracy and freedom and brotherhood? They don't have any meaning any more. I have nothing to write about any more . . . You look at me as if I'm talking in a foreign language. Didn't it hurt *you* to read about the murder of the Jewish Anti-Fascist Committee in the Soviet Union? . . . What's happened to us? Were we cheated or did we cheat ourselves? I just don't know, God in heaven, I just do not know! Can you understand what it is suddenly not to know? And the terrifying thing is – I don't care either . . .

His predicament is real and we do not have to have been committed Marxists to share it, for the speech echoes a prevailing disillusion with politics in general. The rhetoric is, in part, forceful; yet with how dull a thud does that allusion to 'the Jewish Anti-Fascist Committee in the Soviet Union' fall. The reality was horrible, we agree; the allusion is relevant to the argument; a play of this sort, presenting our own dilemmas, needs to point at real events. But the effect here is to drop us from drama into a leading article. We are brought up short; the dramatic perspective is narrowed; the symbol is too limited to work properly.

And here is part of the play's conclusion:

SARAH: There will always be human beings and as long as there are there will always be the idea of brotherhood.
RONNIE: Doesn't mean a thing.
SARAH: Despite the human beings.
RONNIE: Not a thing.
SARAH: Despite them!
RONNIE: It doesn't mean . . .
SARAH: All right then! Nothing then! It all comes down to nothing! People come and people go, wars destroy, accidents kill and plagues starve – it's all nothing, then! . . . Despair – die then! . . . You don't want to do that, Ronnie. So what if it all means nothing? When you know *that* you can start again. Please, Ronnie, don't let me finish this life thinking I lived for nothing. We got through, didn't we? We got scars but we got through. You hear me, Ronnie? . . . You've got to care or you'll die.
RONNIE: I – I can't, not now, it's too big, not yet – it's too big to care for, I – I . . . Too big, Sarah – too big, too big.
SARAH [*shouting after him*]: Ronnie, if you don't care you'll die.

Beatie Bryant's tirade at the end of *Roots* is also worth quoting to show the sort of way Wesker's work is relevant and stimulating. She is talking to her stolid and uncomprehending relatives:

. . . Do you think we really count? You don' wanna take any

notice of what them ole papers say about the workers bein' all-important these days—that's all squit! 'Cos we aren't. Do you think when the really talented people in the country get to work they get to work for us? Hell if they do! Do you think they don't know we 'ont make the effort? The writers don't write thinkin' we can understand, nor the painters don't paint expecting us to be interested. . . . 'Blust', they say, 'the masses is too stupid for us to come down to them. Blust', they say, 'if they don't make no effort why should we bother?' So you know who come along? The slop singers and the pop writers and the film makers and women's magazines and the Sunday papers and the picture-strip love stories—that's who come along, and you don't have to make no effort for them, it come easy. 'We know where the money lie', they say, 'hell we do! The workers 've got it so let's give them what they want. . . . Anything's good enough for them 'cos they don't ask for no more!' The whole stinkin' commercial world insults us and we don't care a damn. Well, Ronnie's right—it's our own bloody fault. We want the third-rate—we got it!

We won't consider the touching climax—that Beatie suddenly realizes that she is talking, not quoting, 'articulate at last' (salvation through communication), the content of her speech. It may be objected that this is a tract but there is nothing necessarily wrong with tracts, though they don't of course make the greatest sort of drama. Wesker is adapting Shavian methods; and this speech—there are many such throughout his work—presents a theme and a situation well fitted for class involvement and discussion. His work is sometimes sentimental, his characters conventional, and their motivation arbitrary. (One cannot, for example, really believe that Dave Simmonds, in *I'm Talking About Jerusalem*, would have taken the lino without his employer's permission.) But his deep concern and sincerity come through it all with a kind of rough power.

I think Osborne's *Look Back in Anger* still retains enough vitality to be interesting. It turns out on inspection to be much more ironic, much less committed to the Jimmy Porter rhetoric than its legendary fame would imply. His speeches, nevertheless, give splendid voice to the adolescent impulse for spitting in authority's eye, and its precarious conclusion, the pathetic flimsy game of squirrels and bears, points, as it is intended to do, the weakness of the Porter stance, and, beyond that, the defects of the society that fails to use him. We are here on difficult ground, where we have to try and distinguish the modish, the temporarily stimulating, from work tough enough to stand the dull handling we must in our conditions inevitably give it.

His *Luther* seems to me a far more interesting work than *A Man for All Seasons*. In this play, and in *The Entertainer*, he tries to bridge the gap between auditorium and stage, to achieve the kind of direct address to the audience that we find, for example, in *Richard III* and *Hamlet*. He makes us the congregation for Luther's sermon, the crowd around the Pardoner's stall. Letting Archie Rice step out of the play and take us into his confidence involves us doubly in what is going on, and gives his plea 'Don't clap too hard, ladies and gentlemen. We're in a very old building' an eerie resonance. Osborne's merits, I am convinced, are solid, though sometimes difficult to discern through the fog of publicity that surrounds him and that he, on occasion, takes delight in thickening. He seems to me humane and compassionate, very concerned for the old building we all inhabit. His energy is at times misguided and ill-controlled, and when he fails he crashes badly. But he remains one of our most interesting talents.

The American dramatist whose work seems to me to suit our needs is Arthur Miller. *Death of a Salesman* is hard to read, because its form depends on the use of a multiple setting, and what is clear to the eye in the theatre is not always clear on the page. But this can be got over. The sort of work we are thinking of must include hints on how to read a play, how to visualize what is going on. Groups who have read some Shakespeare should have no difficulty about this. Here is a short quotation from the scene where Linda, the Salesman's wife, is exhorting her sons to show their ageing and ailing father some love and respect:

LINDA: ... I don't say he's a great man. Willy Loman never made a lot of money. His name was never in the papers. He's not the finest character that ever lived. But he's a human being, and a terrible thing is happening to him. So attention must be paid. He's not to be allowed to fall into his grave like an old dog. Attention,

attention must be paid finally to such a person. You called him crazy—
BIFF: I didn't mean—
LINDA: No, a lot of people think he's lost his—balance. But you don't have to be very smart to know what his trouble is. The man is exhausted.
HAPPY: Sure!
LINDA: A small man can be just as exhausted as a great man. He works for a company thirty-six years this March, opens up unheard-of territories to their trademark, and now in his old age they take his salary away.
HAPPY [*indignantly*]: I didn't know that, Mom.
LINDA: You never asked, my dear! Now that you get your spending money someplace else you don't trouble your mind with him.
HAPPY: But I gave you money last—
LINDA: Christmas-time, fifty dollars! To fix the hot water it cost ninety-seven fifty. For five weeks he's been on straight commission, like a beginner, an unknown!
BIFF: Those ungrateful bastards!
LINDA: Are they any worse than his sons? When he brought them business, when he was young, they were glad to see him. But now his old friends, the old buyers that loved him so and always found some order to hand him in a pinch—they're all dead, retired. He used to be able to make six, seven calls a day in Boston. Now he takes his valises out of the car and puts them back and takes them out again and he's exhausted . . . And what goes through a man's mind, driving seven hundred miles home without having earned a cent? . . . And you tell me he has no character? The man who never worked a day but for your benefit? When does he get the medal for that? . . .

Miller is writing a tragedy. To this death 'attention must be paid'. His play is part of that tradition which begins with Ibsen, and which tries, without the aid of poetry, to express in drama based on the realities of bourgeois life the range of experience, of feeling, which the novel had taken over from the great renaissance playwrights. Willy Loman stands for modern man; his salesmanship for the civilization he lives in and by; his death arraigns the values of that civilization. It is interesting to inquire how far the action, characters and language of the play can support the tragic burden; interesting, too, to reflect on the gap that separates 'A small man can be just as exhausted as a great man . . .' from 'A sight most pitiful in the meanest wretch/ Past speaking of in a king!'

The playwrights I have mentioned so far build on traditional methods; they present few linguistic or technical difficulties to anyone who has read, shall we say, *Major Barbara*. I can imagine entertaining and stimulating work being based, for example, on *A Man for All Seasons*, *Luther*, and *The Crucible* or *Galileo*, examining their treatment of history, and the way their authors have made the dilemmas and conflicts depicted emblematic of those in our own society. *Look back in Anger*, the Wesker *Trilogy*, and *Death of a Salesman* could be discussed as examples of the dramatist presenting aspects of contemporary life; and made perhaps the jumping off ground for comparison with and critical appraisal of current television and screen offerings. One of our aims if we are to read the drama of our own day must be to lead on to such appraisal, and to the beginnings of critical discrimination applied to experience outside the classroom.

We have now to look at the third kind of modern play, the surrealist, absurd sort, which exploits the mysterious and the irrational. To start with we can I think omit those like Ionesco's *Amédée, or How to Get Rid of It*, which convey their meaning so largely through stage effects. If we can't see the corpse, the mushrooms and Amédée 'flying up out of reach of the policeman' we are left with the words alone, and they are not, by themselves, at any rate in translation, very interesting. We might note here that there are similar objections, from our special view-point–I am not considering their value as plays– to such works as Wesker's *Kitchen* or Henry Livings's *Nil Carborundum*. '. . . the growing corpse in *Amédée*' says Mr Esslin in his preface to the Penguin selection of *Absurd Drama* 'can best be understood as a poetic image. It is in the nature both of dreams and of poetic imagery that they are ambiguous and carry a multitude of meanings at one and the same time, so that it is futile to ask what the image of the growing corpse stands for.' I agree, as I suppose we all do, about the 'multitude of meanings' in the poetic image; but I cannot follow Mr Esslin's deduction, that it is *therefore* 'futile' to ask what it means. And, indeed, Mr Esslin does not rest in futility, for he goes on to suggest several things the corpse *might* mean. Later he tells us that 'Narrative or discursive thought proceeds in a dialectical manner and must lead to a result or final message. . . . Poetry is above all concerned to convey its central idea, or atmosphere, or mode of being; it is essentially static', and that in the old drama we have come to expect 'neat resolutions'. I do not understand what Mr Esslin means by saying that poetry is essentially static. This is not a term I would apply to the *Ode to Autumn* or 'I wake and feel the fell of dark . . .' or *Among School Children*. Nor do I find any 'neat resolution' in *Lear*, *The Tempest*, *Le Misanthrope*, *The Wild Duck* or *The Three Sisters*. But the main point is clear: these plays are 'poetic'; and they are as they are and not otherwise because the rhetoric of naturalism will not convey their authors' vision of a world without purpose, filled with beings who live solitary, incommunicable lives. They look back, according to Mr Esslin, to the 'ancient tradition of ritual drama', 'a poetic image of an archetypal event brought to life through a series of symbolic actions'.

We should not take too seriously talk about communication being impossible for anyone who really believed this would be silent. Our age has no doubt its special difficulties, and we have been hearing about them for a long time now. It was Prufrock who lamented 'It is impossible to say just what I mean . . .' and the exasperated Sweeney who grumbled 'I gotta use words when I talk to you . . .' (Don't forget *Sweeney*. The avant-gardists come and go, but *Sweeney* soldiers on, very much alive.) Our immediate problem is to decide whether any of the absurd theatre will do for us.

Certainly, I think, Beckett. Readers of *Waiting for Godot* need to be sympathetic. This is not an author to try on groups who have not read much, or are inclined to be hostile to, or resentful of, literature, because it's not factual, or practical, or even 'true'. But any group which is prepared to let its imagination be acted upon, to experience the play, can gain insight into what is after all an important aspect of modern writing.

Brecht, Wesker, Osborne take society seriously. They do not deal with naked unaccommodated man, and their characters are, as it were, draped in moral systems, ideologies, loyalties. Beckett strips these all off. His play is difficult to quote from, because the writing is seamless, and has a rhythmic flow which imposes assent. Waves or pulses of intensity energize the flood and die away, and if one isolates them one distorts the pattern. Perhaps this section from the tramps' talk near the beginning of the first act will give some idea of its quality.

ESTRAGON: What did we do yesterday?
VLADIMIR: What did we do yesterday?
ESTRAGON: Yes.
VLADIMIR: Why . . . [*angrily*]. Nothing is certain when you're about.
ESTRAGON: In my opinion we were here.
VLADIMIR [*looking round*]: You recognize the place?
ESTRAGON: I didn't say that.
VLADIMIR: Well?
ESTRAGON: That makes no difference.
VLADIMIR: All the same . . . that tree . . . [*turning towards the auditorium*] . . . that bog.
ESTRAGON: You're sure it was this evening?
VLADIMIR: What?
ESTRAGON: That we were to wait.
VLADIMIR: He said Saturday. [*Pause*]. I think.
ESTRAGON: You think.
VLADIMIR: I must have made a note of it. [*He fumbles in his pockets, bursting with miscellaneous rubbish.*]
ESTRAGON [*very insidious*]: But what Saturday? And is it Saturday? Is it not rather Sunday? [*Pause.*] Or Monday? [*Pause.*] Or Friday?
VLADIMIR [*looking wildly about him, as though the date was inscribed on the landscape*]: It's not possible!
ESTRAGON: Or Thursday?
VLADIMIR: What'll we do?
ESTRAGON: If he came yesterday and we weren't here you may be sure he won't come again today.
VLADIMIR: But you say we were here yesterday.
ESTRAGON: I may be mistaken. [*Pause.*] Let's stop talking for a minute, do you mind?
VLADIMIR [*feebly*]: All right. [*Estragon sits down on the mound. Vladimir paces agitatedly up and down, halting from time to time to gaze into distance off. Estragon falls asleep. Vladimir halts before Estragon.*] Gogo! . . . Gogo! . . . GOGO!
[*Estragon wakes with a start.*]

ESTRAGON [*restored to the horror of his situation*]: I was asleep! [*Reproachfully.*] Why will you never let me sleep?
VLADIMIR: I felt lonely.
ESTRAGON: I had a dream.
VLADIMIR: Don't tell me!
ESTRAGON: I dreamt that–
VLADIMIR: DON'T TELL ME!
ESTRAGON [*gesture towards the universe*]: This one is enough for you? [*Silence.*] It's not nice of you, Didi. Who am I to tell my private nightmares to if I can't tell them to you?

There is no certainty of place or time or status, and we, the onlookers are firmly reminded that we share this uncertainty; we, too, wallow in this bog. We cannot communicate, for when we try, our fellows refuse to listen. If we take the words 'I had a dream', and the accompanying ironic query about the (dream) universe 'This one is enough for you?' to be spoken by the artist, then we have here the refusal of the masses to respond to the imaginative vision, or heed the warnings of the private nightmare, or console those whom it rides, for there is 'Nor hate of what's to come, nor pity for what's gone. Nothing but grip of claw, and the eye's complacency . . .' Beckett's stylized, bare dialogue has subtle rhythmic inflections: see how the melting cadences of Estragon's last speech in this passage reinforce the irony, for these tramps are pilgrims with nowhere to go. Whether Beckett's gloom, summarized in the famous 'They give birth over a grave . . .' is too unrelievedly nihilistic for the classroom is not for me to decide, but an approach to 'placing' him might come from a reading of *Lear*, considering how much *more* that fable includes; and some of Yeats, notably *Meditation in Time of Civil War* and *Nineteen Nineteen* is relevant.

Pinter, too, exploits a barren idiom, 'the dreary intercourse of daily life', and he peddles a special brand of paranoiac terror. I think he promises more than he pays for his plays seem more interesting while one is watching them than they do in retrospect. One wonders, for example, whether the horrific conclusions of *The Room* or *The Dumb Waiter* are justified, but *The Birthday Party* and *The Caretaker* are well worth our attention. What is interesting about his dialogue is not its 'naturalness', or tape-recorder truth but its rhythm. Here is a passage from the second act of *The Birthday Party*.

PETEY: Oh hullo, Stan. You haven't met Stanley, have you Mr Goldberg?
GOLDBERG: I haven't had the pleasure.
PETEY: Oh well, this is Mr Goldberg, this is Mr Webber.
GOLDBERG: Pleased to meet you.
PETEY: We were just getting a bit of air in the garden.
GOLDBERG: I was telling Mr Boles about my old mum. What days. [*He sits at the table, right.*] Yes. When I was a youngster, of a Friday, I used to go for a walk down the canal with a girl who lived down my road. A beautiful girl. What a voice that bird had! A nightingale, my word of honour. Good? Pure? She wasn't a Sunday school teacher for nothing. Anyway, I'd leave her with a little kiss on the cheek – I never took liberties – we weren't like the young men these days in those days. We knew the meaning of respect. So I'd give her a peck and I'd bowl back home. Humming away I'd be, past the children's playground. I'd tip my hat to the toddlers, I'd give a helping hand to a couple of stray dogs, everything came natural. I can see it like yesterday. The sun falling behind the dog stadium. Ah! [*He leans back contentedly.*]
MCCANN: Like behind the town hall.
GOLDBERG: What town hall?
MCCANN: In Carrikmacross.
GOLDBERG: There's no comparison. Up the street, into my gate, inside the door, home. 'Simey!' my old mum used to shout, 'quick before it gets cold.' And there on the table what would I see? The nicest piece of gefilte fish you could wish to find on a plate.
MCCANN: I thought your name was Nat.
GOLDBERG: She called me Simey.
PETEY: Yes, we all remember our childhood.
GOLDBERG: Too true. Eh, Mr Webber, what do you say? Childhood. Hot water bottles. Hot milk. Pancakes. Soapsuds. What a life. . . .

We will want to think about the play, ponder the relationship between Stanley and the mysterious strangers, but meanwhile it is a pleasure just to listen to Goldberg. The speech generates energy: character and situation (we know by this stage that nothing Goldberg says is 'true') are created in the words, which ask, as all good dialogue should, to be heard, and there is not much in the plays I have been reading recently of which I could say the same.

N. F. Simpson is the most immediately appealing of the 'absurd' writers, and this piece from *A Resounding Tinkle* will show what I mean.

BRO: Was it still raining when you went to the door, Middie?
MIDDIE: There's a slight drizzle. It's not much.
BRO: I'll give it a few minutes longer. I don't suppose Nora will mind. I don't go out in the rain oftener than I need these days, Uncle Ted. My old hat isn't up to it.
UNCLE TED: That's what you're always saying, Bro. Isn't he Middie?
MIDDIE: Hats aren't everything in this world. There are other things besides hats.
BRO: We know they aren't everything.
UNCLE TED: I dare say there are plenty of people who wouldn't mind having a hat like yours, Bro. all the same.
BRO: It isn't so much having the hats as knowing how to make the best use of them.
MIDDIE: We can't all be blessed with hats.
UNCLE TED: I suppose plenty of people do get by without hats, but it's rather silly to pretend they don't matter.
BRO: Look at Mrs Blackboy's husband and the showers he's got through in his time with that green plastic bag he carries round on his head.
MIDDIE: That's not a hat.
BRO: Or Bella for that matter.
MIDDIE: Bella overdoes it. The time she spends on millinery she could spend on something else.
UNCLE TED: She gets through the rain though.
MIDDIE: A lot of those who are supposed to have such wonderful hats go around half the time in other people's. . . .

and so on. It has been said that Simpson's work derives from Lear and Carroll, and that it is typically English nonsense, but I think this view makes his work sound too cosy. To me it is full of overtones of unease and discomfort. The classical aim of comedy, said Shaw, was to chasten morals through ridicule. Perhaps a portentous dictum to apply to Simpson's work, but I think this is what his plays do. They are funny; in their absurdity we see ourselves; above all they make us listen to ourselves, and hear how ludicrously inadequate our everyday language is. This preoccupation with language and communication is in varying degrees common to Beckett, Pinter and Simpson.

The plays of John Arden are very varied and work on very different levels, and in this variety is one of the things that makes his work so attractive. He is committed to no particular technique, he follows no party line, is prepared to turn his hand to anything and is not afraid to risk falling flat on his face. If we look, for instance, at two comparatively slight pieces, the television play *Soldier, Soldier* and the one-actor *When is a Door not a Door* we have at once a feeling of life and of competence. Of the second play he writes 'I have never been a fanatical upholder of the idea that the inspired writer should not lower himself to commissioned work even when the conditions are so stringent as to apparently cramp his style.' There is a tough common sense in this cool appraisal of himself as craftsman. He has complained how hard it is for 'dramatists and directors . . . to open out the conventions of the drama'; the fact that he has submitted to these conventions, has worked within them and understands their limitations from inside means that he understands what he is doing when he goes outside them.

There is a free play of feeling in his dramas; he does not load his political and moral dice. One has read complaints that such plays as *Live Like Pigs* or *Sergeant Musgrave's Dance* are muddled; Arden, the argument goes, ought surely to side with his unreclaimed nomads or his socialized respectables in the first, or make out a strong unambiguous pacifist case in the second. Instead we see that the antisocial violence and disorder of the Sawneys is balanced the mob-hysteria aroused in their respectable welfare-state-benefited neighbours, and the play ends in unresolved squalor and pathos. So Sergeant Musgrave fails, and we are made to feel why he fails, and the strength of the case against him. 'Tragic' is too large a word, too ambiguous, too loaded with literature and controversy and sterile speculation to be much use today. Yet one is tempted to use it of Arden's serious work, which has a resonance rarely heard in that of his contemporaries. He is trying to find a myth, an action which will stand for what he has to say, and will be at once capable of being elaborated into such intrigue as is necessary for his purpose, and of working as a symbol, and he intermingles prose, ballads and rough verses to suit the different sorts of intensity his developing fable demands. On verse he has an interesting remark, quoted by John Russell Taylor in the introduction to the Penguin volume of plays: 'If people are speaking formal verse with lines that rhyme, the audience does not have to worry whether it sounds natural. They are talking poetry. It's with the half-and-half thing that one is in trouble.'

The end of *Sergeant Musgrave* illustrates these points. The Sergeant's mad scheme has failed, the dragoons have arrived, authority is in the saddle again, and he with his sole remaining companion are in prison awaiting court martial and the inevitable rope. Outside the townspeople dance. Mrs Hitchcock, landlady of the inn, brings the two men a drink. Private Attercliffe accepts with gratitude, but Musgrave refuses. He broods over his failure. 'Numbers and order. According to Logic. I had worked it out for months.' Then he turns to her and demands 'What made it break down?' She regards him with a mixture of pity and mockery, and after further exchanges finishes by saying '... the end of the world and you thought you could call a parade. In control—*you*!' I transcribe the rest of the scene.

MUSGRAVE [*very agitated*]: Don't talk like that. You're talking about my duty. Good order and the discipline: it's the only road I know. Why can't you see it?

MRS HITCHCOCK: All I can see is crooked Joe Bludgeon having his dance out in the middle of fifty Dragoons! It's time you learnt your life, you big proud sergeant. Listen: last evening you told all about this anarchy and where it came from—like, scribble all over with life or love, and that makes anarchy. Right?

MUSGRAVE: Go on.

MRS HITCHCOCK: Then *use* your Logic—if you can. Look at it this road: here we are, and we'd got life and love. Then *you* came in and did your scribbling where nobody asked you. Aye, it's arsey-versey to what you said, but it's still an anarchy, isn't it? And it's all your work.

MUSGRAVE: Don't tell me there was life and love in this town.

MRS HITCHCOCK: There was. There was hungry men, too – fighting for their food. But *you* brought in a different war.

MUSGRAVE: I brought it in to end it.

ATTERCLIFFE: To end it by its own rules: no bloody good. She's right, you're wrong. You can't cure the pox by further whoring. Sparky died of those damned rules. And so did the other one.

MUSGRAVE: That's not the truth. [*He looks at them both in appeal, but they nod.*] That's not the truth. God was with me . . . God [*He makes a strange animal noise of despair, a sort of sob that is choked off suddenly, before it can develop into a full howl.*] – and all they dancing – all of them – there.

MRS HITCHCOCK: Ah, not for long. And it's not a dance of joy. Those men are hungry, so they've got no time for *you*. One day they'll be full, though, and the Dragoons'll be gone, and then they'll remember.

MUSGRAVE [*shaking his head*]: No.

MRS HITCHCOCK: Let's hope it, any road, eh?

[*She presents the glass to his lips. This time he accepts it and drinks, and remains silent.*]

ATTERCLIFFE [*melancholy but quiet*]: That running tyke of a Sparky he reckoned he were the only bastard in the barracks had a voice. Well, he warn't. There's other men can sing when he's not here. So listen to this.

[*He sings.*]

> I plucked a blood-red rose-flower down
> And gave it to my dear.
> I set my foot out across the sea
> And she never wept a tear.

> I came back home as gay as a bird
> I sought her out and in:
> And I found her at last in a little attic room
> With a napkin round her chin.

At her dinner, you see. Very neat and convenient.

[*He sings.*]

> Oh are you eating meat, I said,
> Or are you eating fish?
> I'm eating an apple was given me today,
> The sweetest I could wish.

So I asked her where she got it, and by God the tune changed then. Listen at what she told me.

[He sings to a more heavily accented version of the tune.]
> Your blood-red rose is withered and gone
> And fallen on the floor:
> And he who brought the apple down
> Shall be my darling dear.
>
> For the apple holds a seed will grow
> In live and lengthy joy
> To raise a flourishing tree of fruit
> For ever and a day.
> With fal-la-la-the-dee, toor-a-ley,
> For ever and a day.

They're going to hang us up a length higher nor most apple-trees grow, Sergeant. D'you reckon we can start an orchard?

The pathos and the power of that conclusion have been earned.

There has been much of interest produced in the last fifteen years or so. 'Renaissance' is too grandiose a term, I think, but new modes of expression have been worked out at the Royal Court, in the more adventurous repertory theatres in the provinces, and by many sorts and shapes and sizes of fringe groups. Some of them have had solid runs in the West End. This kind of success is no necessary criterion of value; but when all the theorists of drama have had their say one fact remains: that the medium the dramatist works in is the subjugation of an audience, and we can say of our contemporaries that they have left Yeats's room full of fifty or so sensitive and sympathetic souls to battle it out with the ordinary theatre-going public. In the long run their work can only be the stronger for the struggle.

READING LIST

Robert Bolt: *The Flowering Cherry* (Heinemann). *The Tiger and the Horse* (Heinemann). *A Man for All Seasons* (Heinemann).

Peter Shaeffer: *Five Finger Exercise* (Hamish Hamilton). *The Royal Hunt of the Sun* (Hamish Hamilton).

John Osborne: *Look Back in Anger* (Faber and Faber). *The Entertainer* (Faber and Faber). *Luther* (Faber and Faber). *Inadmissible Evidence* (Faber and Faber). *A Bond Honoured* (Faber and Faber).

N. F. Simpson: *A Resounding Tinkle* (Faber and Faber). *The Hole* (Faber and Faber). *One-Way Pendulum* (Faber and Faber).

Harold Pinter: *The Birthday Party* (Methuen). *The Caretaker* (Methuen). *The Dumb Waiter* (Methuen). *The Homecoming* (Methuen).

Arnold Wesker: *Roots* (Cape). *Chicken Soup with Barley* (Cape). *I'm Talking about Jerusalem* (Cape). *Chips With Everything* (Cape). *The Kitchen* (Cape).

Arthur Miller: *Death of a Salesman (Collected Plays)*, (Secker and Warburg). *A View from the Bridge (Collected Plays)*, (Secker and Warburg). *The Crucible (Collected Plays)*, (Secker and Warburg). *All My Sons (Collected Plays)*, Secker and Warburg). *After the Fall (Collected Plays)*, (Secker and Warburg). *Incident at Vichy (Collected Plays)*, (Secker and Warburg).

Eugene Ionesco: *The Lesson (Collected Plays)*, (Calder and Boyars). *The Bald Prima Donna (Collected Plays)*, (Calder and Boyars). *Amédée (Collected Plays)*, (Calder and Boyars).

Samuel Beckett: *Waiting for Godot* (Faber and Faber). *Krapp's Last Tape* (Faber and Faber). *Endgame* (Faber and Faber). *Happy Days* (Faber and Faber).

Bertholt Brecht: *The Caucasian Chalk Circle* (Methuen). *The Good Woman of Setzuan* (Methuen). *Galileo* (Methuen). *Mother Courage and her Children* (Methuen). *St Joan of the Stockyards* (Methuen). *Arturo Ui* (Methuen).

John Arden: *Sergeant Musgrave's Dance* (Methuen). *Live Like Pigs* (Methuen) *The Workhouse Donkey* (Methuen). *Armstrong's Last Goodnight* (Methuen). *Götz the Ironhand* (by J. A and M. D'Arcy), (Methuen). *Soldier, Soldier* (Methuen). *The Hero Rises Up* (Methuen).

3

Contemporary English and American Poetry
FRED INGLIS

ANY attempt to map out the climate for contemporary poetry commits the cartographer to a number of large statements about the culture of the time and the country. The poetry, like the life of the time, is bewilderingly diverse, and in so far as the poetry *is* the life of its time and country, and that life at its most refined and self-aware, then such an essay as this becomes a sortie into the way a society lives, the reasons it has for remaining alive, and into the peculiar quality of that aliveness. But our society and its historical moment do not only make a poet the man he is (which doesn't mean that a poet, as a political man, may not try to change that moment), they place certain constraints on the way we read our poets. We start to expect that a poet (or any other kind of artist) choose certain kinds of subject and organize them in certain forms. The activities of the trendbenders in colour-supplement England are not without their symptomatic relevance; the rapidity and unbelievable superficiality of the fashionable world has in a curious way become a surrogate for a national Academy.

I don't want to fall into the familiar heresy of attributing all cultural ills to the frivolity of bright young intellectuals-about-television, but their presence and the ambivalent esteem and laughable salaries they are paid must have a place in any diagnosis of the state of poetry. For it is clearly possible to say that the moral and literary life of England is characterized by a deep absence at its centre; from the very little I've seen, I guess that a great many Americans would say much the same about the U.S.A. There is no centre—only a multiplicity of reference points. To say this is not to see history as progressive delapidation: there are strong and good things to be said for both societies. But most people would find it very hard without recourse to a vestigial Christianity to offer adequate answers to the questions: what is the significance of life? What is the worth of an individual life in these societies? The moral confusion is neatly summarized here:

> In discussing Greek society, I suggested what might happen when such a well-integrated form of moral life broke down. In our society the acids of individualism have for four centuries eaten into our moral structures, for both good and ill. But not only this: we live with the inheritance of not only one, but of a number of well-integrated moralities. Aristotelianism, primitive Christian simplicity, the puritan ethic, the aristocratic ethic of consumption, and the traditions of democracy and socialism have all left their mark upon our moral vocabulary. Within each of these moralities there is a proposed end or ends, a set of rules, a list of virtues. But the ends, the rules, the virtues, differ . . .
>
> It follows that we are liable to find two kinds of people in our society: those who speak from within one of these surviving moralities, and those who stand outside all of them. Between the adherents of rival moralities and between the adherents of one morality and the adherents of none there exists no court of appeal, no impersonal neutral standard. For those who speak from within a given morality, the connection between fact and valuation is established in virtue of the meanings of the words they use. To those who speak from without, those who speak from within appear merely to be uttering imperatives which express their own liking and their private choices. The controversy between emotivism and prescriptivism on the one hand and their critics on the other thus expresses the fundamental moral situation of our own society.[1]

In these circumstances, it becomes logical that the two strongest forces in English and American society—the twin forces of capital and individualism—will intercalate at the absent centre. Thus the Academy of our time is staffed by the fashion critics of TV and the weeklies—staffed, effectually, by the helots of competitive possession. The force of capital projects the images of isolated consumption and happy waste as emblems of the good life; the force of the individualist or shopkeeper's ethic projects the criteria of moral commercialism and rulelessness as touchstones of a degraded 'freedom'. One can try out this theory against the advertising and critical pages of the Sunday papers in order to see how the vocabulary and morality of competitive possession are interchangeable between the two forms of writing.[2] Poetry is tested on the one hand by commercial stocktakings: 'let's make an inventory of this poem—rhythm, syntax, images, and so on'; and on the other hand, by pious incantation of a merely private nature but with a certain sociable currency: 'unique compassion' 'poignant ironies' 'marvellous poise' 'beautifully judged ambiguity',[3] and so on. These words are extremely precious; within a shared morality they would have an ascribed and precise meaning; but their habitual employment is in the service of cant. The complementarity of these two verbal systems—stocktaking and liturgy—can be recorded at any public auction of works of art.

It is not idiosyncratic therefore, it is quite central to an understanding of poetry that one acknowledge the invisible constraints placed upon our profoundest ethical responses by the language of economic relations. To see the restraints is to move them by an energy which is potent enough to alter the relations. The perception is itself a positive act; it does not only describe the world, it changes it. Now I have said that in a queer way the cultural commentators of TV and the weeklies have gained an authority analagous to that of a national Academy. It is a great deal more than back-scratching to say that Raymond Williams's television criticism in *The Listener* is exceptionally rare for its 'friction, the sense of pregnant arrest, which goes with active realizing thought and the taking of a real charged meaning'[4]. If his writing sometimes becomes congested, then it is by attempting too much to take the measure of the density of things. What his contrasting presence enforces is the sensational absence of such a strength in other critical efforts, and it would be easy to adduce proof that the weekly reviewers and the TV whizz kids are the opinion-formers where they are not the teachers at the Universities. Any reader of literature—any human being—confirms, chastens and replenishes his humaneness by reference to some shared centre. It is in this way that standards create themselves and a shared, valued body of experience exists in a national memory. It is only in this way that a civilization lives. At the moment, the existing centre of reference is either unbelievably trivial or strained and desperate. It is worth anatomizing a document which offers a classic statement of our contemporary nervelessness, for it may explain why certain poets are so misvalued at the expense of others. For our history may make the work of certain poets possible even though they still go unread; and if they are unread, they have no presence in our culture and they must wither. If, therefore, their poetry speaks up for images of life which need renewing and if it stifles for lack of air and attention, the images themselves will die, and the possibilities of future life constrict once again.

The document in question is the eponymous essay in A. Alvarez' book *Beyond All This Fiddle*[5] ('fiddle' of course means poetry) which first appeared in the *TLS* for March 23rd 1967 and was solemnly applauded by the editorial. Alvarez is an important figure in any discussion of contemporary poetry because his anthology *The New Poetry*,[6] it is true to say, provides much of the contemporary poetry best known to many specialist students and nearly all the others. If it was simply a matter of knowing those poets and no others, one might be less discomposed for, his theories notwithstanding, the editor has allowed some good poems and poets into his volume. But I am principally troubled about the theories that go with the selection, for these seem to me about as dangerous and exclusive as one could wish to find, and their accessibility (endorsed by George Macbeth's repellently named *Penguin Book of Sick Verse* (1965), the recent Corgi Selection *Love, Love, Love* and the stomach-turning cant of the pop scene) and attractive simplifications have given them widespread currency. I would like to spend this essay dismantling the arguments on which the statements rest, for they are gimcrack structures, but the job will be better done by summary and contrast with a selection of poets whom I shall quote from and recommend and who may be taken, in their diverse ways, to stand out against the comfortable recipes of genocide and psychic upheaval which Mr Alvarez prescribes for all those poets tongued with the grace of *Zeitgeist*. And in any case, it is in the restatements of his first essay that Alvarez seems to come nearest to being serious about what he says, or at least to wearing his rather raffish desperation with the air of being able to justify it intellectually. Indeed, part of the interest of the essay is that he has not surrendered to the really unforgivable *trahison des clercs* which lapses nervelessly into the pop world. Though he toys with that world, he does not pretend that it is necessary for human solidarity and breadth to sink yourself in it. In synopsis, his argument is this: at a time when cultural promotion and trend-spotting is big business, the poet is deprived of a working style and is consequently left with the responsibility of psychic exploration. Tradition has lapsed; in the shifting, provisional, glittering world (I do not parody) of pop, mass technology and endless change, privacy is the only truth. In this privacy, the poet–prompted by psycho-analysis–cultivates a cool, transparent honesty, and in the lucidity of verse discovers and explores the world of violence, duplicity, horror and illusion within which, of course, we all live everyday but which is only externalized in concentration camps and H-bombs. Well, as one might murmur, 'John dos Passos could have done it', could have caught in parody the air of persuasive cogency, of logical inevitability with which the thing is done.

Sylvia Plath's is a logical extension of Lowell's explorations: she simply went further in the direction he had already taken. For her, it turned out to be a one-way street from which there was no going back. So she went to the extreme, far edge of the bearable, and, in the end, slipped over ... Extremist art becomes a premonition of the holocaust, while its slightly schizophrenic detachment from its own anguish corresponds to the split in the environment between violence and cosiness, war and well-being ... Given a situation so precarious, internal confusion transmuted into new kinds of artistic order becomes the most possible form of coherence.[7]

The exploitation of such exceedingly delicate terms as 'schizophrenic' seems to me fashionably allusive, as a way of not raising the essential social and moral questions about Sylvia Plath's poetry. And what on earth is that sentence doing of which the key phrase is 'corresponds to the split'? Which split? *Corresponds*? But by this stage there is no checking the trenchancy and illusory vigour, the brisk aplomb with which the essay advances. One may object that all the efforts of psychiatrists are directed towards unifying what is dislocated, to the long and strenuous labour of affirming sanity and centrality, and not of finding ways to lose them, towards discovering and defining again what is meant by humanity, tenderness, patience and love, not towards the dereliction of these qualities. It would seem not so much a matter of courage to pursue extremism, but a matter of self-indulgence and sensationalism, that these are trivial ends sponsored by boredom, and as has been finely said in another context, out of triviality comes evil. In all this, the virtue Alvarez finds himself able to endorse is

a certain Jewishness. I mean Judaism not as a narrow orthodoxy but as a force working perennially on the side of sanity. It is, after all, the one great secular religion, a religion with no belief in the afterlife, and founded on a social ethic of respect, responsibility and family piety. Hence it is empirical in its attitude to experience, pragmatic and hard-minded.[8]

By an extraordinary paradox, Alvarez ends up ratifying those qualities—'sceptical, non-idealistic' which most commend themselves to the English and American capitalist bourgeoisie, and the complementary extremism of his approved *avant-gardistes* comes to sound like an obverse of vulgar exoticism. His argument seems to me trivial, as well as an awful warning against an over-readiness to take new bearings, for the danger is that one charts only what confirms a course to a chosen end and leaves out everything else. This essay proposes some alternative readings. I am aware that all I have said marks me as one who has not had bestowed upon him the grace of the *Zeitgeist*, and that to talk like this is, in turn, to be in danger of grudgingness and tightness of mind. Alvarez (and the host of new-criers, from Marshall McLuhan to Edmund Leach) would tell me that I simply haven't noticed how bad things are, how the old order has decayed and the old standards have cracked and broken outwards. Well, at the risk of these accusals, let me assert that the function of poetry is to fortify and replenish the human spirit rather than to chasten and diminish it, to affirm and celebrate life and ways of living[9] rather than to settle for blankness, fatigue, defeat and misery. *Is* it hopelessly nostalgic and timorous to rejoice in Wordsworth's definition of a poet?

... a man speaking to men: a man it is true, endued with more lively sensibility, more enthusiasm and tenderness, who has a greater knowledge of human nature, and a more comprehensive soul, than

ENGLISH AND AMERICAN POETRY

are supposed to be common among mankind; a man pleased with his own passions and volitions, and who rejoices more than other men in the spirit of life that is in him; delighting to contemplate similar volitions and passions as manifested in the goings-on of the Universe, and habitually impelled to create them where he does not find them.[10]

It is not as though Wordsworth insulated himself from the realities of life. He had, after all, his own horrors to contemplate: a child and lover lost, the shocking brutalities of the Terror, mad mothers and idiot boys, but he managed to rejoice in them. Wordsworth, as any serious poet, searched and spoke out for 'a central, a truly human point of view', and, greater than 'a point of view', made real in his poetry a robust moral sanity, that eager and spontaneous response to life which comes only from long, disciplined labour and habits of reflection. If such a poet has been superseded in the drift to the destined apocalypse, then Heaven help us.

His supercession (which I shall contest) is happily accepted by the admirers of Philip Larkin, the normative poet–if for the moment we set aside the troubadours of Courtly Love on Merseyside[11]–for those who do not traverse the galaxies of inner space. Rather, his verse interlocks with the extremists. His casual smallness is the social corollary of an intense subjectivism: both forms of poetry prevent the dimensions either of the metaphysical, the political, or the non-human pressing upon us. The *only* claim admitted is to human interest. Sometimes the interest is smart and wry, and suffused with a vague poeticism, as in the much-admired *Church-Going*[12]; sometimes it is more knowing and ambivalent:

> The fathers with broad belts under their suits
> And seamy foreheads: mothers loud and fat;
> An uncle shouting smut; and then the perms,
> The nylon-gloves and jewellery–substitutes,
> The lemons, mauves, and olive-ochres that
>
> Marked off the girls unreally from the rest.

'Notice', as the poet might say confidentially, 'notice how neutrally I register this quite impossible and revolting vulgarity.

I don't say these good people are vulgar, now do I? Don't impute to me . . .' and he spreads out his hands in mock helplessness. But though he so often is, he mustn't be allowed to get away with such crude caricature. There is no edge or extensiveness of experience felt to be present here in a way that would permit selection of this order–none of the fineness of feeling which justifies Eliot's vision of desolation in *The Waste Land* (though that too has its mean-minded stereotypes: consider the typist's seduction, and see how far Larkin falls below even *that*). In spite of what Charles Tomlinson savagely and rightly calls Larkin's 'tenderly nursed sense of defeat'[13], Larkin won't really allow alternative actions even where he sees his own–ruefully, of course–as stunted and ungrateful. So the man in *Dockery and Son* has to be a bonhomous and unselfaware oaf if he can already be father to an undergraduate, while Larkin himself is still wandering about in the bachelor cold. And he only gives himself the chance to write with a greater opulence and fluency in order to deny that it can be done. For example, in *Love Songs in Age*, a widow coming across old songbooks has felt herself pierced by a brilliant nostalgia.

> But, even more,
> The glare of that much mentioned brilliance, love,
>   Broke out, to show
> Its bright incipience sailing above,
> Still promising to solve and satisfy,
> And set unchangeably in order. So
>   To pile them back, to cry,
> Was hard, without lamely admitting how
> It had not done so then, and could not now.

Larkin has certainly an ear for cadence and for easy, unforced utterance, but he cannot leave noble images alone without rigging them to do his dirty work for him. Love, you see, is 'much mentioned' (and therefore an evasion); it makes the same old promises which turn out to be the same old frauds. The most cursory reading of the folksongs in *The Idiom of the People* will make it clear that Larkin fiddles his definition of love into a final 'solution', an 'unchangeable order'. 'Unchangeable'? As soon love the pepper-pot. But the fraud Larkin works on us is hidden behind the modulation into a richer poeticality which gives off an aroma of significance without needing to have any.

> We slowed again
> And as the tightened brakes took hold, there swelled
> A sense of falling, like an arrow-shower
> Sent out of sight, somewhere becoming rain.
>
> *(The Whitsun Weddings)*

The lines are rather beautiful—vivid and haunting in cadence and in the experience caught. But they are bogus; they move us to nowhere in particular. They do not clinch the poem; they just stop it, *rallentando*.

Larkin takes large subjects—the 'significance of contemporary living'—and walks around them. His desolate report on the living is fatal only to himself, because he bodies forth no image of what fineness of living or value might be like. The mild neutrality of tone comes to seem studied, and the shallowness of feeling evidences a writer who does not earn his rueful, oblique and sometimes ugly perception of emptiness. Even Betjeman's suburban nostalgia means more than Larkin's predominant listlessness; it is much more generous. But not all contemporary poetry is either confessional [*sic*] or low-spirited and it is worth turning to those poets whose strategies, in language, rhythm, form and decorum make some kind of continuity honestly credible.

I could briefly begin by urging upon English attention three American poets who have real claims to be grouped with the pioneers of the modern movement when that phrase means Eliot, Pound, Yeats and Lawrence. American literature just now is going through a period of drastic overvaluation which is intensified by the cult of contemporaneity in new University courses. None the less, there are fine poets nothing like well enough known from American literature since 1920, and the three with whom readers might begin are Wallace Stevens, W. C. Williams, and, less considerable but neglected, E. A. Robinson. Stevens and Williams are coming into their own a little now, and Stevens indeed is becoming in need of a much sharper treatment in discrimination for he was a copious writer and did not blot enough of his lines. What is tending to happen is that as he comes under the full footnoted and variorum treatment from the scholars and his smallest poems are quarried for statements of his strange epistemology, the main body of his work is simply not assimilated into the texture of people's reading. It does not soak into the bone of our reading, as I think we can say Eliot's work has. Stevens has not penetrated to the centre of our literary intelligences, and it is high time that he did.

He was shaped by the wealth and connections of New England and Connecticut, by the Harvard of the Genteel Tradition, and his poetry, though often peculiar and exotic and drenchingly perfumed, is deeply traditional while it makes something new of its traditions. The fundamental theme of his poetry is grave and permanent; it is the problem of sorting a coherent world out of the chaos of particulars which remain when religious belief is withdrawn. The world is sensory, it has its delights, its disorder, and it is mortal. But the human intelligence is restless, and would make its own order. In the following poem, Stevens describes an intellectual experience known to us all. The reader, alone and intent, becomes absorbed in his reading in such a way that the book becomes transparent in the realization of its truth. In this way, we say, literature becomes a part of us; the book soaks into the mind, it alters the mind, it reshapes the life around us. The language of the poem is plain, the tone serene and imperturbable, the rhythms lovely and right.

> The house was quiet and the world was calm.
> The reader became the book; and summer night
>
> Was like the conscious being of the book.
> The house was quiet and the world was calm.
>
> The words were spoken as if there was no book,
> Except that the reader leaned above the page,
>
> Wanted to lean, wanted much most to be
> The scholar to whom his book is true, to whom
>
> The summer night is like a perfection of thought.
> The house was quiet because it had to be.

> The quiet was part of the meaning, part of the mind:
> The access of perfection to the page.
>
> And the world was calm. The truth in a calm world,
> In which there is no other meaning, itself
>
> Is calm, itself is summer and night, itself
> Is the reader leaning late and reading there.
> (Untitled, 1946)

One could turn to this endlessly to particularize its virtues. The voice of the utterance is distinctively Stevens' own. He has taken what he had to learn from the past, but the speech is our speech. Stevens needs setting in the canon of the greatest modern poets, and he is not often to be found there by many of our students and teachers. Stevens, like Eliot and unlike Yeats whose efforts so often collapse inwards in a heap of old fabrication, found for himself a centre of unity. He is able to move difficult abstractions from philosophy into the opulent, fecund, dandified but *accessible* speech of his poetic. From *Sunday Morning* (1915), one of the greatest poems of the century, Stevens moves imperturbably onward, constantly checking and resettling his profound and beautiful vision of a world robbed of religious unity and superhuman meaning. He remains steadily open to the creation of the new images by which we need to steer, and when he experiences despair, he does so with a dignity and assurance that re-forms despair into something positive and possible.

> There was a crush of strength in a grinding going round,
> Under the front of the westward evening star,
>
> The vigor of glory, a glittering in the veins,
> As things emerged and moved and were dissolved,
>
> Either in distance, change or nothingness,
> The visible transformations of summer night,
>
> An argentine abstraction approaching form
> And suddenly denying itself away . . .
> (From *Reality is an Activity of the Most August Imagination* 1955)

Stevens purchases his superb eloquence at the cost of leaving out too much of the everyday world and all of the political world.

The omissions are very serious. He managed to build a credible metaphysic but the fabulous wealth of Hertford insurance prevented his ever looking outwards to the large motions of societies, and he remained blind to the most urgent reality of international contradiction. Yet homage is due to much: along with what is overwritten or emasculate, there is a solid body of work which in precision, magnificence, and intellectual sense surpasses a lot of Yeats and all of Pound, and his solutions to moral and theological problems are a good deal sounder than Yeats's.

W. C. Williams is getting a good deal of attention now; his name is better known in this country than ever before. He has a good deal to answer for, in the feckless obscurity of some of his verse, in his mischievous irresponsibility whenever he made one of his rare statements about writing, and the way in which some of his theories and a few of his poems have been used by younger writers to defend their own wilful unintelligibility. I am not being silly if I say that I do not understand a line of many poems by Louis Zukovsky and Charles Olson. But at their best, Williams's poems have a lean, sinewy fidelity to voice and feeling, the curve of the poem drawn tight by the unaffected, laconic drawl of the voice. He is then a stylist, minute and finished, and he controls the free verse movement by the succinctness of his line lengths, the touch which places sensory detail and brave statement delicately alongside each other.

> They enter the new world naked,
> cold, uncertain of all
> save that they enter. All about them
> the cold familiar wind–
>
> Now the grass, tomorrow
> the stiff curl of wildcarrot leaf
>
> One by one objects are defined–
> It quickens: clarity, outline of leaf
>
> But now the stark dignity of
> entrance–still, the profound change
>
> has come upon them: rooted they
> grip down and begin to awaken.
> *(By the road to the contagious hospital)*

Williams rarely fails to treat his world with affection and dignity. The subject here, spring and the growth to the life, is important, the writing plain and intense, the speech humane. The treatment is less traditional than in Stevens, but the poem looks and behaves like a poem, and one can understand it. Williams worked a style which is less eloquent than Stevens's (whose was the heritage of Harvard, Tennyson and Keats) but in which the poet's work may push onward through everyday experience.

The last of the three hostages named as belonging to the pioneers of modern poetry in summary does not look a pioneer at all. E. A. Robinson kept mostly to the pentameter, he wrote (for goodness' sake!) Arthurian romances and sonnets, and he believed in the power of reason. But he could match Yeats for piercing loveliness of cadence and, again, his moral statements are a good deal more defensible. They amount to what sometimes looks like a rather grim if courageous endurance, but the stoicism is suffused with an elegance of movement, inflexions of such sweetness and dignity that much more than mere endurance is embodied in the total effect. As here:

> When we parted
> I told her I should see the King again,
> And, having seen him, might go back again
> To see her face once more. But I shall see
> No more the Lady Vivian. Let her love
> What man she may, no other love than mine
> Shall be an index of her memories.
> I fear no man who may come after me,
> And I see none. I see her, still in green,
> Beside the fountain. I shall not go back . . .
>   If I come not,
> The Lady Vivian will remember me,
> And say: 'I knew him when his heart was young,
> Though I have lost him now. Time called him home,
> And that was as it was; for much is lost
> Between Broceliande and Camelot.' (*Merlin*, 11, 757–81)

Robinson is slighted for his crypto-Victorian effects, but if this kind of verse is dated Victorianism, so much the worse for the moderns. It is quite as difficult now as then—as for Shakespeare in the sonnets—to write pentameters which are firm, upright, graceful and more than just mellifluous. Robinson can write such verse, and we cannot afford not to read it. This is why I include in this brief and eclectic guide the work of a poet who died long before 1945, my approximate starting point. Robinson shut his mind to the revolutionary effects of Pound's and Eliot's poetry, but this does not mean that he lost himself in a doomed attempt to recover the past. What, after all, do we mean by 'modernity'? Too often, it becomes a matter of making things look new at all costs, which in turn sets up a reflex resistance to anything which appears in Robinson's kind of dress.[14] His world is not one which reaches into a dark nexus of fear; it is not impending or violent. On the contrary, his sense of order, gracefulness and clarity are called to the service of traditional concepts. At his best, he does not baulk the difficulty of doing this; his poems are often about the disjuncture between those resonant images and the defeats they now suffer. He gives us the defeat and victory possible when you hold by the old terms, and this is his modernity. It is worth adding that some of Robinson's short poems which celebrate in a wry way, the solitude and toughness of various derelicts and down-and-outs—I am thinking of poems like *Mr Flood's Party* and *Aaron Stark*—are convenient entrances for students in that they take what at first sight looks like social conscience-stricken subjects. The anxious clichés marshalled by the surface appearance of the poems are struck away by the poet's mocking sharpness. Robinson's irony is an altogether more astringent matter than Philip Larkin's.

An essay like this can lapse into a smart review dispatching every volume with brisk facility into its proper slot. There is a colossal flood of poetry cascading from large and small houses alike, and from the quarterlies. It's hardly surprising that, in so bewildering and contradictory a crowd, it should seem a relief if the critic (and the student) can manage to recognize a set of mannerisms which recur, which are describable and which may be classified as a style. It is the fault of pedagogic habits of mind that students (and critics) look for schools and movements in poetry, for tendencies and revolutions. Thus they typically learn to describe the Romantic qualities of the Romantic poets, and more narrowly, the Keatsishness of Keats. They do not learn how to discover and describe the good poems, nor what is to be said in favour of Keatsishness. The basis of too much literature teaching is historicism, and the result is that the readers of poetry think of the poems they study as 'representative' of this or that, as possessing certain qualities appropriate to their time which may be catalogued but not understood. Typically, the reader learns to understand a poem *in terms of* its context and never to understand it as a unique performance of special intentions.[15] He is consequently helpless to identify the differences between Goldsmith and Crabbe, both as to treatment and as to intelligence, though in some unexamined way he feels that there must be something wrong with a poet who goes on writing heroic couplets when he must have noticed that he had been superseded by the revolution. The same situation obtains in discussion of contemporary writing, which is treated in the same way as the object of this academic historicism. The result is a kind of determinism, which teaches that poetry reflects the subject-matter of its time, and where it does not it may be derided as genteel or backward-looking. The facts of literary history are real and should be a part of a study. The poetic revolutions and innovations are part of the facts, and we need to understand them if we are to do our work. But the historical facts too often are a refuge for those who are unable to discover a good poem, or they are a refuge for those (there are many) who are frightened of a good poem and find protection in an historical relativism which insists on the difference and the insulation of man from man, and age from age. A desirable determination to find out exactly what Shakespeare meant can involve a refusal to accept that he ever meant what we would mean or that his feelings were ever like ours. Similarly, a settled determinism in the face of twentieth-century violence breeds not a wise but a cosy passiveness. With the same effortless fluency, the historical critic may absolve himself from responding to Shakespeare or to the poetry of his own time. Empson deals all the smacks necessary:

> Waiting for the end, boys, waiting for the end.
> What is there to be or do?

What's become of me or you?
Are we kind or are we true?
Sitting two and two, boys, waiting for the end.

Waiting for the end, boys, waiting for the end.
Not a chance of blend, boys, things have got to tend.
Think of those who vend, boys, think of how we mend,
Waiting for the end, boys, waiting for the end.

(Just a Smack at Auden)[16]

In the theories parodied here, we are waiting for the last revolution, and trend-spotting becomes the game played by the same rules as end-spotting. One looks out for revolutions since innovation remains the only light in the gloom of ennui. Making it new can be the only interest in a world deprived of its fixed points. Let me protest. The greatest poems in English have more in common with each other than with the schools to which they belong. One would be grateful if someone could do for literature what the genius of Dr Pevsner has done for art, and write an essay called 'The Englishness of English Poetry' (the relations to which of key American poets would not exculpate them from peculiar responsibilities to an American tradition). The Englishness lives distinctly in the poetry of a central line of men. It is not falsifying their historical context to say that their Englishness transpires in the distinctions of declaration, the steadfast, hard density of language and utterance in these plain, sturdy voices[17]: in Shakespeare's *Sonnet 64* and *73*, in Ben Jonson's *Farewell to the World* and *To Penshurst*, in Johnson's *Vanity of Human Wishes*, in Pope's stirring vision of a great metropolis in *The Use of Riches*, in much of Crabbe, in Wordsworth, especially in the tale of Margaret from *The Excursion*, in *Ode to Autumn*, in Hardy's greatest poems, such as *After a Journey* or *Neutral Tones*, in Edward Thomas's *As the Team's Head-Brass*, *Home* or *Lights Out*. A close comparison of such poems suggests a way of coming at the living centre of the English language; this configuration embodies the vitality of our moral history. This is what that difficult word 'tradition' may mean. Not some hopefully Platonic dance of ideal poets, for all these men are of different stature and enormously different contexts, but their essential speech, the gravity and upright dignity of

ENGLISH AND AMERICAN POETRY 77

their utterance rings in each case strikingly alike. Here is the history of our poetry, and if we believe that continuity is possible and important, that there is no inevitable need to relinquish civilization to a chaotic flux whose only value is change, then it is worth sorting amongst the bewildering host of poetry volumes for voices which sound something like those we listen to as to masters.

It's odd, therefore, that a teacher who would want to urge innumerable and radical changes all through our society, is none the less vocal in the interests of reaction and conservatism in literature. I believe there are a number of teachers who feel that way, to their surprise and amusement; who, without at all subscribing either to the apocalyptic movement or to an obstinate nostalgia for a lost age, urge the pressing need to take from the past what it has to give, to labour in recovery of what is lost and irreplaceable. It's important not to be misunderstood here. We cannot recreate the past. But our language is a constant mediator between past and present. It takes in (or neglects) the radically new concepts and in absorbing them the reciprocal pressures of old ideas and forms displace and redistribute themselves. They are not crudely usurped; they take new outlines. Historical dialectic generates movement by dynamic contradictions between its parts. One might cite the pentameter. I suppose it is a heresy to say there is only one correct form: certainly there are beautiful poems in free verse, and I shall quote some. But the pentameter embodies centuries of craftsmanship and wisdom; it is capable alike of conversational ease and of majesty; it can move with unrivalled loveliness. It is suicidal to throw away the traditional forms now when we need their sanctions and order more than ever. It is also a heresy to suppose that in writing like this a full half-century after *Prufrock* came out the pentameter is beyond resurrection. It is there, living and moving in our everyday speech. One does not need a formal training in prosody, but one does need an ear. Few people are tone-deaf. If we train ourselves, we will hear the pentameter, and when we can hear it, we may use it.

The following pentameters come from an English poet, who, in his single-minded courage as well as his command over his rich traditions, is doing much to sustain continuity and to comprehend unprecedented experience, to discharge, in other words, the function of the poet. His subjects are great ones; without blinking the horrors of life, the subjects permit affirmation and beauty, and the treatment is unfailingly large, noble and compelling. The poet is F. T. Prince.

> Drenched in the silver of old olive-trees,
> The little bay lies empty, in a trance.
> I watch the far sea bathed in pale blue light,
> And on the rough sea-wall the tone of time
> Comes out, and on the fundamental rock
> Scored over, lights and shadows pause and pass;
> And there the memory of some one face
> Yet living, some transparent thought at gaze,
> And looking from deep lids where it had nested
> As if it were a breath, a truce, a peace,
> Safeguards our happiness, that is and needs
> Nothing but a deep gazing on our love.
> *(Gregory Nazianzen)*

The quotation should suffice to establish that in recommending the pentameter, I have not got in mind the chatty and chattering use made of it by John Wain, nor the flatness of Elizabeth Jennings. This writing has a resonance and an impersonal seriousness where theirs is amateur. Nowadays it takes courage as well as great gifts to launch on statements of such gravity, and beside this, as most of Prince's work, the familiar poets of the anthologies and Poetry Book society are so slight as to be invisible. Saying this, there are a dozen misunderstandings to guard against. There can be fine poems written in a less stately style; there can–there must–be poems of harsh stricture against what is deathly or repulsive; there can be comical poems and throwaway poems. But unless the language and music of a national poetry are capable of nobility like this, then we are living in an un-serious world.[18] Such a world may be right in regarding 'confessional' poetry as the best it can do, but it ought to know what has been lost. As long as Prince writes all is not lost. At the level of sensuous perception, the poem is very lovely–the movement liquid, the details haunting and serene. But the poet charges the details with intense moral significance. The adjective 'fundamental' and the piercing phrase 'the tone of time' advert us that this charging is happening, and then Prince gives us the steady peace of the closing six lines. Where else can one find such lazy eloquence in the maintenance of such full life in the present? Prince maintains life, with intelligent resolution and with human faith. This poem takes divine love for its subject; many of his other poems treat human love, and treat it as something solid, hard of discovery, but actual. No one would deprecate the pressures human love has to bear (has always borne), but one may work to create it and it is good. It needs such help as Prince gives it. Not, however, that either kind of love is his only subject. *The Old Age of Michelangelo* is what it says it is: a monologue by the greatest European sculptor about his art and himself. It utterly outstrips Browning's and Pound's (and Lucie-Smith's) similar efforts and, while facing the harshness and desolation inevitable to an artist, realizes again his function. One simply cannot say that the force for life in Michelangelo which Prince honours and reviews are no longer relevant to our living. And the method here and in a comparable poem, *Strafford*, is a great deal more direct and available than that of (say) *The Cantos* or *Paterson*. He takes actual historical subjects and, recounting details of their lives with great beauty, is at liberty when he likes to generalize. The subjects are important; they touch civilization at its centres; they repose at a suitable historical distance, and they permit generalizations of great power about art and politics. No doubt there are flaws in the writing, but the method is unimpeachable and deserves imitation. I would like to quote extensively, but there is not room. The standard of writing in this volume is amazingly consistent. Prince, I would say, is unrivalled in England. Those who find they can share my admiration should go on to read Seamus Heaney's volumes *Death of a Naturalist* and *Door Into The Dark*. Heaney is only just over thirty and he is not at all a 'follower' of Prince (he may well not have read any of his verse); I have put the argument against the taxonomy of poetry. But Heaney, perhaps more luckily equipped than most of us in coming from rural Ireland, takes familiar subjects— churning milk, brambling, his family, his marriage–and honours them. The tenderness and actuality with which he treats them are the subjects of the poems, and if his gifts are less large than those of Ted Hughes, whose poems are already well-known, he is less wilful and less mistaken about the springs of his inspiration and the nature of his insights. Hughes in fact is a critical subject, for his second volume *Wodwo*[19] contains only a very small amount of writing in which he does not succumb to that incomplete and violent parody of the *Zeitgeist* celebrated by Alvarez. These few poems—poems such as *Full Moon* and *Little Frieda*—are successful but his long silence before publication and the extreme patchiness of the result implies that he now does not know where to turn for his subjects and is too honest to jack up his generous talent in the production of such non-poetry as wins the Poetry Book Society nominations. Comparably, Heaney is going to have to work extremely hard if he is not to shrink into an agreeably domestic poet. I'd like to go on record as saying I think that he will take the honourable risks.

I would like to set two American poets firmly beside F. T. Prince, and in a modest way, as part of the main English tradition I described. Yvor Winters and J. V. Cunningham, once Winters' pupil, are both poets who have, as a matter of programme as well as temperament, set themselves to reanimate traditional patterns. There is no illicit trading in their verse with a rejected rhetoric; their poems are at once modern and powerfully conventional. Their voices are modern while their poems specify the potential of their traditions. As in this love poem of Cunningham's, where the daring use of octosyllabic blank verse excites both astonishment and recognition.

> The night is still. The unfailing surf
> In passion and subsidence moves
> As at a distance. The glass walls,
> And redwood, are my utmost being.
> And is there there in the last shadow,
> There in the final privacies
> Of unaccosted grace,—is there,
> Gracing the tedium to death,
> An intimation? Something much
> Like love, like loneliness adrowse
> In states more primitive than peace,
> In the warm wonder of winter sun.
> (from *To What Strangers, What Welcome*)

It is a poem of some metaphysical sternness. It moves with pensive hesitation to its elusive end, yet the cadences and diction are firm, wonderfully precise, and elegant. The poem's surface is smooth and tight, and though the thought is not easy, Cunningham renders immediate an experience anyone over sixteen must know; the scaring, seductive tension on the edge of a relationship which is about to become keener than was expected. The poem comes from a sequence which describes a love affair as it moves from loneliness through knowledge to intimacy, loss and painful regret. In *Las Vegas*, the poet records the disgusting and comic ugliness possible in human desire,

> Her ass twitching as if it had the fits,
> Her gold crotch grinding, her athletic tits,
> One clock, the other counterclockwise twirling,
> It was enough to stop a man from girling.

And in the end, with a fully adult disenchantment, he faces the loss of what must be lost. The wisdom accrues to life in spite of the pain.

> I sit in the last warmth
> Of a New England fall, and I?
> A premise of identity
> Where the lost hurries to be lost,
> Both in its own best interests
> And in the interests of life.

Cunningham's unusual strength reposes in his unfettered use of big, blunt words, 'life' 'grace' 'wonder' 'love', all netted in the ease of his speech. The love affair comes actual in the verse, but Cunningham also makes the reader know the press of extra-human moral sanctions at the back of the individual's actions. The poetry sets itself to make a morality, and its potentiality bulks larger than its quiet courtesy releases.

Winters' verse sometimes has a slightly more ponderous step, a less delicate touch, but it is the work of a strong man, deeply engaged. It is significant that when the *Collected Poems* were published for the first time in this country in 1963 the *New Statesman* reviewer felt that all he need do was quote the deliberate archaism of the sonnet to Melville, lean on the solidarity of fashion and wait for laughs. Well, risibility at the expense of lines like these may be left to itself; the damage done is so obviously not to the poet.

> Incarnate for our marriage you appeared,
> Flesh living in the spirit and endeared
> By minor graces and slow sensual change.
> Through every nerve we made our spirits range.
> We fed our minds on every mortal thing:
> The lacy fronds of carrots in the spring,
> Their flesh sweet on the tongue, the salty wine
> From bitter grapes, which gathered through the vine
> The mineral drouth of autumn concentrate,
> Wild spring in dream escaping, the debate
> Of flesh and spirit on those vernal nights,
> Its resolution in naïve delights,
> The young kids bleating softly in the rain—
> All this to pass, not to return again.
> And when I found your flesh did not resist,
> It was the living spirit that I kissed,
> It was the spirit's change in which I lay:
> Thus, mind in mind we waited for the day.
> When flesh shall fall away, and, falling, stand
> Wrinkling with shadow over face and hand,
> Still I shall meet you on the verge of dust
> And know you as a faithful vestige must.
> And, in commemoration of our lust,
> May our heirs seal us in a single urn,
> A single spirit never to return.
>
> (*The Marriage*)

The constellation of fixed points in this universe are marriage and children, literature and the University. The manner of the poem is heroic: to win a certainty for poetic statement, to cut away all ambiguity from around the lines so that the statement is clear, hard, definite. The statement gets its density from the force and conviction with which Winters re-creates his poetic context. Within the poems one feels the push of a particular history (*John Day, Frontiersman, John Sutter*), an opulent beauty

ENGLISH AND AMERICAN POETRY

of landscape in which poet and history are rooted (*On a View of Pasadena, In Praise of California Wines*) and an accurate morality (*The Marriage, Time and the Garden*). If, as Hopkins said, it is the vice of distinctiveness to tend towards oddity, it is a cost weighed, paid and worth paying by Winters. In their turn, two men now about forty have built on what they have learned from Winters and Cunningham, and have made the buildings their own property. The work of John Williams and Alan Stephens (in *The Necessary Lie* and *Between Matter and Principle*) bears honourable witness that it is as profitless to generalize about the U.S.A. as about anywhere else, and that the work of John Berryman may well be as unrepresentative as I believe it to be bad.

One piece of neat mockery by Alan Stephens summarizes the difficulties of writing poetry just now. It is written in syllabics; that is, the only rule is that the lines contain a given number of syllables, here seven (an even number would sound normally metrical). The poem is a parody on the method.

> After he concluded that
> he did not wish to raise his
> voice when he spoke of such mat-
> ters as the collapse of the
>
> Something Empire, or of things
> the folk suffer from, he sim-
> ply set in words such meanings
> as were there, and then, when he
>
> finished the final verse, van-
> ished in the blank below it . . .
>
> <div align="right">(<i>syllabics for T.G.</i>)</div>

I would like to end by calling attention (with the odd digression) to two poets who do try to speak of such matters as the things the folk suffer from. The men I choose are Charles Tomlinson and Edward Dorn and although of a number of candidates they seem to me the best, I am as much interested in the directions their work points at as in their achievement at the mid-point of their careers. Tomlinson's name is well-known; Dorn, an American of forty, is slowly gathering a reputation after publication of two handsome volumes by the new (and admirable)

Fulcrum Press. Both men, I am sure, have read pretty closely in the main line twentieth-century poetry, in Stevens and Williams as well as Eliot and Yeats, and Tomlinson at least has had something to learn from Hardy's tranquillity and toughness of spirit. But I am not trying to chart influences here[20]: it is always a chancy and rarely an illuminating exercise in clairvoyance. What I am trying to do is to point at the ways these poets have opened themselves to the multifariousness and complexity of modern poetry, and can show for it that rare saturation in experience which must precede imaginative insight of any stamina. Negative capability, yes; but also a sure, astonishingly rapid apprehension of moral form in experience.

Tomlinson is the stronger of the two poets, though a mixture of sardonic callousness and a denial, at times, of a necessary involvement vitiate some poems. In his case, I am more concerned that students may confine their reading to a few early poems, and miss among other his sharpness of judgement and active humour in *American Scenes*. He points his satire by ironic allusion to the beauty of art, architecture and life which he knows and feels as possible elsewhere. The comic play in the following lines between the desert motel with its photograph of Roy Rogers, the cowboy myth-hero, and the faultless selection of rich gestures controls and judges the poet's repugnance before the irreducible nastiness of modern American townscape.

> Nervy with neons, the main drag
> was all there was. A placeless place.
> A faint flavour of Mexico in the tacos
> tasting of gasoline. Trucks refuelled
> before taking off through space. Someone lived
> in the houses with their houseyards wired
> like tiny Belsens, The Gotterdämmerung
> would be like this. No funeral pyres, no choirs
> of lost trombones. An Untergang
> without a clang, without
> a glimmer of gone glory
> however dimmed. At the motel desk
> was a photograph of Roy Rogers
> signed. It was here
> he made a stay. He did not

>   ride away on Trigger
>   through the high night, the tilted
>   Pleiades overhead, the polestar low, no
>   going off until
>   the eyes of beer-cans
>   had ceased to glint at him
>   and the desert darknesses
>   had quenched the neons. He was spent.
>   He was content. Down he lay.
>   The passing trucks patrolled his sleep,
>   the shifting gears contrived
>   a muffled fugue against the fading of his day
>   and his dustless, undishonoured stetson rode
>   beside the bed,
>   glowed in the pulsating, never-final twilight
>   there, at that execrable conjunction
>   of gasoline and desert air.
>
>   (*At Barstow*)

The slight internal rhymes consolidate the masterly tightness of the free verse. The light comedy of the tone plays upon the surface of deep feelings. Not that Tomlinson may be thought of as at all limited by his satirical intentions. The satire is confidently poised to take off into the angry hatred of a poisoned English landscape bonded into the rich evaluation of a given human life such as we find maturely balanced in *John Maydew, or The Allotment*. Tomlinson when he is not mannered is very good indeed. He is capable of celebration of ways of life which would invite an easy nostalgia of a lesser poet, while he offers them justice and wisdom (*Return to Hinton, The Churchyard Wall*); he can be harsh and chastening when it is called for (*On the Hall at Stowey*); he can be very funny; he can be haunting and lovely in his cadences (*At Wells: polyphony*). Best of all, he can see and revere the otherness of things, the mysteries or godlessness of non-human creation; in his plainness and clarity and decisive carriage, his absence of self-obsession, he is a far more truthful and trustworthy poet than the R. S. Thomas and Geoffrey Hill with whom he has been disadvantageously contrasted for their more dramatic feelings.

Edward Dorn's nerve-ends are more exposed, and though

directly an imitator of William Carlos Williams, he tangles himself occasionally in tiresome vulgarities and indecency. One may applaud the attempt on Dorn's, Olson's, Williams's part (and Whitman's) to let the humdrum, messy, squalid world in upon their sensibilities, without condoning messy or vulgar writing. The messiness is partly inevitable when you attempt, as Charles Olson taught the gifted students of Black Mountain College, to let in so much of the outside world upon yourself. I ought probably to have spent some time upon Olson's *Maximus* poems for when you have found your way into them (which is remarkably hard to do)[21] they are bold, ambitious-minded projects as well as maddeningly obscure. But Olson's is a big name in the States and one can't talk about everybody. Dorn is much younger and I hope it is not parochial to say that a real source of interest in his second volume *The North Atlantic Turbine* springs from the contact between this odd, honest imagination and contemporary England. Sometimes he throws a line away because he doesn't want the reader to notice that he can do nothing with it; other times he is just flip and bothersomely offhand. But his most marked source of energy is the powerful anger of a strong man, anger which may issue as irony or laughter or controlled and taut severity but in which no one could mistake the presence of those full and living positives whose mutilation by the ugliness and distortion of society causes this quick and scalding sympathy. (The poem was written, I gather, after a mining disaster expropriated the miners to the profit of the mine-owners.)

> No hesitation
>   would stay me
> from weeping this morning
> for the miners of Hazard Kentucky.
>   The mine owners'
> extortionary skulls
> whose eyes are diamonds don't float
> down the rivers, as they should,
> of the flood
>
>   The miners, cold
> starved, driven from work, in

> their homes float though and float
> on the ribbed ships of their frail
> bodies,
>
>> Oh, go letter,
>> keep my own misery close to theirs
>> associate me with no other honour.
>
> (*Morning Letter*, March 29 1963)

There seems to be a slight waywardness here (*why* no fullstop after 'flood'?), but the free verse is close and firm, the laconic tone manages to convey both anger and tact, and he handles the whole poem with a combination of eloquence and easiness worthy of Thomas Campion. The poem (like *At Barstow* or Winters' *On the Despoilers of Learning*) is an act of intelligent political courage–greater, to make the point, than one will find in Sylvia Plath or Antony Hecht. For comparable kinds of interest in the States I would set by Dorn some of the work of Gary Snyder, Denise Levertov and Robert Duncan. Dorn and Snyder can write muddily; in several poems, after long acquaintance and hard work I have still no idea what they are talking about. But they are fully alive, they have lived through a full and thick experience, they have a sense of history and geography. And they have made convincing efforts to reconcile their light and spontaneous American talking to the baffling, coagulated stuff of technical living. Their constant effort is to be easily and spontaneously truthful about the muffled, complicated society they record and judge. They may bring it off. And with their masters, they have helped to sponsor the derivative but distinctly English beginnings of J. H. Prynne and Elaine Feinstein.

There are of course dozens of names which do not appear in this essay, and some of them deserve reading. Apart from Stevens and Williams, I offer no discussion of older poets whose reputation is pretty well-established or whose work is well-known (Tomlinson though well-known is only forty-three), and it is my experience of those two that they are little read outside one or two university departments. Of the older poets who have published very much in the past twenty years in England, I cannot think there many poems worth turning up. Graves is the obvious exception, and his impressive but closely limited poetry sets greater problems of diagnosis than there is room for here; in any case he is widely read. Hugh MacDiarmid also poses large problems, but he demands an essay to himself, and his best work, the *Hymn to Lenin*,[22] has been with us a long time now. Robert Lowell I shall have to leave to himself and to history. His best poetry is perhaps his early work. Since *The Mills of the Kavanaghs*[23] he has so often chased himself farther and farther into his own head; some recent poems about Vietnam only serve to emphasize this. (I cannot begin to estimate the vast and still growing body of poetry on that terrible subject.) Yet difficult and erratic as he is, he can be magnificent; can be the greatest poet alive.

Finally, of those distinguished poets I would have liked to treat but cannot, I would mention Theodore Roethke whose posthumous collection *The Far Field* was comfortably his best, and who wrote the gladdest love poetry since Yeats's. I think that with William Stafford he will get his reward, and the audience they both deserve. Those I have discussed here are not getting their deserts, or are being in part misunderstood. The ignorance and the misunderstanding arise from theories which are wrong-headed and complacent. The theories are inherent in our cultural fashions and in so far as literature is a part of our morality, then the theories, which are widespread, trivialize our experience. The conceit and sensationalism of the best-selling poets are mistaken for inspiration, and their vulgar rhetoric for afflatus. There is a determined variety of poets who still make sense of transmitted and continuous values, but unless they are more widely read, then the apocalyptic theories will prevail and we shall lose all grasp upon our continuity, and upon the memory of our race. A number of spokesmen have welcomed this rupture as accomplished and irrevocable, and quite a number more have decided to genuflect resignedly to the new world in their company. I am certain the attitude is wrong, and I evidently share this conviction with the poets I mention. If I am right, we need on the part of the teachers and students the most strenuous efforts to throw off corrupt theories and decadent poetry, and to maintain the life and growth of our literature. If we do not make these efforts, we deserve the poetry we get. But the failure would mark a miserably low stage in our history.

A poet's function is to find the points of growth possible to a race and an age, and to nurture them. It is of a significance I cannot take in here that the energy and directions for an English poet at the moment are likely to come from the U.S.A., though this is not necessarily so, and it is by no means axiomatic that the results should appear determinedly 'modern'. In spite of the dismal quality of so much poetry today, in spite of a lowering and maleficent climate ('where does one start in the cold and wet?') poetry is better placed than, temporarily, the moribund novel, because it *can* assimilate the new, arcane language of a technical culture into its poetic diction. Eliot, Stevens, Williams, have shown it how. The novel does not command a language which can integrate the complexities of large economic change and of tiny psychological manœuvre. Poetry can recover these concepts for a literary and spoken language; the men I discuss, in a harsh and stony atmosphere, have launched upon such work. This is not to revive the arid rivalry between poetry and the novel; it is to say that this kind of literature *could* be more likely, as things are, to find an available language in which to create and refine those radiant, fine images by which a civilization must live if it is to know what its treatment of itself is worth. Whether, when spoken, this language will be listened to is another matter.

NOTES

[1] Alasdair MacIntyre, *A Short History of Ethics* (Routledge, 1967), p. 267.

[2] I paraphrase at this point the *May Day Manifesto*, Raymond Williams, ed. (Penguin, 1968), p. 41 ff.

[3] These quotations are all taken from C. B. Cox and A. E. Dyson, *The Practical Criticism of Poetry* (Arnold, 1965), pp. 82-4.

[4] F. R. and Q. D. Leavis, *Lectures in America* (Chatto and Windus, 1969), p. 17.

[5] A. Alvarez, *Beyond All This Fiddle* (Allen Lane, Penguin Press, 1968), pp. 3-21.

[6] A. Alvarez, ed. *The New Poetry* (rev. edition) (Penguin, 1966).

[7] Alvarez, *Beyond All This Fiddle*, p. 17.

[8] Alvarez, op. cit., p. 8.

[9] These admirable formulations are provided by Donald Davie in 'England as a Poetic Subject' *Poetry (Chicago)* 100, 2, 1962, p. 122.

[10] W. Wordsworth, *Preface to Lyrical Ballads*, 1802.

[11] *Their* representative collection is *Poetry of the Underground*, David Horowitz, ed. (Penguin, 1970). These poems are the equivalent of Victorian sentimentalists: the poetaster as bedwarmer. Alvarez was bitterly sharp about the collection (*Observer*, October 31st 1969).

[12] Philip Larkin: *The Whitsun Weddings* (Faber and Faber, 1964). *The Less Deceived* (Marvell Press, 1956).

[13] Charles Tomlinson 'Poetry Today' in B. Ford, ed. *Penguin Guide to English Literature*, Vol. 7. *The Modern Age*, p. 471.

[14] Denis Donoghue to whom I am in debt says some interesting things about Robinson in *Connoisseurs of Chaos* (Faber and Faber, 1966), p. 129 ff.

[15] I paraphrase Quentin Skinner in 'Meaning and Understanding in the History of Ideas', *History and Theory* (U.S.A.) March 1969.

[16] William Empson, *Collected Poems* (Chatto and Windus, 1955), p. 62.

[17] I paraphrase myself here, in *The Elizabethan Poets* (Evans, 1969), pp. 161 ff.

[18] The essential argument about a serious style is made by Ian Robinson, 'Religious English', *Cambridge Quarterly*, 2, 4, Autumn 1967.

[19] Ted Hughes, *Wodwo* (Faber and Faber, 1967), *Crow* (Faber and Faber, 1970): a sequence which does not modify the judgements offered in this paragraph.

[20] cf. Quentin Skinner, 'The Limits of Historical Explanations', *Philosophy*, XLI, July 1966.

[21] I am most grateful to Mr Tom Cain for his guidework here. He advised me that the essential preliminary readings are Olson's *Mayan Letters* (Cape, 1968) and *Call Me Ishmael* (Cape, 1967). A useful history of Black Mountain College by Michael Weaver has just been published.

[22] Hugh MacDiarmid, *Collected Poems* (Oliver and Boyd, 1961).

[23] (Harcourt, Brace and World, New York, 1946). A sequence of poems, *Power*, in *The New York Review of Books*, April 24th 1969, is possible proof of my last assertion about Lowell's gifts.

READING LIST

J. V. Cunningham: *The Exclusions of a Rhyme* (Alan Swallow). *To What Strangers, What Welcome* (Alan Swallow).

Edward Dorn: *Geography* (Fulcrum Press). *The North Atlantic Turbine* (Fulcrum Press).

ENGLISH AND AMERICAN POETRY 91

Robert Duncan: *The Opening of the Field* (Grove Press).

Elaine Feinstein: *In a Green Eye* (Goliard Press).

Denise Levertov: *The Jacob's Ladder* (Cape). *The Sorrow Dance* (Cape).

Robert Lowell: *Poems 1938-1949*. (Faber and Faber). *For the Union Dead* (Faber and Faber). *Selected Poems* (Faber and Faber).

Charles Olson: *The Maximus Poems* I-IV (In Progress) (Cape).

F. T. Prince: *Doors of Stone, Collected Poems 1938-1962* (Hart Davis).

J. H. Prynne: *Kitchen Poems* (Goliard Press). *The White Stones* (Grosseteste Press).

E. A. Robinson: *Collected Poems* (Macmillan). *Selected Poems* (New Directions).

Theodore Roethke: *Collected Poems* (Faber and Faber).

Gary Snyder: *A Range of Poems* (Fulcrum Press).

William Stafford: *West of Your City* (Harper and Row). *Travelling Through the Dark* (Harper and Row).

Alan Stephens: *Between Matter and Principle* (Alan Swallow).

Wallace Stevens: *Collected Poems* (Faber and Faber). *Opus Posthumous* (Faber and Faber). *Selected Poems* (Faber and Faber).

Charles Tomlinson: *Seeing is Believing* (O.U.P.). *A Peopled Landscape* (O.U.P.). *American Scenes* (O.U.P.). *The Way of a World* (O.U.P.).

John Williams: *The Necessary Lie* (Verb).

William Carlos Williams: *Collected Early Poems* (New Directions). *Collected Later Poems* (MacGibbon and Kee). *Pictures from Breughel* (MacGibbon and Kee). *Selected Poems* (New Directions).

Yvor Winters: *Collected Poems* (Routledge).

4

The Contemporary American Novel

SEYMOUR BETSKY

My aim is to convey to a British audience more a sense of the community of America's better writers than anything approaching even a rough hierarchy. The sum is stronger–and ought, in our time, to be stronger–than the parts. We cannot today think in terms of a James, a Lawrence, a Conrad, though, a writer of stature can appear at any time. At least we can 'place' the achievement of a novelist against some of his predecessors whose work enters into his own. And at the same time we ought to look in our better writers for Saul Bellow's 'colony of the spirit', a community of intelligences, whose shared achievement as writers, shared insights, shared formulations, even shared fates can become part of the way we see ourselves and our difficult world. No single writer begins to be adequate to America's industrial culture. Or even adequate to the way that culture shapes the writer's personal relations in love, or sex, or family; or elusive identity; or loneliness; or approaching death. We live, all of us, among fragments, and the best we can do is, through joined effort, to piece them together. Put more affirmatively: If the collective perceptions of the better novelists fail to be adequate in our day, whose voice is more adequate?

I

Saul Bellow is America's most distinguished novelist. He is the urban Jew novelist of immigrant origins who, in his own words, inhabits a

> universe . . . without the comforts of community, without metaphysical certainty, without the power to distinguish the virtuous from the wicked, surrounded by dubious realities and discovering

dubious selves. . . . Things have collapsed about us . . . and we must each of us try to put together some sort of life.

He conceives of fictional characters as

oddly dispersed, ragged, mingled, broken, amorphous creatures . . . bathed in mind . . . and impossible to circumscribe in any scheme of time . . . a quaintly organized chaos of instinct and spirit.

In that view, ranges of the comic or the ironic prevail. Further, his protagonists

stand outside society and, unlike Gatsby, have no wish to be sentimentally reconciled to it, unlike Dreiser's millionaires, have no more desire for its wealth, unlike Strether, are not attracted by the power of an old and unknowing civilization.

As a professional to the bone, Bellow has avoided the 'didactic purpose', and has insisted that he be judged entirely as a novelist, 'in a scene, in a dialogue, a mood, an insight, in language, in character, in the revelation of a design'. In short, Saul Bellow has, novel by novel, devised an original strategy for creating fictional meanings for a changing, erudite, comic self, moving, in the urban disorder of American life, towards inevitable death: from the fictional autobiography of *Dangling Man*; to the novel as dramatic poem in *The Victim* and *Seize the Day*; to the wholly original, unexpected *Adventures of Augie March* and *Henderson the Rain King*, each practically unprecedented in American fiction; to a return, in *Herzog*, to a transmuted form of *Dangling Man*, this time with a lifetime's professional expertise and critical reflection showing.

Dangling Man (1944), *The Victim* (1947) and *Seize the Day* (1956) are traditional novels (the latter a novella) well-known enough to require little commentary. But nothing in Bellow's previous novels prepares the reader for the virtuoso performance of *The Adventures of Augie March* (1953). Its impact comes, first, from the rhetoric of the fiction, where style is theme: a framework allowing for maximum openness of the protagonist to the individuality of his American experience, largely urban, from childhood, through the Depression, World War II, and its aftermath – all within the structure of a picaresque novel. Augie is narrator, compulsively talkative, with a command of racy idiom, who muses, recalls, digresses, asserts, associates freely, employs a special vocabulary and turn of phrase. He is by turns 'larky and boisterous', witty, elusive, graphically observant, often idiosyncratic in notation. His erudition is an extended lecture, virtually, in the Humanities, American-style, where World History and World Literature strive – and fail – to enhance characters and events. Bellow picks up Emerson and Whitman in his celebration of America's variety; Melville in the energy of observation and in the principle of resistance to the terms of American society; *Huckleberry Finn* in much of the tough comedy and the way the protagonist moves through damaging adventures, absorbing blow after blow without essential damage and with resiliency, lighting out, finally, for the European territory; Fitzgerald and Dreiser, especially the latter, in the depiction of the American success-ethos in Chicago; even Joyce's Leopold Bloom in the humorous stream-of-consciousness and self-humour. Again, Bellow's dramatic gift shows to even greater advantage and command: some eighty characters move through the novel, most of them individualized. Style, then, is Bellow's means for keeping alive, for 'seizing the day' as novelist, for capturing people and the world in variety. Style, so conceived, appears more important in Bellow's eyes than any patterns he might discover. *Dangling Man* talked about a strategy. *Augie March* carries it out:

> Whereas, to him, judgement is second to wonder, to speculation on man, drugged and clear, jealous, ambitious, good, tempted, curious, each in his own time and with his customs and motives, and bearing the imprint of strangeness in the world. In a sense, everything is good because it exists. Or good or not, it exists, it is ineffable, and, for that reason, marvellous.

Augie March is the second of three sons of a poor, half-blind Jewish woman (the 'Jewishness' of *Augie March* is even more special and unrepresentative than of *The Victim*) whose husband has deserted her. The boys live in Chicago, brought up by their 'Grandma' Lausch, later, in one of the better scenes in the novel, institutionalized as old and indigent. The youngest

March is made feeble-minded, for no ascertainable reason. The eldest, Simon (a continuation of Amos of *Dangling Man*), whose story Augie relates in counterpart to his own, is ambitious, brilliant, unscrupulous, and becomes rich and powerful. The core of the novel which belongs to Simon is entirely successful, partly in itself, partly in the way it assimilates, implicitly, other approximations of success and failure, American-style, in the novel. The rest of the book suffers in comparison. Augie's adventures are many, and in sheer variety would appear to follow no thematic pattern. Still what emerges cumulatively, perhaps unintentionally, is Augie's responsiveness to American life in a way that continues, and reinvigorates, the explorations of Fitzgerald and especially Dreiser. The great achievement of the book is the achievement of the American *ambience*, sixteen pounds to the square inch. In that world Bellow registers, as taken for granted without need for comment, mutual exploitation and misuse, beginning in the family; the use of any means to justify the end of success—trickery, bribery, corruption, meanness, force, threat. The ethics at the top—Simon's story and Einhorn's story—permeate all of society. It is an ambience, also, that, of itself virtually, produces constant betrayal in personal relations.

Augie exemplifies the principle of resistance, the obstinate passion for the freedom of non-commitment. Yet, again as in *Dangling Man*, this principle seems to make impossible, also, any attachment to people, to place, to functional job, to institutions. The novel is least successful in depicting a viable relationship of men and women. Bellow is at his best where women become deadly antagonists or where, like Mimi Villars, the women make no demands.

The weaknesses of *Augie March* quite equal its strength. Even more than Asa Leventhal, Augie has no centre. We do not know where the principle of resistance comes from, why it takes root, how it functions psychologically. Bellow's intellect, again, loves to play with Ideas, but it avoids the reflective intelligence. Augie, thus, functions as passive recording instrument, Bellow's puppet. The master's voice, therefore, wills Augie March into being, energy of style and all. The question remains whether such a style is equal to the effective capturing of the American experience, and here it is a matter of differing judgement.

Whitmanesque exuberance strikes one as willed vitality which distorts the quality of that experience. Ranges of naturalism and surrealism would seem more appropriate.

Henderson the Rain King (1959) picks up the rhetoric of *Augie March*, though protagonist and setting are so radically different that one's response is fresh and new. Henderson is an original in a different way. The comic note is, much of the time, close to farce, to burlesque, to the fantastic. The special quality of the novel derives from Henderson's special quality: he is in all respects outside. Physically enormous, he is given outsize wilfulness, impulsiveness, boisterousness, violence, tenderness, with powerful, though unfocused, psychic and emotional cravings. The novel's comedy is adjusted to that size. Henderson comes from an old New England family, is a latter-day Henry Adams, eager to serve. He is, through inheritance, many times a millionaire. He is bookish (the authentic Bellow touch), zany, given to playing the violin with large insensitive hands. His first wife, remote and neurotic, now laughs at his quixotism, and he has now reached a point of dissatisfaction with his second marriage and his way of life.

At odds with his American world (Henderson is another Bellow 'resister'), Henderson escapes to Africa in an effort to be reborn, as it were, in a world in every respect different from his own. The novel is, at one and the same time, a parody of, and tribute to, Hemingway. Bellow creates a special Africa, a country he has never seen, in rich detail—a considerable *tour de force*. In America, Henderson, escaping from people, had been involved with pigs, cats, a chimpanzee, an octopus, a seal, and an old brown bear. In Africa he first encounters frogs, and then lions. In the energy of observed details, Africa reminds us of the Mexico section of *Augie March*, though that it is far more effective. Among Africans, Henderson is another Augie March, highly adoptive. But he brings disaster to the first tribe he tries to help, he destroys the water supply on which both people and cattle depend. Henderson is, indeed, an Anglo-Saxon *schlemiel*.

In the second African community, Henderson becomes even more fantastically involved in tribal politics based on magic, totemism, and belief in the transmigration of souls. He ends up by being made king, the rain king. Here Henderson tries to discover an access to reality which Western culture ignores because it has not learned 'to encounter death'. He discovers forces stronger than death in the natural world, in the animals, and in the Africans. Prince Dahfu is his tutor, a tribal chief who studied medicine in Europe. He teaches Henderson how to encounter a lioness by learning to be still yet active, how to come alive in dignity and courage in the presence of the lioness. Dahfu is torn to pieces by it, finally, but Henderson has had his lesson. Bellow's description of the relationship of Dahfu and Henderson is one that can bear comparison with that of Queequeg and Ishmael of *Moby-Dick*. Melville, too, lies behind this novel. Henderson's unfocused dissatisfaction with humans; his restlessness; his self-humour; his search for adventure which will reinvigorate; his respect for the civilization of a barbaric people as, in many respects, superior to Europeans and Americans; his acceptance of pain and death; his respect for sources of life in the natural world, in animals, and in African human beings–all evoke Melville. Bellow achieves the most effective realization of friendship of which I know in contemporary American fiction. Still, what Henderson learns is hardly translatable to America; so that the book's ending must be as inconclusive as that of *Augie March*. But the book is, on its own terms of fantasy-comedy, *sui generis*, and a pleasure in itself.

Herzog (1964) is Bellow's most ambitious, yet least satisfactory, novel–a retreat from life. The attempt is original. Bellow wishes to create an intellectual of distinction and sufficient national recognition in the academic field of, presumably, the History of Ideas. He is a Joseph of *Dangling Man*, come to fruition; thinly disguised autobiography. Moses Herzog has not only been betrayed by his second wife and her lover, Herzog's former friend, who is, and remains, married. He has been betrayed in a manner which makes him in his own eyes, as well as in the eyes of individuals within his circle, a ludicrously comic figure. The comedy–*Herzog*, like *Seize the Day*, is painful comedy–is generated by the distance between achievement in the academic world (*Who's, Who,* for example) and Herzog's scarcely bearable anguish, one that moves in the climax to intended murder, in the world of close relationship. He is aware of the impotence of intellect, especially where a professed historian ought to see his own condition within a meaningful historic frame, when the personal wound festers.

Herzog is another of Bellow's erratic heroes: moody, impulsive, wilful, distraught, unpredictable, even slightly mad. In *Dangling Man*, Joseph sought relief in a journal. In *Herzog*, the protagonist uses unposted letters to famous people in an attempt to clarify his needs, his resentments, his quarrels with his age and his society. Some of the letters reflect emotional turbulence. Others sound like lectures for the Department of Social Thought of the University of Chicago, Bellow's own academic post. Herzog can perceive his own egotism, narcissism, self-righteousness; his loneliness, his sorrow, his sense of waste. But he fails entirely at coherence, and the serenity at the end of the novel is willed, spurious.

Herzog's attempts at self-understanding, or understanding of 'the age', fail. Again there is no centre to a principal character of a Bellow novel. And the novel is written from the inside of Herzog's head and emotions, claustrophobically. Nowhere is there clarification of the betrayal itself, the nub of the novel. And the style of *Herzog* is incapable of arresting experience, interrogating it, ordering it, judging it. Instead, like *Augie March* and *Henderson the Rain King*, it captures the flux of experience, associates freely, catalogues, gains separate, fragmented insights. The subject-matter is, by now, the familiar one: the betrayal of all relationships, including family feeling (the best scene of the novel depicts Herzog's return to his Canadian ghetto neighbourhood). The context is also familiar: the urban worlds of Chicago and New York City. Once again Bellow appears to locate the enemy in 'Reality Instructors': individuals who accept the terms of America's self-interested way of life and can be heartless in their relationships to others. But the 'Reality Instructors' are far less forceful than Simon of *Augie March* or than the characters of *Seize the Day* who combine to destroy Tommy Wilhelm.

Bellow's principal concern appears, in *Herzog* as in *Augie March* and *Henderson the Rain King*, to keep alive individuality in a culture too complex to begin to know; one, moreover, that seems to be going the way of spiritual death; to keep alive and yet to feel all the compassion of intelligence towards those deserving of it.

Few critics underestimate Bellow's gifts. Yet they qualify recognition of his achievement in ways that, cumulatively, deny him secure status among the better novelists in the tradition. No single, damaging critique has appeared. If anything, we witness critical acclaim. But critics outside America are, rightly, cautious. In a period of economic ascendancy and world power, there is, especially in a nation as culturally active as America, an inevitable tendency for a great nation to claim a great literature. Critics participate in that feeling, deep in the national psyche, more than they realize. American critics have convinced themselves, too, that writers like Fitzgerald and Dreiser, for example, are 'great' writers, a claim that a cultivated Englishman or European rightly finds untenable. Still, it is easier for Americans, given this perspective, to make claims for contemporaries who appear, in original ways, to bear comparison with such predecessors. Besides, the world outside America is by now familiar enough with the huge academic industry where young scholar-critics have reputations to make and tenure to secure, by publishing books and articles, especially on contemporary American writers. There are more books and articles on Bellow than on any other living American novelist. Yet the curious withholding of 'major' recognition persists.

Partly it is a realization that Bellow's fiction offers protagonists who search for durable relationship; yet the fiction has not yet created a single memorable image of such a relationship, even within families. The relationship of men and women, especially, suffers from damaging immaturity without Bellow's being able to reveal in his novels the reasons why immaturity is almost inevitable, or why the relationship might be, in the Laurentian sense, impossible. Again, Bellow moves in society and is intelligent about that society. But Bellow has not himself descended into the destructive element as, say, Mailer has. He is curiously remote, a spectator, as one critic has put it, 'accurate, informative, aware—everything but authentic'. Bellow's fiction, too, is learned, full of Ideas. But he is, finally, violated, victimized, by them. He cannot order them coherently. Nor do they illuminate, or penetrate, his characters. Above all, we find it difficult, in most of his fiction, to penetrate to the centre of character, to the ruling passions, to psychic compulsions. And much of the time Bellow strains at, will, fictional life. Then, too, Bellow is, recognizably, a Jewish writer, one of the few with an expert knowledge of Yiddish. Yet he makes only eccentric use of his Jewish materials. If his characters are, like Bellow himself, second-generation Jews, then the fiction never illuminates the special hold of their Jewishness. The roots appear to have dried up.

The fiction of Norman Mailer offers a corrective to Bellow. It constitutes a descent into the maelstrom, the work of a writer who has immersed himself directly into the main stream of 'the American experience'. Mailer has been a combat soldier in the Pacific; has been active in politics; has been involved in forms of violence, where, in one instance, he stabbed one of his former wives; has taken drugs; drinks heavily; has, in times even more difficult than they were for, say, Hemingway or Fitzgerald, made a living as a writer in the industrial marketplace for letters (Mailer has avoided academia in all its forms), but much of his writing has paid the price of exhibitionism, meretriciousness, and journalistic gimmickry. Like Hemingway, Mailer joined–and is known to be part of–the American Celebrity world. Like Hemingway, again, Mailer is proficient at boxing (at one point he even 'backed' a fighter, José Torres, who became lightweight champion of the world); like Hemingway he has put his life deliberately in jeopardy in order to test his courage, his manhood. Like Bellow, Mailer–though mostly outside his fiction–offers himself as an intellect, where he succeeds occasionally in setting off sparks. His recent book of prose, *Armies of the Night* (1968), does more than that. It is a description of the March on the Pentagon in 1967, where a various army combined to halt a nation involved in the costly and criminal war in Vietnam. More than Bellow, then, and more than Hemingway, Mailer has been a 'witness' of his times. But his case is peculiar, for, only with his recent novel, *An American Dream* (1965), has Mailer found a suitable frame within which to interpret that American experience effectively.

The Naked and the Dead (1948), written at twenty-five, describes infantry action in the invasion of the island of Anapopei, and the ascent up Mt Anaka, in the Pacific area. It remains, with the exception of the unconventional *Catch-22* (strongly to be preferred), perhaps the best novel to have come out of World War II–itself a commentary on the difficulty of writing successfully about war in our time. Mailer's novel offers the implied judgement that war is somehow a reflection of the society that wages it, but the gap between what is offered and what convinces is large enough to accommodate several infantry divisions, complete with tanks and planes. Only two realized characters stand as fictional 'proof'. One is General Cummings, intellectual fascist, latent homosexual, with a genius for organization and tactics. Yet that genius is entirely undercut in the end by an episode that might well have come out of the hilarious *Catch-22*, where a ludicrously incompetent officer, Malleson, performs the decisive operation inadvertently and gets the credit. The other is Sgt Croft, a Texan, equal, so far as one can judge, only to the demands of successful combat, and who cannot in any significant way be moved out into American life. What is successful is the way Mailer conveys the sense of impotency in anyone, officer or enlisted man, when intimidated by power. The two 'liberals,' Lt Hearn and Pfc. Valsen, are invested with that impotence, a supposed reflection of American fascism. The members of the platoon are only fictionalized Hollywood—for all Mailer's use of Dos Passos' techniques— except for the way they reflect deadly antagonism to each other and the way they carry the insight that the least privileged members of American society, already failed and beaten in civilian life, must bear the brunt of combat. Much of what is effective in the novel had already been done by Hemingway: the 'natural history of the dead', the scenes of action, the sense (as in Stephen Crane before Hemingway) that one is plunged into combat without being able to understand or to control one's destiny, and always in an inconsequential military action. *The Naked and the Dead* exhibits an impressive command, however, of soldiering itself, as well as of Pacific island topography.

Like Bellow, Mailer has shown the courage of experiment, particularly in view of the runaway best-seller success of *The Naked and the Dead*. *Barbary Shore* (1951) continues Mailer's political preoccupations. It is, in effect, a Cold War novel and conveys a sense of collapse in the political Left after disillusion with Russia. Again the more forceful character in this claustrophobic work lives on the right hand of power: Hollingsworth, the fascist-like secret agent of the State Department. Once again impotency characterizes the opponents of power, this time the hunted ex-radical, McLeod, and the narrator, Lovett, who, as the voice of the author, is almost a cipher. In *Barbary Shore*, further, Mailer explores the relationship of sex with forms of power and forms of powerlessness. But the story is tedious, its quality that of unrelieved melodrama. We can see in the perspective of *An American Dream* the reason for Mailer's failure. It was the failure to see 'politics' within the totality of American culture; specifically the failure to imagine how the total culture works in relation to forms of power.

The Deer Park (1955) is a novel about the way in which power works in the Hollywood entertainment industry which manufactures America's fantasies (a theme done far more effectively in a novel by Walker Percy, *The Moviegoer*). The underlying metaphor in the title enforces a comparison with the court of Louis XIV and implies decadence before disintegration. Again it is a novel which shows Mailer struggling, and failing, to find a structure which would transcend simply the political dimension, one that might reveal the American way through the lies it manufactures.

But *An American Dream* (1965) is Mailer's *Augie March*, a kind of picaresque comedy, with good pace and the compression of *The Great Gatsby*, a novel that could not have been predicted from his previous fiction. Anticipations, however, can be found in his prose journalism, *Advertisements for Myself* (1959) and *Cannibals and Christians* (1965). (That journalism is so compounded of some of the finest perceptions we possess about the quality of American life in our time, as well as of so much that is cranky and half-baked, that the job of sorting out seems positively Herculean.) Remarkably, Norman Mailer, less gifted than Saul Bellow, has in *An American Dream* found the framework for which he has been searching, one that is more satisfactory than any Bellow has found, and one that enables him to engage his American culture–politics and all–at dead centre. Compared with the Mailer of *An American Dream*, Bellow strikes us as academic. And the fact that there is so much that is objectionable in this book does not impair its achievement.

An American Dream fuses two traditions in American imaginative life, one represented by Dreiser, Fitzgerald, Hemingway, and Mark Twain; the other, the world of the popular, or national, imagination: Hollywood, detective fiction, *True*

Pornography, *Time* magazine, and *TV*. In *An American Dream*, further, we realize that American national culture is distinctive and differs radically from the 'English' or the 'French'. The 'American Dream' is basic to the way many Americans think and feel about the American experience. There is no comparable 'English' or 'French' dream. Again, *An American Dream* is about forms of power in American life. The way power has expressed itself is distinctive, too, in any comparison with its forms in Europe.

The whole structure of the novel, including the climax prepared for in its opening pages, dictates a confrontation between the hero, Rojack, half-Jewish, and the character who, like Cowperwood of Dreiser's trilogy (*The Financier*, *The Titan*, and *The Stoic*), or Tom Buchanan of *Great Gatsby* (Fitzgerald's radical failure, seldom pointed out, to give us *representative* 'power'), must bear the greatest responsibility for what has happened to the American Dream. Barney Oswald Kelly is a kind of Joseph P. Kennedy (the 'Oswald' suggests that the elder Kennedy must, indirectly, bear responsibility for the assassination of his son), crossed with any representative of an American interlocking corporate directorate out of *Time*, or its equivalent in film. Kelly belongs to the enterprising social-climbing, speculating, ruthless, power leadership, a Jay Gatsby without the 'dream'; and the ethics he personifies interpenetrates American society, again as in *Gatsby*.

Now, towards the end of the book, we perceive Mailer's fictional point. Kelly lies behind the war Rojack fought. Now he is behind the next war that the new Rojacks will fight: he works with the C.I.A. in the Cold War. Like the Buchanans, Kelly and his daughter belong to High Society, corrupt and bankrupt of any standards for manners. He represents American 'justice': the tie-up of the police and the judiciary with the world of power. He might easily be a behind-the-scenes member of the Board of Trustees, responsible, finally, for Rojack's losing his university job, and defining the limits beyond which teaching cannot go. He might easily, again, be an owner or advertiser in the TV corporation that fires Rojack. He ties in directly with Mafia's organized gangsterism and its extensions. Most of all, he represents the ethos of the society itself, where success remains the sole standard, whatever the means utilized; so that every talent, like Rojack's, is forced, first, to seek success, and, second, to seek success in terms dictated by Kelly or his like.

The portrait of Kelly shows felicities which had not appeared in Mailer's 'power' explorations in previous novels. He is shown, like Simon March, to be caught up in the iron vice of freedom that competitive success dictates. He is linked with a consumer society, and his power is adjusted to its every mean demand. His fate depends on market fluctuations, and he acknowledges that the real work must be done by managerial technocrats, on whom he is dependent. He inhabits a world of threat and counter-threat. And his personal world is a shambles.

Mailer now shows intelligence in the way he portrays the influence of Kelly's world. One might wish to alter the terms appreciably. One could visualize Kelly as a character as much produced by the demands itself of the industrial machine to produce high living standards, as a power imposing his will on his society in so many ways. Still, what Kelly represents is as strong as Mailer suggests. In the end, all serious opposition to it must be broken as, in effect, one sees opposition broken in each industrial society. The only opposition which cannot be broken, in Mailer's eyes, is the act of personal courage. In an act of Hemingway-like courage, Rojack endangers his life by walking on a parapet of Kelly's apartment building, with Kelly looking on, himself not daring such an act, and, at one point, attempting to kill him. At the end of the novel however, Cherry and Shago Martin are dead. Rojack is beaten. Mailer has him light out for the territory, first, ironically, for the malignant west in Las Vegas, Nevada, then, finally, Mexico.

An American Dream ought to be a pointer for future writers. His special achievement is that he has utilized effectively the materials from the media of America's popular imagination. Yet there are weaknesses. The framework he employs is right, but the protagonist as a living character within that framework is no more intelligent than Mailer, the prose journalist. Rojack's response to each event is a compound of metaphor doing the work of 'feelings' and generalized and quirky 'thought' doing the work of needed discriminations. *An American Dream* is, therefore, as claustrophobic as *Herzog*: we live in Rojack's skull. Further, the fiction concentrates so heavily on the pathology and psychopathology of the American experience as shaped by the Barney Oswald Kellys that the novel comes to be an indulgence where the possibilities for health are given no play. There ought, too, to be more possibilities for human compassion which appear in the best short story Mailer did, *The Man Who Studied Yoga*, which deals with lives of quiet desperation of a few Jewish ex-radicals. Unquestionably there is a certain resiliency in the language which rejects what appears to have gone rotten, but Mailer fails to reveal all the roots of that rottenness. As with Bellow, then, the reader is dealing with willed health. Moreover, Mailer has been corrupted more than he knows by his need to 'make it'. The element of autobiography permits much that is only reckless, exhibitionist, and meretricious in this novel, however much he tries to control these elements with comedy.

Bellow, Mailer and the overwhelming majority of American writers grapple each with a special, personal responsiveness to their culture, however objectified in the successful work. Vladimir Nabokov, on the other hand, utilizes every instrument available to defeat the critic who would press him into that category. Mostly he plays with 'point of view', contriving his fiction in a way that makes it impossible to identify novelist with protagonist: disguises, masks, chess strategies, involved allegory, trick-mirror effects, parody and self-parody, anagrams, language-play involving many languages, unlikely protagonists, mystifications. These contrivances—learned, witty, complicated, devious—sever all links between the writer and his creation (Nabokov sees his role as 'anthropomorphic deity *impersonated* by me' (italics added) except for the one link that claims his exclusive attention: 'Given these characters in these relationships, and within this special fictional structure and world', he seems to say, 'have I succeeded in writing the successful work of fiction? The critic's job is to comment on narrative pace, dialogue, variety of tone, qualities of the comic and tragic, special uses for language: the work of art.' But the critic in turn, accepting such terms, answers: 'Only *Lolita* and *Pnin* are relatively successful.' Each is realized in a special way. But felt realization locates itself at points where the reader's personal responsiveness has been aroused. That is to say, as the cumulative effects of each novel—the result, indeed, of Nabokov's discussibly complex art—begin to tell, the critic can focus on certain fictional nodes. Then he perceives that each novel offers a powerful image of the way lonely death in our time comes to Nabokovian characters with whom the author has made us sympathize. Nabokov's extraordinary learning, sophistication, use of parody, tough common sense, and, above all, sense of the poignantly comic–tragic are all subordinated to the demands of a theme that moves us. There is, besides, in each novel the comedy of the anthropological, in Nabokov's case a balanced fusion, at once satiric and celebratory, in his view of America. We are kept engaged, kept agile, kept entertained from start to finish. We even anticipate re-readings where we can take in more and more–no mean achievement. But in all the other novels, and in different degrees, the element of fictional play–elaborate, intricate, tricky–destroys engagement and calls attention to 'technique'. Nabokov then assimilates to the Joyce of *Finnegan's Wake* and the more tedious portions of *Ulysses*.

The triumph of *Lolita* is the character of the fictitious Humbert Humbert, who takes possession of a twelve-year-old nymphet, travels with her across America, loses her to a rival, Quilty, meets her very briefly when she is seventeen, married, and pregnant, loses her permanently, murders Quilty, suffers a heart attack in prison and dies, leaving his 'confessional' to another fictitious 'John Ray, Ph.D'. Nabokov tells the reader that he has 'impersonated' both.

Like Leopold Bloom, Humbert is a comically conceived, dramatic creation from the inside. His compulsion is sexually perverse: an attraction for nymphets between the ages of nine and thirteen, though the perversion is interchangeable, almost, with a form of homosexuality. He inhabits the terrible prison of his perversity, his psychic disturbances showing at times in the contrivances of style. Humbert is a clever, conscionable compulsive with a sense of humour whose object is mostly himself, who yet suffers tortures and debasements as he tries to protect himself against society. The novel is a Nabokovian exercise in multiple disguise, planned also as a parody of the confessional, or the literary diary. Humbert tries to explain, never to excuse, himself. The irony is that he is sensitive, intelligent, has sophistication, learning, and is, indeed, in all ways superior to those with whom he must live, especially to the nymphet, Lolita, who, at the age of twelve, seduces him.

Though subordinate, Lolita comes alive too. The prose becomes fussy through repetitiousness as the novel progresses, yet Nabokov captures the sexual attractiveness of the nymphet, especially the transience of the potential attractiveness and delicacy of the young, in Lolita's case violated by inner and outer vulgarities. Best of all, Nabokov has an ear and an eye for the sexually sophisticated American Philistine girl of twelve, whose humour is as natively American as–at its level–the American G.I., who can be clever at school and among friends but is enslaved to the crudities of the culture. Through Lolita Nabokov offers his exhilarating satire of America: motels, popular songs, tourist attractions, progressive schools, the tyranny of the teenager, the essential loneliness of the elders, the pathetic attempt to escape suffering and death. He uses America's very physical geography by way of pointing up the degree to which it has been debased. Yet the comforts, the conveniences, the luxuries, the country itself, seen through the eyes of a European *émigré* like Humbert, are seen with a celebratory zest. Nor is the European way of life offered as superior.

The success of *Lolita* is one that comes, first, from the quiet cumulation of effects: the wheels-within-wheels of ingenious disguises; the narrative pace and variety; the complex sympathy for Humbert as the reader comes to see the world from his point of view, a mixture of self-torture, perceptiveness, and comedy; the painful comedy of the relation with Lolita. Then, at a certain point, Lolita escapes from Humbert with his rival, Quilty, whom, later, Humbert murders. The next time he sees her she is a married woman of seventeen, heavily pregnant, living in squalor and debt with an undistinguished, partly deaf, ex-G.I. husband. In that confrontation Lolita makes clear to him that she would face almost any consequence rather than return to him; and Humbert realizes the depth and tenaciousness of his love. Like Tommy Wilhelm in *Seize the Day*, Humbert weeps quietly for himself and for the defeated of the world. At this very point the novel conveys the poignancy of lost love, picking up a very early episode of the book, Humbert's love when a boy for Annabel Leigh (Shades of Poe) who died; the imprisoned loneliness of Humbert and the foreshadowing of his death; the awareness, controlled by comedy, at once of his own absurdity and of his loss; and quiet acceptance and a sense of inevitability. Having been brought to a pitch of sympathy for Humbert, the reader is aware of compulsions alive in this man which all his urbanity, learning, and charm cannot control, compulsions malign and demonic in their consequences, and inaccessible in psychic origins. Further, the novel sustains its power as it moves through a scene where Humbert murders his rival, one of the best in the book. It is a conscious parody of the detective novel and film, but the farce which controls the description of that murder fuses brutal details with a sense of futility, again inevitable.

Pnin (1957; *Lolita* was written in 1955) is closer to Nabokov's own world of Russian intellectuals, scholars in exile, and the American academic community. Timofey Pnin is an Assistant Professor (i.e. untenured) in Russian literature at Waindell College, roughly of Nabokov's age, who parallels Nabokov's pattern of exile. Like Humbert Humbert, Pnin is a figure of tragi-comedy, though much of it is the comedy of eccentric normalcy not, as in *Lolita*, of psychopathology. Pnin is a Dickensian figure, whose refusal to submit—not even to recognize—the ordinary American world involves him in a series of endless crises with American routines. After years in America he speaks like a Russian immigrant learning the language; is absent-minded and often inaccurate in his dedicated scholarship; is easily manipulated by students and is a butt of satire at faculty meetings; devises ingenuities out of all proportion to the simple need to cope with American noises, regularities, and vulgarities. But Pnin's genuine integrities, consequently his dignity, prevail for the reader.

What is most extraordinary in *Pnin* is this: Nabokov, in the fictional presentation of Pnin, offers no dramatic posturing: the *stance* of dignity, the *stance* of stoicism, the *stance* of transcendence. Pnin, like Humbert Humbert, acts out his fictional character, in dialogue, in gestures, in outward movement, in a series of highly comic scenes, without the need to *declare*, or for Nabokov to *underline*, certain attitudes. Only in retrospect does the reader register this extraordinary achievement. Perhaps the most striking quality is the absence of any impulse to attack, directly or indirectly, individuals or the culture. It is an example of maturity not to be found among other American authors.

Nabokov's case is difficult, critically, given his formidable credentials, so much worthy of our esteem. There is, first, the command of language which invokes comparison with Joseph Conrad: some twenty years' publication in native Russian; over twenty-five years' in English, to the point where he is now respected as an American writer in a way Conrad was respected as an English writer; a small output in French; a command of German, Italian, and Spanish. One admires, too, the steady stream of writing: poetry, novels, short stories, plays, translations, memoirs, scholarly and critical articles. Nabokov, one recalls too, was at one time Fellow of the Museum of Comparative Zoology at Harvard, a specialist in Lepidoptera; and he had at one time been chess editor of an *émigré* paper.

More, one learns to admire certain attitudes, many of which enter his fiction. Like Bellow, Nabokov appears to have a photographic memory and almost total recall which have enabled him to transform personal experience from early childhood into the terms of his art, including his memoirs. Again like Bellow, he exemplifies the writer for whom the work of art constitutes not only a stay against confusion, disorder, and chaos, but also a means of controlling the terrible effects of time and suffering and death. I have also called attention to his special quality of maturity. The very wealthy patrician family suffered exile when Nabokov was ten. He lost a much respected, deeply loved father through political assassination, a man who in his native Russia had belonged to an élite of committed politicians of signal intellectual distinction. And for years Nabokov made a precarious living writing for *émigré* publications. Then, with the Nazi threat, he suffered exile again, this time to America, where he held, again precariously, academic posts, until the publication of *Lolita* made him accidentally well off. Yet what we admire in Nabokov's best fiction is a combination of virtues: the absence of self-pity or complaint, of recrimination, of meanness, of vindictiveness; a highly active sense of the absurd and the humorous; a capacity for compassion; a tough, no-nonsense astringency when aroused.

Bellow, Mailer and Nabokov have, each in his way, produced a body of work within which there is fictional achievement demanding close attention. The situation for American critics is such, however, that differing critics will readily produce other candidates. The best hope lies in exchange. One expects, still, that there would be general consensus that Bellow has been the best American novelist since World War II. The meaning of such a cultural circumstance may be, first, as already pointed out, that the culture has become too complex for any single talent to be adequate. The best one can do is to call attention to a number of good novels, trusting that a consolidation of critical work 'in the common pursuit' waits to be joined. Evaluation is complicated by the awareness on the part of cultivated Europeans that the achievement of American predecessors on whom present novelists draw is hardly 'major'; yet American novelists and critics now take such 'major' status for granted. I should myself not wish to make a case for the following as better than second-order, or, in certain cases, even below, when compared with European counterparts: Hemingway, Fitzgerald, Crane, Dreiser, Faulkner, Twain and Melville are special, recognizably American, and the job of sorting out realized significance in their work is yet to be done within the framework of comparisons with Europe. Cooper and Hawthorne are more important for historical reasons than for reasons of intrinsic stature. And that leaves the lonely figure of Henry James, half-European, about whom there is least question.

2

Bernard Malamud's best novel, *The Assistant* (1957), is an attempt in its way to do for the twentieth-century Jew in America what Hawthorne did for his Puritan ancestors who settled in America over two hundred years before *The Scarlet Letter* was written. What Hawthorne's novel conveys is the power of Puritanism to conquer a wilderness, tame the savages, build a closely-knit theocratic community. Puritanism was fanatical, self-righteous, intolerant, militant, repressive, cruel, superstitious. Yet it demanded integrity of conscience in the eyes of God, the necessity of a certain openness and communion within that community, respect for learning dedicated to God's purposes, and a conviction of the sanctity of married life (the subject matter of the book deals with the effects of adultery). A whole people lived by these beliefs, and died by them. But these religious convictions were quickly transformed by the push of secular life, so that, by Hawthorne's time, they had been attenuated almost out of existence.

The Assistant is a novel as tight in its structure as Bellow's *Seize the Day*. It is the story of a different kind of failure. A recognizably traditional Jew, Morris Bober, is a failed grocer to whom a young Italian, Frankie Alpine, attaches himself as, in fact, an assistant in suffering. With the death of Bober, and after Alpine has fully earned that assistantship, he lets himself be circumcised as a Jew.

Morris Bober thinks and feels and speaks in Yiddish, and Malamud captures—lucidly, transparently, directly—Yiddish speech rhythms with an impeccable ear. But the burden of Bober's speech conveys, with the traditional Yiddish humour rooted in accepted suffering felt to be the lot of Jews, the sense of miserable economic failure, culminating in bankruptcy; of physical suffering, Bober's weak lungs leading to pneumonia and death; of resignation and endurance; of failure in relation to those closest to him, the members of his family. Bober's daughter, Helen, thinks and feels in accents of the American feminine genteel, yet remains in touch with the world of her father, borrowing from that world self-respect, self-dignity. She is the Jewish daughter but one step removed from the force of traditional modes. Frankie Alpine, the Italian assistant, uses idiomatic American speech where it is still in touch with ghetto life.

What distinguishes Bober for the reader is the way he lives out much of the traditional assumptions of the diaspora Jew, though divorced in his case from doctrinal religious ties. Bober's bedrock is honesty; cheating would produce unbearable psychic explosions; he can only trust others who, in turn, cheat him; and he must give value for the money, even though he must count that money in nickels and dimes. He is, therefore, a born victim in an environment where what he represents of traditional conduct is doomed—an environment deeply and naturally competitive, where customers are thought of as suckers, where the supermarket takes over, and where crime itself—in this book petty crime—is built into a way of life. So Morris Bober suffers for the Law, he cannot do otherwise. He is beaten, and he dies.

Malamud, like Hawthorne, achieves a balance in presentation, though his own sentiments are far more sympathetic to traditional Jewish belief than Hawthorne's were to early Puritanism in America. Helen's affection and respect for her father is tempered with criticism: he accepted his role as victim passively; he retreated claustrophobically from American life and was unimaginative about the possibilities it offered; he encouraged life-denying proclivities. She is aware, too, of predispositions: the expectation that life will inevitably mean hard work, early decay of one's powers, failure, and persecution from the Gentiles. Bober, sacrificing himself to these implicit convictions, sacrifices his wife and son, and almost sacrifices his daughter.

The implication of the book is that traditional Jewish modes of thinking, feeling, and acting are doomed to evaporate quickly in America: the time-span for the disintegration of such belief is enormously compressed in any comparison with the Puritans. In *The Assistant*, the fictional environment is no longer even the Jewish ghetto. Bober lives in an ethnically mixed neighbourhood. Even more, the implication is, too, that Italians have somehow remained closer to their traditional order than the Jews. At the end it is Frankie Alpine who takes on the burden of the Jews.

Malamud's latest novel, *The Fixer* (1966), is historical fiction, worth reading and, in its way, a legitimate extension of *The Assistant*. Malamud moves back to the Jewish community in Europe, as though Hawthorne might have been impelled to trace his own Puritan roots in historic England. *The Fixer* follows Malamud's single-minded pursuit of the same theme, though in transposed terms.

The novelists we have so far considered are not only older men. Each in his best work–even Mailer–has been able to use what we have in the past called the 'traditional order'. Bellow's fiction searches for durable relationship among men and women, or in friendship; for a 'colony of the spirit'; for compassion and tenderness and charity; for the devotion of one's life to a principle that includes, yet transcends, merely decent living standards (which Bellow respects); for respect for learning; for common justice as the French Enlightenment, say, would support the belief; for integrity itself in the act of fiction as a process, at the same time, of integrity of consciousness, a form of truth-telling that would be a disaster for a culture to lose. The strength of Mailer's fiction is the strength of attack: on the impulse to dominate in powerful leaders; on the ethos itself of success, where competitiveness, ruthlessness, exploitation, inhumanity, crime itself, are all built into the system. Nabokov discovers a principle of transcendence in early family life and in the fresh aliveness of childhood and youth. His awareness takes in, without concerning itself to fix blame or even to assess causes, the shocks that flesh and spirit, in our special times, are heir to. But he is an attitude of quiet, humorous, almost uncommented-on acceptance, without complaint or self-pity (however different is the effect of the writing of each, there is a resemblance between Nabokov and Hemingway at his best). And he shares with Bellow both a love of learning and a devotion to the intrinsic value itself of the pursuit of letters in its many forms. In Malamud, the principle of righteousness in a world of persecution and suffering, the ancient heritage of the Jew, lies behind his best work.

John Barth, on the other hand, is a younger novelist, born in 1930. He enjoys the responsiveness of an audience largely of the young, as do others whom one may conveniently link with Barth: Joseph Heller, J. P. Donleavy, William Burroughs, John Rechy, Ken Kesey, Hubert Selby. (The link is intended to be 'sociological' and is not here concerned with effective fiction.) That is to say, each is in his way a black humorist. Barth is an *academic* black humorist, while writers like Burroughs, Rechy, Selby, Kesey and Heller resemble Mailer in the way their fiction grows out of a dead-centre engagement with the American experience, untempered by the subtly softening effects of the academy. The arrival of a large number of such writers may, in fact, signify that a radical turning point has come. What does black humour mean? In our day it means that its exponents no longer feel even the vestigial force–this is, of course, a matter of degree, adjustable for each writer–of traditional values as Americans have tried to live them out. Yet they contemn, often enough with violence, the commitments of an industrial culture. Indeed they seem perversely to celebrate the underground life of that culture as preferable. Problems of 'alienation' and 'identity', thought to have reached almost a breaking point in Bellow and Mailer, are now far more acute. We inhabit the fictional world of the madhouse, of nightmare surrealism, of monstrous distortion, often played against effects of realism and naturalism. Nor has the work of a single writer shown awareness of a glimmer of light at the end of the tunnel.

Barth's first novel, *The Floating Opera* (1956), remains his best. One's reading of *The End of the Road* (1958) suffers from a sense of thematic repetitiveness, though it remains highly readable. *The Sot-Weed Factor* (1960) and *Giles Goat-Boy* (1966), virtuoso performances, one in historical, the other in science fiction, are sizeable failures (806 and 710 pages, respectively). Each is boring; the humour forced, the style undistinguished. While Barth's philosophical themes remain the same, they are now attenuated almost out of existence. In *The Sot-Weed Factor*, history is interpreted in the light of fashionable modern ideas which only shrink those historical dimensions, not enhance them. *Giles Goat-Boy* is a sophomoric allegory.

3

The Negro novel belongs within a separate category, recognizably 'Negro'. Almost all novels written by Negroes have Negro characters within a Negro setting. The Negro novel deserves serious consideration partly for reasons which belong to sociology, since the fate of America depends so much on the fate of its Negroes. More importantly, however, Negro writers have come of age. The best of them, Ralph Ellison, deserves comparison with the better non-Negro novelists. Besides, the achievement of James Baldwin and Ralph Ellison in making available to future Negro writers a framework within which their fiction can develop augurs well.

The complex problem of the Negro is that he must be equal to two cultures: his own; and the white culture that has so shaped Negro culture that the Negro writer's very sense of identity begins with his awareness of the differences. Both Baldwin and Ellison begin with this awareness. From this indispensable point of departure, each has made available to Negro writers their full humanity as integral human beings; coming from particular families, or, more often, non-families, or hopelessly fractured families; having their own sexual experiences; developing, usually, within ghetto communities (one of the finest Negro novels, however, depicts the lower middle-class Negro: *Maud Martha*, by Gwendolyn Brooks (1953)), Northern or Southern, characterized by crime, violence, drug-addiction, heavy drinking, evangelical religion, unemployment, or else the 'garbage' jobs of society, unbelievable squalor; inheriting a special history, originally of slavery, but now, after a number of permutations, at a great turning-point. Understandably, the pressure on the Negro novelist to use his talents in the service of his people is almost irresistible, and Baldwin has succumbed. At the same time the example of the better writer in America and Europe figures as the example to the Negro where fiction, and the language of fiction, becomes an indispensable instrument in the search for identity. Through the language of fiction he can search for honesty in consciousness and in feeling. The Negro writer's strength lies in his Negro identity, a rich and compelling subject-matter, unavailable for almost all white writers. His weakness lies in the perplexities he faces as the result of so many contrary pressures.

It is astonishing that no American critic has captured the nature, the scope and the limitations of Ralph Ellison's achievement, a revealing symptom of the degree to which a sense of belonging to community and specific tradition has so deserted America's influential critics that their antennae fail to respond to its persuasive presence in Ellison. Ellison has written only one novel, *Invisible Man* (1952). While the reader registers the gap between clearly articulated intention (Ellison has been as lucid as any critic) and what the novel realizes (again Ellison remains the best, the most modest, guide), still *Invisible Man* remains the most successful novel by an American Negro.

The novel demonstrates the way a Negro writer can begin to dominate both inheritances, white and black, as well as the more difficult, more complex relations between them. The opening section describes the nameless protagonist living underground in a basement coal-cellar in Harlem which is a source of heat, light and power supplied from tapped lines of Monopolated Light and Power. He plays five copies simultaneously of Louis Armstrong's record of 'Black and Blue', and eats pink and white vanilla ice-cream, covered with sloe gin. The novel then offers a flashback review, 'recollected in tranquillity' (in a sense like Ishmael of *Moby-Dick* after a disaster – a race-riot), of what his life of passive resistance (much like *Augie March*) has come to be as he has tried, like Augie, to escape entrapping forces. The section reminds us of Dostoevsky's *Notes from Underground*, as well as of Kafka in its surrealist conception.

Next, the structure acts out the contributions of both Eliot, Joyce and Dreiser. The novel describes the Negro individual talent (the protagonist in his underground cellar is a writer) growing up within Negro southern society, itself shaped by white society. The opening episode describes a Negro scholarship boy, together with other young Negroes, spotlighted in a ballroom where a blonde stripper dances in the nude. Blindfolded, the Negro boys fight each other, with the drunken whites urging them on. We follow him later to the Negro college which he attends; then to the rural backwoods, accompanied by a white member of the Board of Trustees from the North. Ellison then recapitulates the movement of his race, from southern community, in places still feudal, to the industrial north, where he is, symbolically, given a job in a paint factory. His job, supervised by a Negro, is carefully to add black paint to white, the paint itself intended for a national monument. From here Ellison moves him to the Harlem ghetto; to involvement within a Communist Brotherhood; to a race riot; to a description of Negro Protean man, Rinehart, coping with chaos, change, and instability; back to the underground. Eliot and Joyce lie behind Ellison's attempt to flesh out in the living details of the novel what Negro inheritance, inseparable from one's very skin, means. But *Invisible Man* enacts, from start to finish, a sense of entrapment by 'forces' (as in Dreiser) that brutalize, degrade and humiliate him in the South, and, in the North, lead to violence, crime, drug-addiction, radical politics, and race riots in the ghettos.

Ellison modulates effects of realistic writing with surrealist touches, and with symbolic episodes. He borrows from Faulkner in the part of the novel dealing with the South, especially the awareness of the symbiotic relationship of white to Negro; from Melville's *Confidence-Man* in his depiction of the most effective character in the novel, Rinehart; from *Huckleberry Finn* the balance he achieves of humane strength with crippling weaknesses in the Negroes he presents. The presiding spirit, however, is Hemingway: the attempt of the writer, as writer, to portray what the Negro truly is and truly feels, not what he is encouraged to feel, or is supposed to feel, and not what enraged conscience alone might compel him to feel.

The life of the novel conveys its pervasive note of affirmation, while the structures itself, Ellison's tactical error, submits to 'forces' that constrict. *Invisible Man* utilizes the most intimate materials from Negro life, especially its speech: oratory in its many forms (graduation speech, funeral sermon, political harangue, demagoguery supporting riot, revival meeting); dialects of the rural South, as well as the special forms of Negro-genteel; the language of Harlem: jazz, blues, jive, Bible, the numbers racket, voodoo, spiritualist cure, sports, verbal play for its own sake, and the idiom of the streets in ordinary exchange. The novel is, too, a tragi-comedy, much of it leavened by the special quality of Negro humour in variety-burlesque, farce, the surreal, and the traditional humour of an oppressed people who learn to live with terrible realities. The Negro inheritance, described in *Invisible Man*, is in so many ways grim and appalling. At the same time it is rich in possibilities of life: a varied community sharing American experiences in ways unknown to, unavailable to, the whites today.

Moreover, the theme is about the special condition of the Negro: a search for identity that is special to him, yet one he shares with articulate whites. Black invisibility (Faulkner's insight which Ellison borrows) is easier to fictionalize: that is to say, the whites, especially in the South of *Invisible Man* (Ellison mostly eliminates the whites in the North, a grave error in strategy), see the Negro in a way that, in the perception itself, denies him humanity. That perception sub-humanizes, brutalizes, humiliates, simplifies him. At the same time the novel shows how the white muddies his own identity in that process. At this level of the novel he is entirely successful. When the novel moves North, the search for identity of the Negro assimilates again to that of the whites. Each is in danger of losing his identity in an industrialized culture where the work he does is subhuman and devoid of relationship with people, with the industry, and with the society; where he lives in a condition of urban agglomeration; where family disintegrates; where religion offers no help; where education is not equal to the burdens placed upon it; where political leadership provides no solution. Admittedly, the problem of identity for the Negro is at once special and more acute. The point is, however, that Ellison is equal to that absolutely essential insight.

Invisible Man is important for what it has achieved for Negro writers as a model. The irony is that the achievement may have come at precisely the time when Ellison, who now articulates the role of the writer more powerfully than any white writer, may have arrived at a time when the role of the writer himself is threatened with extinction. He seems curiously old-fashioned.

The basic structural flaw of *Invisible Man* has been alluded to. That novel, like *Augie March*, offers us a protagonist (in Ellison's work he is even nameless) who can only resist passively. It is Ellison, then, who responds, as it was Bellow who responded in *Augie March*. The protagonist is the puppet. In order to give us society as an iron cage, Ellison cripples full responsiveness, a major flaw.

In this sense, Ellison's one book of prose, *Shadow and Act*, provides us with what *Invisible Man* lacks: precisely the intelligence which begins to be adequate to a Negro writer's inheritance. It is by far the best book of prose written by a Negro writer. In rich particularity it conveys pride in race and the affirmation of possibilities in Negro life. Ellison the writer, trained, incidentally, as a jazz trumpetist, musicologist, and composer, gives us the Negro in his various economic activities; in food, dress, dance, song, humour, folk culture, patience, endurance, sense of timing. He covers the full range of American Negro humanity in a way that includes, yet transcends, outraged conscience, Baldwin's present stopping-point. These essays follow Negro history carefully, from early slavery, through the most terrible crime of the whites, as he sees it, in Reconstruction South, to the Great Migration to the North, finally to Harlem in the present. He describes what has been gained, but also what has been lost, in the movement from South to North as the culture of industrialism shattered family life, splintered churches, and deprived the Negro of the degree of stability he had possessed. Ellison is perhaps best of all on the complex interaction of Negro and white society, both in the South and in the North, and, in particular, in the present danger of the

Negro losing what is significant in his tradition. *Shadow and Act*, finally, is the best account describing what the function of the Negro writer ought to be and he uses what he can learn from the white writers and white culture towards the end of describing accurately what Negro life comes to. The sensibility of the better Negro writer becomes the sensibility of his people:

'a way of feeling, of seeing and expressing one's life. And the process of acquiring technique is a process of modifying one's responses, of learning to see and feel, to hear and observe, to evoke and evaluate the images of memory and of summoning up human values in the ways which have been established by the great writers who have developed and extended the art.'

Ellison is the more impressive writer. But James Baldwin became the talent whom his race (and the whites) chose to represent them. Baldwin's talent is more narrow, more concentrated in the fierce intensity of the experience of injustice. He is much closer to the present mood of the American Negro. Baldwin, like Ellison, is aware of the degree to which the quality of self- and community-awareness has been moulded by whites. But his writing lacks detachment, impersonality, hence dimensional understanding.

Baldwin's first novel, *Go Tell It on the Mountain* (1953) remains the best fiction he has written, and it is a minor work in the tradition of conventional fictional autobiography. The story covers one day in the life of a fourteen-year-old bastard child, Johnny Grimes, who lives in Harlem with his mother whom he loves and a stepfather whom he must battle all the time. Part I deals with the present. The last section, 'The Threshing Floor', describes his 'birth in Christ'. The evangelical religious experience was central for Baldwin, as Negro music was for Ellison. The middle part, with a Southern setting, is a flashback covering the histories of his stepfather, Gabriel, his Aunt Florence, and his mother Elizabeth and her lover Richard. The novel is at its best in half a dozen scenes where Baldwin captures the speech of each differentiated character, allows each to present himself, dramatically. Baldwin controls these scenes with touches of humour and irony, adjusted to specific Negro realities. The weakest parts of the novel—most of it, unfortunately, and, indeed, most of the novels that follow—attempt psychological introspection and a capturing of feelings. The language is cliché-ridden, or portentous, or overblown, rhetorically. That language is expressive of generalized emotions, utilizing all the excess or banalities of best-seller prose in ladies' magazines. Where the dramatic scenes fail to utilize Negro speech and action out there, the convention is that of inferior film. The imagination is then unoriginal, the reverse of experimental, filtered often through mass-media stereotypes. The final section, 'The Threshing Floor', is a *tour de force* description of religious conversion: hysterical, apocalyptic, top of the lungs. It soon becomes repetitive, impenetrable, claustrophobic.

The achievement of the novel lies in a certain balance: much irony, little self-pity or sentimentality, and an understated control of the realities of Harlem life without the need for overt social protest, presented in the speech of characters who face up to those realities. Best of all, perhaps, is Baldwin's handling of the way in which the whites have imposed themselves on the Negroes. No whites appear, and each Negro is allowed his special response. The name of the protagonist, Johnny Grimes, suggests psychic dirt for which he blames himself. The surrounding evil: the squalor, the rats, the urine-smelling, congested houses, the family disruptions, the sense of degraded manhood, the criminality and the violence, all are felt by each Negro to stem from himself. Religion is a form of consolation and revenge, dignity in the eyes of God and promise of a better life to come; and a conviction that Negroes are the children of Moses, enslaved now to the white man, but promised both deliverance from, as well as destruction of, the enemy.

4

At the end of this brief survey of American fiction since 1945, the perspective should be made clear. First, nothing is gained by 'covering' the field with names, titles, dates, and potted summaries. This survey has been evaluative in nature and has focused on what has emerged for one critic as the better fiction since 1945. Implicitly it invites differing critics to register other evaluations and to propose other candidates, for example,

William Styron, Philip Roth, J. D. Salinger, John Hawkes, Flannery O'Connor, or John Updike. The best work of these writers deserves to be read: Styron's *Lie Down in Darkness* and the *Confessions of Nat Turner*; Philip Roth's short stories, *Goodbye, Columbus*, and his novels, *Letting Go, When She Was Good*, and *Portnoy's Complaint*; Salinger's best short stories and *Catcher in the Rye*; John Hawkes's *The Cannibal* and *Lime-Twig;* Updike's *Rabbit, Run* and *Couples*.

Further, there are single books that can be recommended. Some have already been mentioned: Walker Percy's *The Moviegoer*, Joseph Heller's *Catch-22*, Gwendolyn Brooks's *Maud Martha*. Others are: William Burroughs, the *Naked Lunch*; J. P. Donleavy's *The Ginger Man*; Ken Kesey's *One Flew Over the Cuckoo's Nest*; John Rechy, *City of Night*; Hubert Selby, Jr's *Last Exit to Brooklyn*; Terry Southern's *Magic Christian*; Vance Bourjailly's *The Violated*; John Horne Burns's *The Gallery*; Evan S. Connell, Jr's *Mrs Bridge* and the (1969) *Mr Bridge*; Herbert Gold's *The Man Who Was Not With It*; Thomas Pyncheon's *V*; Paul Goodman's *Empire City*; Jack Kerouac's *On the Road* and *Desolation Angels*; Wallace Markfield's *To an Early Grave*; James Purdy's *Cabot Wright Begins*; Edward Wallant's *The Pawnbrokers*, and *Children at the Gate*; John Williams's *Stoner*; Richard Yates's *Revolutionary Road*.

Given more space, one could summarize readily the achievement of each writer who has produced single books, or a body of work, deserving closer attention. That way, one could answer somewhat more adequately to the intention announced at the outset: to provide the total responsiveness of a 'community' of novelists (and their critics and audience).

There is a possible way, however, in which the present survey might be rounded out. That is to provide a rough category of novels along 'cultural' lines, i.e. literature as cultural document.

What has been described, implicitly, has been the response of gifted writers to their American culture of industrialism, science and technology, and democracy. One group of writers, then, shows a commitment to that culture, whatever the depth and range of criticism. It would include, first, writers who feed the entertainment industry, as well as the out-and-out best-sellers (Sloan Wilson, Leon Uris, Harold Robbins, Herman Wouk, Cameron Hawley, Allen Drury). Of the writers since 1945, only

Updike would be a significant addition, though many of the older and competent writers continue to produce: James Gould Cozzens, Louis Auchincloss, John Cheever, John Hersey, John O'Hara, Irwin Shaw, Peter de Vries, and others. Significantly the 'political' novel, or the novel of social protest, in the tradition of Norris, Upton Sinclair, Sinclair Lewis's *It Can't Happen Here*, the proletarian novels of the 1930s, John Dos Passos, John Steinbeck, and others, appears to have lapsed. Only in the Negro novel do the possibilities remain: a continuation of the tradition of Richard Wright. Even here, the better work lies in prose journalism: the work of James Baldwin, *The Autobiography of Malcolm X*, Claude Brown's *Man-Child in the Promised Land*, Eldridge Cleaver's *Soul on Ice*.

In the next category we find writers who refuse to give their full support to American culture. They stand outside society, as it were, and yet offer appraisals deriving from the traditional culture. In this respect they resemble the English minority tradition critical of industrialism whose work Raymond Williams has considered in *Culture and Society* 1780–1950 (e.g. Wordsworth, Coleridge, Arnold, George Eliot, Ruskin, Morris, Lawrence, Orwell, Leavis, T. S. Eliot). These would include: Saul Bellow, Vance Bourjailly, Mary McCarthy, Paul Goodman, Bernard Malamud, Norman Mailer, Evan S. Connell, Jr, Walker Percy, George P. Elliott, Ralph Ellison, Herbert Gold, Howard Nemerov, Grace Paley, Carson McCullers, Flannery O'Connor, William Styron, Vladimir Nabokov, Wright Morris, Philip Roth, J. F. Powers, J. D. Salinger, Robert Penn Warren, Richard Yates. Many of these are older writers.

Finally there are the writers, mostly the young (though a few of the older ones may be found here: Mailer, Salinger, Paul Bowles, William Burroughs, Kerouac, Purdy), who reject the vision, the goals, the dedications of American culture. They are, in fact, 'alienated', and attempt to convey what it feels like to inhabit, usually in an urban agglomeration or suburban facelessness, American culture, in its latest phase: neo-colonialism; the atom bomb; electronics, computers, space exploration; continued extensions of necessary bureaucracies to handle mass production, distribution, consumption, government; continued triumphs of technology and the machine; visual media in film and TV challenging the existence of print; intensification of the rat race; radical changes of a kind that have altered sexual, family, and other personal relations beyond 'traditional' recognitions; the dynamic rate itself of accelerating changes, too complex and bewildering to follow.

These writers not only condemn the way of life of present American culture. Even more, they no longer appear to feel the powerful promptings of traditional values and attitudes; or are hesitant, defensive, ambiguous and tend to build masks, disguises, ambiguities, uncertainties into the very structure of the fiction they write. The group is various, is splintered, allows for much overlapping. The best one can do is to suggest stress and modulation. There is, pervasively, an emphasis on the difficult search for identity itself. Next, one encounters writers who convey a powerful image of nightmare: John Hawkes, for example. But nightmare effects combine in others with realistic accounts that resemble, in the transposed terms of the 1960s, the Elizabethan underworld; while many writers employ effects of black humour in their fiction. Here we inhabit the world of the homosexual and the homosexual hustler, the lesbian, the drug-addicted, the criminal, the hopelessly lost, the mad. I refer to the novels of Burroughs, Rechy, Selby, Ken Kesey, Jack Gelber, Sanford Friedman, Alfred Grossman, Bert Blechman, and many others. I have already alluded to some of the black humorists: Donleavy, Stanley Elkin, Irwin Faust, Bruce Jay Friedman, Terry Southern, Joseph Heller. Often the note of compassion for the failed, the lost, the outcast, takes predecence: in the work of Edward Dorn, Wallant, William Gass, Kesey. At times, too, one encounters the apocalyptic vision, despairing and nihilistic, or even revolutionary in the political sense, where the writer appears to wish for the breakdown of existing society in all its evils, while unable to envisage what might take its place: Pyncheon, Heller, Jeremy Larner, Susan Sontag, Kesey, Kurt Vonnegut, Jr.

It is possible at this time to view the American novel in two ways. On the one hand we perceive the existence of a large, various, and splintered group of young writers whose beliefs are tenuous, or nihilistic, or uncertain. Whatever else they convey, they do not convey fresh and healthy possibilities within the culture. The combined audience for these writers appears to exist mostly in the colleges and universities; while the industrialized marketplace for letters seems to exclude them from a large public. In short, we may be witnessing the disintegration of the novel as a form – the often foretold death of the novel.

On the other hand, we may hope. A very large number of young writers, supported by a very large audience of young readers – the activity of imaginative work in the Universities is prodigious, almost unbelievable to a European until he goes to America – is exploring what life comes to for them in their American culture. Out of this great stir of activity may come those writers who will carry on in the tradition of America's better writers and help to shape contemporary sensibility. They will help to articulate an ordered response to the complex experience we designate as American culture in the present.

5
An Introduction to Reading in Culture and Society
RAYMOND WILLIAMS

EXPERIENCE is divided into subjects, in every known academic curriculum. When these subjects are called, as so often, disciplines, it seems easy to believe that an understanding of the definitions and boundaries of the subjects is a condition of seriousness. And since academic institutions, almost necessarily, are self-reproducing and self-perpetuating, any questioning of subject divisions—the internal organization of academic studies —can be made to seem an attack on serious study of any kind and even, paradoxically, on academic freedom.

Yet it must always be clear, not only that the division of experience into subjects is arbitrary, but that any particular division is an expression of a particular way of seeing the world: usually a selective combination of past and present. Classification is arbitrary in itself, and the habit of classification, because it lends itself to a particularly straightforward kind of teaching and learning, is deeply rooted in academic method. But the particular classification into subjects has its significance far beyond the walls of academies. It is a prepared, defining framework for the understanding of all experience. To be educated at all is to submit, at least temporarily, to that prepared system. Like everyone else who is writing or reading this book, I have made this submission, to be in a position to work at all. It is then necessary to explain why I now reject the system, in a crisis of experience, and as a condition for continuing and developing my own work.

My centre of interest, from the beginning, had been imaginative literature. I had understood this, since I was a boy at school, as writing novels and plays. And I thought for some time that an academic course in English would be mainly a way of reading other people's novels and plays and poems, and learning what was necessary to understand them. I had two surprises in the course of my education. First, I discovered the shadow line between writing and the study of literature. It amazed me to discover how many teachers of literature regarded writing as something that had already happened, at a safe distance in time, rather than as something that is still happening and that we ourselves can give our main energy to. I found that a critical essay on another writer is taken more seriously, as a contribution to the study of literature, than a piece of what is called–with a slight sideways smile–original or creative writing. Now, in a university, when I tell my scientist colleagues that I am writing a novel they understand me at once; it is what they expect me to do–a practical, experimental, ongoing activity. From most of my colleagues in the arts I more usually get that same sideways smile; it is perhaps no harm that I spend my time in that playful way, but they would like me to know that meanwhile they are getting on with the serious business of editing or collation or criticism. This profound bias against practice, in academic minds that have been trained in what are still called the humanities, is a matter of great significance in the present unrest in education. I do not want to see our arts departments teaching creative practice; in a hierarchical system there is something inescapably absurd about that. But I do want to see the centre of any arts course as practice; free and where necessary co-operative practice; as the only way of defining, at the heart of our studies, the seriousness and the difficulty of the central discipline.

Our present system is against that. And this is not surprising. For its delicate internal balances depend on the exclusion of certain kinds of practice and experience. This, many years ago (I have become hardened now) was my second surprise. To understand works of literature meant necessarily, I thought, understanding the times and societies they had been written in: not as 'background', an inert two-dimensional staged society; but as active experience, of the kind I know in my own life in a particular society at a particular time. This is where the division of subjects fell as a second shadow-line. For I was given to understand that only certain kinds of what were called extra-literary facts were relevant to the study of literature. And at a certain point these extra-literary facts became something else:

were called politics, sociology or economic history; and there were quite other departments of the academy which dealt with them. Might one then go to those other departments? Well no, you must make your choice. And of course, if you're *more* interested in those other things than in literature . . .

This was the point at which I discovered a very curious twentieth-century formation (it was assumed, of course, to be universal or permanent). Just as, once, people were born either little Liberals or little Conservatives, so now people were born, or in early life were confirmed, as having the literary or the sociological mind. And this curious fate, as I explored it, came to resemble more and more the world of party politics. The contempt of each kind of mind for the other—'a *literary* treatment', '*sociology*'—was equalled only by their combined contempt for anyone who belonged to neither party as by law defined; who had not realized that this was the crucial choice any serious man must make.

But I refused, and continue to refuse to make it. For two reasons: one academic; the other from experience. I will make, from politeness, the academic point first. Literature has always been divided into kinds, and in certain periods these kinds have been defined by rules. Literature, needless to say, has gone on in its own ways: sometimes respecting the kinds; where necessary disregarding them or inventing new ones. After two hundred and fifty years of major works, some people still wonder whether the novel is a kind; or they try to classify it under epic or romance. After a hundred years of successful practice, some people say there are no modern tragedies; they know from their definitions what tragedy is, and the dramatists presumably do not. It was not very difficult for me, as a writer, to see what was going on here. Literature, from the habits of a particular kind of study, had become an essentially predictable activity; if it were not predictable, the classifications themselves would be threatened. Some remarkable ingenuity has in fact been forthcoming, revising the kinds when inescapably new works made their appearance. Or, as it became more difficult, some people gave up kinds altogether; only at once to construct an even more formidable system: the division between 'imaginative' literature and the rest.

This was really very neat. It separated novels, plays and

poems from all other kinds of writing; and by doing so it separated them from other kinds of concern. If you look at the actual history of literature, it cannot be sustained for a moment. In every period there are major writers who write work other than poems, plays or novels. From Montaigne to Ruskin, from Bunyan to *The Children of Sanchez*, this is an evident literary fact. The dividers, of course, can get some of their own way. They can invent that last saving category of the 'miscellaneous'; call these men essayists, or 'where appropriate' philosophers, historians, social critics and so on. Anything, in fact, to break the unity of literature; to keep it away from those critical points where its indissoluble concern with the general life is undeniable.

For in fact it is not just in the miscellaneous category that their sharpest difficulties occur. Once we look at what Shakespeare and Swift, Milton and Byron, Blake and Dickens, Wordsworth and Lawrence were writing about, it is only by an act of will (but of a will which is already provided for; a last testament, with substantial endowments) that we can refrain from looking at the general life of men and societies. The literary structures of the works themselves are still of the first importance. Unless we know and study these we have nothing, in their light, that we can look at or say. But as we discover their human importance, we come to know that this does not stand in some separable imaginative sphere. On the contrary, it is through the exercise of imaginative creation and re-creation that we learn and relearn and reshape an always general reality. We have then to put our experience of literature into an active relationship with all the other ways in which we experience and interpret our widest living reality. It is in this finding of active relationship that the study of culture and society can be said to begin.

Necessarily we find our own ways to this point. I want to describe my own way, not as autobiography but as experience. For it was indeed unplanned and was as far as it could well be from the application of preconceived notions and dogmas. I was born into a working-class family which respected education. I went to grammar school and did the work that was set me, mostly with great pleasure and interest. But at the same time, all the time, I was a person in a particular social situation, of which, as an inseparable part of my intellectual growth, I was increasingly and intensely aware. I could see, for example, the intellectual frustration of my father and his neighbours: not from a want of intelligence—that was at least as keen as my own—but from a simple social failure to provide opportunities to connect that intelligence with the work and findings and methods of scores of generations of educated men: men who themselves belonged to no particular class or nation. But this intellectual deprivation was not an isolated fact. It seemed to me to connect very clearly with many directly experienced social and economic facts.

My father was a man doing obviously responsible work. He was a railway signalman; one week out of three working at nights. When I would lie in bed, having finished my homework, hearing the trains going through the valley and knowing my father was alone in his box seeing them safe, I learned two things, as sharp and hard as anything in my textbooks: first, the sense of a society, of a complicated mutual dependence, to which men gave their strength; second, a denial of this society, this real mutual dependence, by the forms of an existing and powerful economic and political system.

For I was already reading about 'lower-class people', and I knew the facts of money and had enough arithmetic to estimate my father's fifty shillings a week. Part of my father's interest in my own education was that I should get a job which carried more respect and more money. It was always an irony, but I have never blamed him for it. He had learned the realities of this society too hard and too long. Respect and money can be dispensed with as aims when you have got used to both. For me, as for him, this particular ambition was a necessary conclusion from our actual social position. The usual cant against it still makes me very deeply angry. But at the same time, always, there was something else. Education was insight into a world that was known to be too difficult, without its aid, to understand and control. It meant very much to him that I should gain this insight; that I should get outside the box where he had to do his prescribed duties, outside the world that was its simple reflection, and get to know enough to come back and change it: if not for him then for hundreds of thousands like him and after him. This was often expressed as a simple political and trade-union aim; but it was deepened, consistently, by the sense of a wider human purpose of which these were the instruments; a sense that through education the general life could be enlarged and liberated.

I won a scholarship to Cambridge, to read English. I supposed, at the time, that it would mean what I expected. It didn't, and still doesn't. But there was something else that I had never foreseen: a profound shock that I suppose has been the basis of all my subsequent work. It was not only that literature was not presented to me as the human experience which, gained so hard and in so many different places and ways, indicated our living perspectives and their difficulties. That, after all, I could remedy for myself; I could read the books—the libraries much more important than the teaching—and go on to relate them to the general life. What really shocked me, much more than the luxury, the snobbery, the fantastically different scale of money-values from that fifty shillings a week, was the use of literature, the use of learning in general, to ratify just this economic and social system and its immediate ways of life. I had to listen to most people being talked about as ignorant inferiors and to learning being prized as the mark which set certain men above others. And this was not, I soon saw, an admiration of learning in itself. These men and their institutions fitted in very easily with a world that had little to do with learning, but that had shared with them the same schools and colleges; that perhaps even more crucially shared the same incomes, the same investments, the same attachments to property.

I did not then have to invent a relation between literature and the general life. I found one in existence, an active working relationship; both practically, in the ways these people lived when they were not reading books; and, more subtly, in schemes of values, approaches, tones, which had as their cumulative effect the teaching of certain decisive attitudes towards other men.

My book *Modern Tragedy* is the record of one such scheme and of my revolt against it; a revolt that took many years to become intellectually articulate. There are similar cases in all the main fields of literary study, some of which I am still working to get clear. All through the sixties I have been trying to understand the relation between the development of the English novel from

Dickens to Lawrence and the very complicated relations between, first, a popular and an educated culture, and second what I have called, looking back to my own experience, educated and customary ways of thinking and feeling. This is a study of literature: the most important English literature of its time. But it cannot be studied only as literature, in the narrowing sense that now has. Dickens's positive relation with a new urban popular culture seemed to me of the greatest importance here. But there was also that consideration indicated when a middle-class critic called George Eliot, Hardy and Lawrence 'our three great autodidacts': for no other reason, that I can discover, than that their fathers were a bailiff, a builder and a miner and that none of them went to public school or to Oxbridge. The central tradition composed in varying ways by Dickens, George Eliot, Hardy and Lawrence had to be grasped socially, in its profound relations with ordinary life and with the problems of growth and change, before it could be again fully valued as the great literature it is and rescued from the anxiously narrowing versions of a self-conscious minority.

Modern drama and film are other related cases. They have been connected, throughout, with the development of society: in the nature of audiences, the social purposes of theatres, the universal popular character of cinema. What I have been trying to discover there is the way in which dramatic forms and conventions embody the actual relationships between a dramatist and his society and especially a dramatist and his audience. I tried to work some of this out in *Drama in Performance* and *Drama from Ibsen to Brecht*, and in the work on film I recently started in Cambridge.

I give these examples of work now mainly accepted within orthodox studies to show how in a particular case, in which I can speak from experience, virtually everything that was presented in existing educational ways seemed to me to require radical re-examination: not only as a way of getting its achievements clear, but more crucially as a way of separating the art from the irrelevant and narrowing social values in which I found it embedded. The study of culture and society, as I came to it, was in this sense severely practical: a study of relationships between works of art and the societies in which they were made: not because I thought this was in the abstract a useful kind of inquiry, but because I knew in immediate experience that the works had been absorbed into a local and temporary society which had very little in common with the worlds of the creators but which now, through its command of education, presented the works, almost invariably, as aspects of itself or at least in its own terms. I could challenge this in two ways. Historically, by going back to the works and their times and showing their real structures. Critically, by putting questions which the works raised in their connections to our own experiences and times: questions which then necessarily went beyond the limits of orthodox literary studies.

I put the point in this way to emphasize that my own approach to the study of culture and society – the only approach of which I can speak with any authority – was through imaginative literature and its connections with social experience. I want to stress, of course, that this is only one among several possible roads. But it was from asking these questions, prompted by literature and experience, puzzled by the immediately available critical and intellectual tradition, that I went on to anything that can be called a theory of culture and society, of a more general kind; the work represented by *Culture and Society*, *The Long Revolution* and *Communications*. Those were books written in an area where I was living and thinking rather than in a 'field' or 'discipline' in which I had been trained. And of course, as it happens, for reasons deeply connected with the whole history of our own kind of society, there was in any case no established field, no formed discipline, within which those questions could have been put in those ways.

I read a good deal of sociology, history of ideas and social philosophy while I was writing those books. Not enough, I dare say; they could of course be made better. But it was very interesting, when the books came out, how some of the narrower sociologists, and related people, started a sort of agitated flag-waving, boundary-drawing and discipline-calling. In Britain, as it happened, much more than anywhere else. From many other parts of the world – from France, Italy and Scandinavia; from Japan and the United States – I found an immediate recognition of the sort of work that was being done, and there within the frontiers of known intellectual traditions. In Britain it was different. Many thousands of people, it was perfectly clear, wanted to put these questions in very much these ways (which of course doesn't mean that they would find or be satisfied with the same particular answers). Something like a new 'subject', a new 'discipline', started growing around the work of four or five people, and is indeed now common in British universities as an element of several kinds of course.

But it is still necessary to record that what is known in Britain as the 'culture-and-society' approach is quite widely distrusted within the curious organization of British social studies. From within that organization, it had better be stressed, none of this work has been done or even attempted. A whole central area of social life – the creation and communication of art and of ideas – had been effectively and (one is tempted to say) deliberately neglected. This is undoubtedly related to the general neglect of ideas and theory within the small area of British sociology: a neglect which has its counterpart – in some ways its redeeming strength – in the emphasis on social survey and inquiry: sometimes the gathering of facts within an existing administration, of which the ideas are assumed; sometimes, of course, independent and radical and reforming, an opening-up of dark areas. But however this was, the fact remained that the work was not getting done, and – which is more controversial – that to get it done would require different approaches, different methods, different minds, if it was to be seriously undertaken. I think in the coming generation there will be extensive and serious work in this whole area, by people originally trained over the whole spectrum of now separated studies, from literature to sociology. There are already encouraging signs of this, and as it develops the work will undoubtedly mature. But still at the present time it is worth recording that the incomprehension and hostility which 'greeted' the culture-and-society emphasis seemed very similar, to one of its authors, whether it came from within official social or official literary studies.

And this does not now surprise me, for what was being challenged – and the note of challenge was always explicitly there – was much more than the orthodoxy of a particular subject. It was the set of habits and assumptions of the English educational system as a whole; the set habits and assumptions, I have already said, of an existing class which has the definition of education within its power and which found professional or pseudo-professional reasons for keeping existing definitions and separations of interests in their known and operative forms. The men who crossed the known frontiers and tangled with the existing system were committing much more than an academic offence. The offence was social, at a very significant time.

Many men before this had crossed the frontiers of that particular system which in England links education with social class. But what became evident after 1945 was that a generation was crossing, and the point of a generation—as opposed to mere numbers—is that it is conscious and in touch with itself, apt to emphasize and pursue its own interests as opposed to merging or qualifying its own interests within an existing establishment. The pressures of course were often severe. But in a number of ways—in new approaches to literature, in a revaluation of working-class history, in a persistent concern with issues affecting majorities, in the study of learning and education, in the new emphasis on cultural history, and in linking ways in matters of style and emphasis—something recognizable as a generation began to form in the 1950s and is now, though of course still not strong enough, making some evident changes of several kinds in the culture as a whole.

It is still, in general, a radical rather than a revolutionary generation, and even as such it is weakened, continually, by elements of exploitation within the general culture. For while this generation has been forming the whole society has been changing: superficially in some of the same directions, in the increasing importance of popular culture and opinion, but also, very powerfully, in ways of exploiting and controlling these increasingly important areas: ways which require, as recruits, people who in different circumstances, or with a different morality, would belong to the radical generation because that has been their experience. Richard Hoggart and I were virtually forced to the study of contemporary communications—in the papers and magazines and in radio and television—because of the altering importance of just this phenomenon. For the communications system continued and continues to be run by a political establishment and by minority capital, with only qualifying though important conceptions of a public service. Yet in form if not always in content this minority system had to appear to be popular: had to adopt popular tones and satisfy, often cynically, popular tastes. In every generation of school-leavers, in every class of new graduates, I find myself wondering (I have given up predicting) which young men and women will use their special experience to fit into this system, and which will go on from their experience to change it.

Britain has, in this sense, never been more interesting and exciting culturally: for there are vital new forces which can remake our culture and society, in very various ways; and at the same time there are very deep pressures on just these people to preserve an old system by superficial alteration, to settle for less than half just because the pull of capital and the established forms are so strong, so beguiling, so apparently welcoming, so temptingly practical. I think the conflict between these two roads, which is now very intense, will be seen, from the future, as historic. This is only one of the many reasons why these years are the most exciting and challenging I could have chosen to live through: an intense, often apparently slow-moving but continuing crisis, of a quite fundamental kind.

These then are my own perspectives. They have to be borne in mind as I go on to suggest reading, for of course it is obvious that I am not pretending to make recommendations in a neutral way. But then, if any part of my argument has been accepted, it should be obvious that there aren't any neutral recommendations. When I came to Cambridge I found myself stranded among partisans: not exactly passionate partisans, it is true, but this was mainly because there were so many of them and they were so like each other, and the things they said and believed fitted into a local and temporary system—evidently local, if you went to other countries; evidently temporary, if you knew any history—but still, with all that national capital and prestige behind it looking very solid and permanent—even 'timeless' to use one of their favourite words—so that even their most extreme prejudices and exclusions took on a local air of normality, and anything else seemed partisan. I think, and have tried to show, that definitions of a subject, of methods of study and of materials of study, embody, necessarily, certain fundamental and chosen values and emphases. I have set mine out directly, and that is the only real difference.

There are several possible starting-points, but the order I

suggest, which can of course be varied, relates to my own sense of how these questions have been formed, within our own culture and society.

READING LIST

A. CULTURE AND SOCIETY—The English Tradition

1 William Cobbett: *Rural Rides.*
Thomas Bewick: *A Memoir.*
Edmund Burke: *Reflections on the Revolution in France.*
Tom Paine: *The Rights of Man.*
Robert Owen: *A New View of Society.*
Robert Southey: *Colloquies with Sir Thomas More.*
Thomas Carlyle: *Signs of the Times. Chartism.*
William Blake: *Songs of Experience.*

2 William Wordsworth: *The Prelude. Preface to Lyrical Ballads.*
S. T. Coleridge: *Biographia Literaria. On the Constitution of Church and State.*
R. B. Shelley: *Defence of Poetry.*
A. W. Pugin: *Contrasts.*

3 Charles Dickens: *Dombey and Son. Great Expectations.*
Elizabeth Gaskell: *Mary Barton. North and South.*
George Eliot: *Mill on the Floss. Felix Holt.*
Thomas Hardy: *Return of the Native. Jude the Obscure.*

4 John Stuart Mill: *Autobiography* (Worlds Classics, O.U.P.).
John Ruskin: *Unto this Last* (Everyman Library, Dent).
Matthew Arnold: *Culture and Anarchy* (C.U.P.).
William Morris: *News from Nowhere* (Monthly Review Press).
Samuel Butler: *Erewhon* (Cape).
W. H. Mallock: *The New Republic* (University of Florida Press).

5 H. G. Wells: *Experiment in Autobiography* (Cape).
R. H. Tawney: *Equality* (Allen and Unwin). *The Acquisitive Society* (Allen and Unwin).
I. A. Richards: *Principles of Literary Criticism* (Routledge).
F. R. Leavis: *The Great Tradition* (Chatto and Windus). *The Common Pursuit (*Chatto and Windus).
T. S. Eliot: *Notes towards the definition of culture* (Faber and Faber).
Q. D. Leavis: *Fiction and the Reading Public* (Chatto and Windus).
Richard Hoggart: *The Uses of Literacy* (Chatto and Windus).

READING IN CULTURE AND SOCIETY

6. Robert Tressall: *Ragged-Trousered Philanthropists* (Lawrence and Wishart).
   H. G. Wells: *Tono-Bungay* (Collins).
   D. H. Lawrence: *Sons and Lovers* (Heinemann). *The Rainbow* (Heinemann).
   Lewis Grassic Gibbon: *A Scots Quair* (Hutchinson).
   Joyce Cary: *The Horse's Mouth* (Michael Joseph).
   George Orwell: *Coming up for Air* (Secker and Warburg). *Critical Essays* (Secker and Warburg).
   Alan Sillitoe: *Key to the Door* (Macmillan).

7. E. P. Thompson: *The Making of the English Working Class* (Gollancz).
   M. K. Ashby: *Joseph Ashby of Tysoe* (O.U.P.).
   Brian Jackson: *Working Class Community* (Routledge).
   Brian Simon: *Studies in the History of Education 1780–1870* (Lawrence and Wishart).
   A. E. Dobbs: *Education and Social Movements* (Kelley).
   Brian Jackson and Dennis Marsden: *Education and the Working Class* (Routledge).
   David Holbrook: *English for Maturity* (C.U.P.).

B. CULTURE AND SOCIETY—The International Tradition
   Montesquieu: *The Spirit of Laws.*
   Saint-Simon: *On Industrial Society.*
   Tocqueville: *Democracy in America.*
   Hegel: *Philosophy of Fine Art.*
   Marx: *Economic and Philosophical Manuscripts. Preface to a Critique of Political Economy.*
   Nietzsche: *Birth of Tragedy.*
   Tolstoy: *What is Art?* (World's Classics, O.U.P.).
   Weber: *Essays in Sociology.*
   Plekhanov: *The Individual in History* (Century Books).
   Trotski: *Literature and Revolution.*
   Hughes: *Consciousness and Society* (MacGibbon and Kee).
   Lukacs: *History and Class Consciousness* (Merlin).
   Gramsci: *The Modern Prince* (Lawrence and Wishart).
   Sartre: *What is Literature?* (Methuen).
   Camus: *The Rebel* (Penguin).
   Charbonnier: *Conversations with C. Levi-Strauss* (Cape).

2 Fischer: *The Necessity of Art* (Penguin).
   Barthes: *Elements of Semiology* (Cape).
   McLuhan: *The Gutenberg Galaxy* (Routledge).
   Fabre: *History of Communication.*

Mao-tse-Tung: *Yenan Talks on Literature and Art* (Foreign Languages Publishing House).
Goldmann: *The Hidden God.*
Benjamin: *Illuminations.*
Benedict: *Patterns of Culture.*

3 Kroeber and Kluckhohn: *Culture, a Critical Review of Concepts and Definitions* (Random House).
Mannheim: *Essays in the Sociology of Culture* (Routledge).
Sorokin: *Social and Cultural Dynamics* (Peter Owen).
Marcuse: *One-Dimensional Man* (Routledge).
Wright Mills: *The Sociological Imagination* (O.U.P.).
Anderson: *Components of the National Culture* (New Left Review).

C. POPULAR CULTURE

A. Cruse: *The Victorians and their Books* (Allen and Unwin).
L. James: *Fiction for the Working Man 1830–90* (O.U.P.).
F. R. Leavis and D. Thompson: *Culture and Environment* (Chatto and Windus).
Q. D. Leavis: *Fiction and the Reading Public* (Chatto and Windus).
L. Lowenthal: *Literature and the Image of Man* (Beacon). *Literature, Popular Culture and Society* (Pacific Books).
S. Mayo: *The English Novel in the Magazine 1740–1815* (O.U.P.).
E. Oppenheimer: *Book Reviewing for an Audience* (Bailey Brothers).
M. Plant: *The English Book Trade* (Allen and Unwin).
Rosenberg and White: *Mass Culture* (Collier-Macmillan).
S. Hall and P. Whannel: *The Popular Arts* (Hutchinson).
R. Hoggart: *The Uses of Literacy* (Chatto and Windus). *Speaking to Each Other*, 2 Vols. (Chatto and Windus).
H. Wilensky: 'Mass Society and Mass Culture' (*American Sociological Review* 29).
D. Potter: *The Glittering Coffin* (Gollancz).
I. A. Richards: *Practical Criticism* (Routledge).
Scrutiny: Collected Scrutiny 1932–53 (C.U.P.). *Selections from Scrutiny*, 2 Vols., ed. F. R. Leavis (C.U.P.).
B. Wicker: *Culture and Liturgy* (Sheed and Ward).
T. F. Eagleton and B. Wicker, eds.: *From Culture to Revolution* (Sheed and Ward).
R. Williams: *The Long Revolution* (Chatto and Windus).

D. FILMS

J. B. Barclay: 'Viewing tastes of Adolescents in Films and Television' (*Public Opinion Quarterly*).

L. Berkowitz: 'Film Violence and Subsequent Aggressive Tendencies', (*Boston Public Opinion Quarterly*, Vol. 27).
British Film Institute: Film Study Materials (On hire).
R. Durgnat: *Films and Feelings* (Faber and Faber).
P. Rotha: *The Film Till Now* (Vision Press).
J. Quinn: *The Film and Television as an Aspect of European Culture*.
P. Wollen: *Sign and Meaning in the Cinema* (Secker and Warburg).
S. Kracauer: *From Caligari to Hitler* (Princeton U.P.).

E. BROADCASTING

R. Baker: *Here is the News* (Leslie Frewin).
A. Briggs: *History of Broadcasting in the U.K.* (H.M.S.O. 1962). *Pilkington Report*, Committee on Broadcasting. (H.M.S.O.).
B. Paulu: *British Broadcasting in Transition* (Macmillan).
J. Scupham: *Broadcasting and the Community* (C. A. Watts).
D. Thomas: *Competition in Radio* (Institute of Economic Affairs).
W. Altmann: *T.V. From Monopoly to Competition* (Institute of Economic Affairs).
W. Belson: 'Effects of Television upon Family Life', *Discovery*, Vol. 21, no. 10.
A. Hancock: *The Small Screen* (Heinemann).
H. Himmelweit: *Television and the Child* (O.U.P.). *Citizenship and Television* (Political and Economic Planning).
J. Trenaman and D. McQuail: *Television and the Political Image* (Methuen). *The Effects of Television on Children and Adolescents* (UNESCO).
M. Whitehouse: *Cleaning Up Television* (Blandford).
H. Wilson: *The Pressure Group: The Campaign for Commercial Television* (Secker and Warburg).

F. THE PRESS, JOURNALISM, READERSHIP

R. Altick: *The English Common Reader* (Phoenix Books).
L. Andrews: *The Problems of an Editor* (O.U.P.).
J. Dodge: *The Practice of Journalism* (Heinemann).
R. Hackett: *Seventy Years of Bestsellers* (Bowker).
R. Hoggart, ed.: *Your Sunday Paper* (London University Press).
L. McColvin: *The Chance to Read*.
M. Nelson: *Freedom of the Press*.
G. Pumphrey: *What Children Think of their Comics* (Epworth Press).
Reports of the Royal Commision on the Press, 1947 and 1962 (H.M.S.O.).
Report of the Commission on Advertising (Labour Party).
W. Schramm: *One Day in the World's Press* (Stanford University Press).

B. Siebert: *Freedom of the Press in England 1476–1776* (University of Illinois Press).

L. Smith: *Unreluctant Years* (Viking Press).

D. Thompson: *Between the Lines* (O.U.P.).

F. Williams: *Dangerous Estate* (Longmans).

The Press: A Case for Commitment (Fabian Society).

G. COMMUNICATIONS STUDIES

B. Berelson: *Reader in Public Opinion and Communication* (Collier – Macmillan).

T. L. Dexter: *People, Society and Mass Communication* (Collier-Macmillan).

L. Fraser: *Propaganda* (O.U.P.).

Free Communications Group: *The Open Secret* (privately circulated).

T. Griffith: *Waist-High Culture* (Hutchinson).

J. D. Halloran: *Attitude Formation and Change* (Leicester University Press). *The Effects of Mass Communication* (Leicester University Press).

M. McLuhan: *The Mechanical Bride* (Routledge).

V. Packard: *The Hidden Persuaders* (Longmans).

T. H. Pear: *The Moulding of Modern Man* (Allen and Unwin).

M. Peterson: *The Mass Media and Modern Society* (Holt, Rinehart and Winston).

W. Schramm: *Responsibility in Mass Communication* (Harper and Row).

D. Thompson, ed.: *Discrimination and Popular Culture* (Penguin).

J. Tunstall: *The Advertising Man* (Chapman and Hall).

R. Williams: *Communications* (Chatto and Windus).

6

Sociology and Culture
IOAN DAVIES

THIS essay includes the word 'culture' in its title because I am not concerned with sociology simply as a subject which deals with aspects of society in some way concerned only with disciplinary competence. For anyone coming to the subject for the first time its significance must in a large measure be in what it represents itself to be, and beyond this, because it is a new 'discipline', how it defines itself in relation to the structure of knowledge and society as a whole. These are 'cultural' acts. In its totality culture can be said to represent the living styles of a society or groups of societies, which is an all-encompassing definition more often used by anthropologists and in need of specification. More particularly it consists of the *technical culture* (the economic and technological instruments of organization); the *symbolic orders* of values, meanings and norms (the ways that social relationships receive recognition in accepted codes of behaviour); and the *expressive manifestations* of the relationship between the technical culture and symbolic orders (in other words the language, art, literature, and knowledge in general). Obviously in no society is there a direct relationship between each of these, and the existence of social divisions based on classes, races, nationalities, religion and so on as well as the transmission of any form of culture from other societies and the persistence of 'historical' features necessarily complicate investigation and simple categorization. The task, however, is a crucial one, particularly if we are to consider the importance of a subject like sociology. For any area of knowledge is necessarily dependent on the technical culture and the symbolic orders for its *raison d'être*. Some subjects—such as many of the sciences—seem close to the technical culture. Whether they have any effect on the symbolic orders must depend on the extent to which they alter the structures on which these orders rest and the extent to which their logic—as with biology in nineteenth-century England—affects the interpretation of values. Other subjects—economics or philosophy—seem in many ways to accord closely with existing symbolic orders: they neither challenge them nor seriously affect them. In these cases the function of knowledge is simply to reinforce the status quo.

Knowledge may challenge the social order in one of two ways: it may contribute to changes in the technical culture in such a way that basic social structures are seriously changed, or it may challenge the symbolic orders by changing the values attributed by people to social order. One doubts if the social sciences can have much impact through the technical culture. (Statistics and computers may have a nuisance effect on our lives and they may make administration easier, but they hardly have much impact on values. On the other hand the technical cultures, particularly mathematics, clearly have important effects on the social sciences.) Their only likely impact is through challenging the symbolic orders, and they can only do this by providing a set of alternative versions of social relationships which affect a wide enough section of a society or its élite to change their values. This does not mean that values only change through knowledge: they obviously do not, but *revolutionary* changes clearly involve changes in knowledge-systems as well, including the formulation of alternative visions of the relationship between culture and society. It is in this context that I want to examine the prospects for sociology.

1. THE BRITISH EXAMPLE

Sociology did not originate in England, though there is enough evidence to claim Scotland as one of the more respectable ancestors.[1] But chauvinistic demands on pedigree are not the reasons for starting with British sociology. The task is a more direct one. We live in Britain and the problems of sociology must be seen in direct relation to the way the subject has developed here and its relevance to the explanation of the culture and social structure of this society. For we must not mistake sociology for a clear-cut discipline like mathematics or even biology: there are few rules, and experiments are difficult to carry out. Sociology is at once the most pretentious and least disciplined of subjects and any attempt at reducing its subject matter to quantifiable proportions runs the risk of making as sociology's patron saint 'Autolycus, that "snapper-up of unconsidered trifles"'.[2] But if it is not a discipline, sociology is at worst a set of methods, a collection of models or even a bag of tricks which allows us to investigate connections which other studies, because of their particularism, have failed to explore. At its most grandiose it attempts to provide a total synthesis of all human knowledge and an interpretation of the development of the entire history of human society. Both these extremes offer something useful, though the methodology is still too crude to be exact enough for the really vital areas of social understanding, while the grand theories frequently pose the important questions without offering us more convincing total explanations than are found in philosophy, religion or history. The problem is, of course, the social setting of sociology itself. As with any other 'discipline' sociology has been affected by the cultures of the societies in which it has developed: one of the tasks of any student of the subject is to distinguish between the stamp of particular cultures and those elements which persist independently of their national roots. This is a familiar problem in philosophy but one which gains its clearest statement in the work of Karl Mannheim and Leon Trotski.[3] In Mannheim the paradox of the intellectuals is that although they are 'classless' and therefore might be able to act as disinterested bearers of knowledge, their own group situation prevents them from being impartial. At present they are constantly identifying themselves with other social classes and in the future although 'it is expected that they will strive to create a forum outside the party schools in which the perspective of and the interest in the whole is safeguarded', their own group structure may generate its own degree of partiality. As with Plato's guardians the problem is who will control the controllers? The Marxist tradition does of course postulate an answer to this problem: while class societies persist there will always be distortion of knowledge. Only after the proletarian revolution and the arrival of Communism will knowledge be Universal and objective. The problem remains, however, of what the universal and objective elements are prior to this change. Apart from crude theorists advocating the proletariat as the singular bearer of this wisdom (and Marx was not of their company), the answer must be the intellectuals. Trotski is the clearest Marxian exponent of this view.

> The intelligentsia . . . is able to give, and does give, a better artistic reproduction of the revolution than the proletariat which has made the Revolution, though the recreations of the intelligentsia are somewhat off line.
>
> In addition the intellectuals act as the bearers of old cultures: their task is to transmit to the proletariat the 'continuity of a creative tradition'.
>
> At the present time the proletariat realizes this continuity not directly, but indirectly, through the creative bourgeois intelligentsia which gravitates towards the proletariat and which wants to keep warm under its wing. The proletariat tolerates a part of this intelligentsia, supports another part, half-adopts a third, and entirely assimilates a fourth.[4]

The issue is a fundamental one for the whole analysis of the transmission of knowledge and simply needs to be spelt out in particular cases. For Trotski is not only describing the process of revolutionary art but offering a thumbnail sketch of the history of culture and knowledge. Substitute any country for the proletariat and the world's reserve of accumulated knowledge and tradition for the intelligentsia and we have ample reasons why Mannheim's paradox must remain Mannheim's personal paradox. Knowledge is acquired and developed according to the internal requirements of a society and because of the transmission across cultures of dominant styles and scientific paradigms.[5] Because of the preferences of publishing houses, of the mass-media or of particular institutions of learning, much knowledge is generated and transmitted which is never 'used' or which does not become part of the accumulated tradition of a society. Equally a fund of learning may not be assimilated in its society of origin but transmitted with devastating effects to other societies (compare the reception of Marxism in Britain with its development elsewhere). This is not simply a question of class differences, as Mannheim and Marx asserted, though they play a crucial part within societies, but of styles of learning which particular societies make their own (otherwise the British industrial working class might be expected to have adopted Marxism as much as the French, Belgian or Russians). How we explain both the national styles of learning and the class differences within societies is a task beyond this essay, but some contribution towards such a study can be made by a brief consideration of the development of sociology in Britain.

Before doing this it is necessary to clarify the premise on which this essay is written. Knowledge develops by being generated within societies and by being transmitted from one society to another. It is clear, therefore, that two levels of explanation are required for these processes. Within a society it is necessary to explain how innovations in knowledge take place, in what structures knowledge is transmitted from generation to generation and therefore how particular forms of knowledge gain dominance. Across cultures the same set of processes must also be explained: what are the sources of knowledge, what are the structures by which knowledge is transmitted internationally, and how are these 'filterings' of knowledge absorbed into receiving cultures.[6] Because it is a relatively recent subject, sociology presents a useful case study of these processes.

British sociology can be said, without much fear of contradiction, to have two major antecedents: the tradition of social and cultural anthropology originating in the late nineteenth century, and the social policy studies commencing perhaps with the Rowntree survey of York in the 1890s (though Engels' *Condition of the Working Class*, written in 1844 is at least as respectable a contender for the title).[7] Three other simultaneous developments—social history, literary and classical criticism, and social philosophy—have, until very recently, played little or no major part in the research of pedagogical development of the subject, and for reasons which will be stated later. The particular bias of British sociology—studies of small communities in non-industrial countries, and the collection of social data as an aid to policy decisions—have clear parallels in the development of British foreign and domestic policy. Anthropology arose directly out of imperial conquest, missionary activities and foreign trade. If in the nineteenth century the Anglican church could be labelled the Tory party at prayer, anthropology came close to being the

Tory party at social research. Throughout the nineteenth century and up to the First World War British sociology was largely represented by anthropologists: meticulously they documented tribes, clans, villages throughout the Empire and its dependancies. The philosophical antecedents of the British anthropologists were almost entirely the philosophers of the enlightenment and the early industrial revolution: Hume, Adam Ferguson, Adam Swift, the utilitarians. Although no anthropology can ignore the eighteenth-century continental philosophers—notably Diderot, Rousseau, Montesquieu and Condorcet—they played no apparent part in the direction of British research until well into the twentieth century. British social anthropology was centrally empirical and only very secondarily philosophical. If it shied away from using anthropology to explore the Human Condition in Rousseau's sense it did attempt a systematic construction of techniques of investigation. This meant, in fact, accepting the premises of British philosophy and the assumptions of the superiority of British culture inherent in the imperialist relationship. The great contribution of British social anthropology was to theories of investigation: the more cultural preoccupations of Frazer and Tylor were by-passed (though exported to America and France) and even Spencer's general theories were ignored in favour of the particular concepts he used to describe society. The social anthropologists saw their task as patiently documenting particular areas of society and investigating the inherent unity of social structures. Their anti-historical bias went hand-in-hand with their rejection of evolutionary theories: ultimately a society was explained in its own terms and functionalism came close to being a circular device for stressing stability and uniqueness. The social anthropologists down to the last great classical figure Radcliffe-Brown were more interested in situations of stasis rather than change and when they borrowed from the French it was Durkheim's functionalism rather than his theories of religion and social change that were used. But the central contribution should not be ignored. Since the beginning of this century and under the powerful influence of Haddon, Malinowski and Radcliffe-Brown British anthropological research emphasized seeing things as they were. Frazer was bypassed not only because of his speculative and cosmic generalizations but because his anthropology was based on documentation, and

SOCIOLOGY AND CULTURE   147

paid slight attention to field work. It was not until the Empire began to crumble and economic and political changes overtook the traditional societies that the emphasis of research and theory slowly began to shift. After the Second World War social anthropology had to face the twilight of Empire and the development of sociology. In many ways its response has been predictable. A discipline with such techniques, traditions and empirical data at its command was well-poised to take over sociology itself. After 1960 a large number of the chairs of sociology were occupied by erstwhile social anthropologists (including Cambridge, Bristol, Manchester, Kent, Sussex, Hull) a tradition set by the London School of Economics which as early as 1907 had appointed L. T. Hobhouse as its first professor of sociology. In part this heralded a change in social anthropology itself,[8] (from the study of 'primitive' peoples to the sociology of 'development', notably at Manchester and Sussex), but it also demonstrated continuity. In spite of the growth of studies influenced by sociological theory and by French (particularly structuralist) anthropology and American cross-cultural analysis, the results of either a more philosophical or of a more critical anthropology have been slow in appearing. A notable development has been the growth of community and kinship studies in Britain employing anthropological techniques.[9] Occasional suggestions of what is possible–such as Tom Lupton's study of the shop floor or Mary Douglas's treatise on rituals of pollution[10]–have to date been minority features. We are left with Edmund Leach's sallies into analysing the Human Condition[11] and the expectation of Peter Worsley's long-heralded *The Present as Anthropology*.[12] Otherwise the community studies continue–in Africa, Asia and Latin America and now in the recently-colonized Mediterranean.

However, social anthropology remains the most coherent indigenous contribution to British sociology, with a body of closely argued evidence far outstripping any other branch of the subject. Its lack of historical perspective, however (which marks even such radical statements as that of Leach), is well matched by the social engineering tradition initiated by the Rowntrees, Booth and the Webbs and dominating what often passes for British sociology. The last decade of the nineteenth century and the first of the twentieth century were marked by a flurry of activity in demography and statistics; the highlight of which was the appearance of Booth's seventeen-volume *Life and Labour of the People of London*. Although the First World War and the subsequent economic depression provided a break on these efforts, the central tradition of British sociology was well established: demographic statistical research with a strong emphasis on technical accuracy, but little interest in theory, and policy oriented research strongly influenced by the Fabians who had, of course, been largely instrumental in creating the London School of Economics. The counterpart to imperialist research was the peculiarly British empirical radicalism of the Fabians: again theory was largely absent. Sociology was centrally about demography and social inequality. When serious work commenced again in the 1940s at the London School of Economics and the Universities of Liverpool and Oxford, social administration, under the direction of T. H. Marshall and later T. S. Simey, Richard Titmuss and A. H. Halsey, was buttressed by population surveys and statistical accuracy pioneered by D. V. Glass at the L.S.E. To a very large extent this remarkable development was a direct result of political policy: the Government set up its Social Survey in 1941 to help it in policy decisions, while the Second World War and the 1945-51 Labour Government stimulated the consideration of 'Social reconstruction'. (The major British sociology publishing series of this period was appropriately called the 'International library of Sociology and Social Reconstruction'.) If the characteristic feature of Statistical surveys was their accuracy, social administration research was marked by its concern with social inequalities and institutional provision. D. V. Glass and E. Grebenik's *Trend and Pattern of Fertility in Great Britain (1954)* and D. V. Glass's *Social Mobility in Britain* (1954) were monuments of precise statistical analysis: the work of Richard Titmuss, Hermann Mannheim and A. H. Halsey was concerned centrally with the relationship between social inequality and the provision of social services, law and education. The characteristic feature of British sociology thus became its emphasis on social stratification: social security was seen in terms of the scope of its coverage; the law and its ramifications examined as part of the class structure (in particular the discriminatory nature of the treatment of working-class children and adults); while education was seen as a structuring of class differences. It would be easy to underestimate this tradition. Academically it improved the accuracy of the subject by concentrating on areas of research where sophisticated measuring techniques could be applied with advantage. Politically it gave focus to plans for changes in social welfare provision, in educational institutions and the treatment of delinquents. There is strong evidence for considering this central British sociological tradition as being the Fabian Society at research: most of its major exponents have not only been members of the Fabian Society but leading members: Richard Titmuss, Michael Young, Peter Townsend, T. S. Simey, Brian Abel-Smith, David Donnison – the list is impressive and without the policy issues which gave them direction it is difficult to see sociology being as politically and socially recognized as it is today.

In spite of this, the failures of this type of activity are equally impressive and parallel the failures of social democracy in Britain. A sociology which attributes single causes to social ills is bound to be in difficulties when those causes have apparently been rectified or where the attempts at rectification fail because they do not call into question other issues, not considered in the first hypothesis. The single characteristic of British sociology to date has been its insistence that the existing institutions do not adequately provide for different levels of the class structure: indeed that the institutions reinforce class differences.[13] This is demonstrably true, but it does not necessarily follow that changes in institutional provision will change the inequalities. The failure of a stratification-bound sociology is that it can only consider institutions in class terms. What is demonstrably absent is a serious consideration of theoretical interrelationships. All that the precise statistical approach can do is to refine techniques of measurement. Crucially, the sense of culture is absent: the matrix of relationships, institutions, ideologies and social classes which, interrelating, comprise a whole system. Up to now, British sociology has been theoretically weak because it has shown no conception of itself as part of a national culture and this is probably because the discipline, like the English, has lacked a sense of history. At best it has explored areas ignored by other disciplines, at worst it has simply provided data for public administrators. It has repeatedly emphasized how institutions control our behaviour. If this is true, the moment for change is upon us. Three major changes affecting sociology have occurred since 1951: the Empire has gone, thus ending the colonial heyday of social anthropology: Britain's international status has been reduced to that of being a shuttlecock between the U.S.A. and Western Europe, finally opening British sociology to the contending influences of American and Continental schools; and in ten years the number of University and Polytechnic departments claiming to teach sociology has increased from three to over thirty.

If it is inevitable that under these pressures the face of sociology in Britain will change dramatically, it is by no means certain in what direction it will change (the international status of Britain is by no means resolved and many of the new sociology departments are too small to make a major impact, and remain wedged between the arid methodology of economics and the policy pressures of social welfare studies and industrial relations). What is certain, however, is that it is already becoming more conscious of theory and of the vast American output. The effects of this are likely to make British sociology very much more self-conscious. At the very least, this should produce a consciousness of culture. But it is worth briefly examining the tradition that it may have to debate with, before considering what that cultural consciousness might fruitfully involve.

II THE SCIENCE OF THE MODERN

T. S. Eliot wrote:

It seems, as one becomes older,
That the past has another pattern, and ceases to be a mere sequence—
Or even development: the latter a partial fallacy
Encouraged by superficial notions of evolution
Which becomes in the popular mind, a means of disowning the past.

(The Dry Salvages)

Sociology has always been concerned with general processes of social change including the problem of long-term change. In many ways it has trespassed on ground usually considered the preserve of philosophers of history, cultural anthropologists and archaeologists. Some of the most important sociological writers of the nineteenth and early twentieth century–Comte, Spencer, Marx, Max Weber and Durkheim–were concerned precisely with the problems of the sequences of social change, and of enunciating theories to explain how societies moved from one level of social and economic organization to another.[14] They were not all entirely convinced that the change was for the better, but unlike the British sociologists and social anthropologists most of them were strongly influenced by biological theories of organic change and to a great degree argued that historical change could be explained by consideration of total processes.

But for the first half of this century sociologists, smarting under the counter-evolutionist and anti-historicist critiques of anthropologists and philosophers, shied away from wide-ranging comparisons on which most of the evolutionary theories depended. History not only had no meaning, it also had no utility for sociologists.[15] It was better to concentrate on middle-range pieces of research: the social system of factories, social mobility or urban ecology. When historians made historical comparisons, like Spengler or Toynbee, they suggested decadence rather than evolution. And in the face of the teleological claims of the Fascists and Communists the humbler task of collecting data and analysing short-term trends seemed the inevitable–and honest–thing to do.

Over the past two decades the picture has changed dramatically. Up to the Second World War the American and British traditions had continued to be so unsure of themselves as to make only occasional references to evolutionary sociology and international comparisons. Now the emergence of new independent states, the preoccupation of industrial societies with economic growth, as well as the continual debates on forms of national co-operation and international conflict, has begun to produce studies which stress comparative approaches to development. The establishment of UNESCO and the increasingly development-minded biases of the large research foundations has given material incentive to comparative sociological studies. Suddenly aware of itself as a world power, America has produced sociologists who have become the theoretical interpreters of that academic tradition which sees 'Plato to Nato' as a viable introductory course for undergraduates. Evolutionary theorists, though thoroughly aware of the functionalist and positivistic critiques of their nineteenth-century predecessors, have found new material to work on, though perhaps with a more narrowly-conceived focus. *Their* task is to demonstrate how societies become industrial, prosperous and *'modern'*, or alternatively to trace the blockages to change.[16] Like Spencer and Comte, they are producing classifications of societies, structures and cultures which are intended to be analytically neutral and abstract. At the same time their social situation demands a contribution to understanding and perhaps influencing real world crises and to producing answers to long-range problems.

Talcott Parsons emerged in the late 1940s as the chief priest of this new tradition. His message of social equilibrium married to a belief in progress has provided a useful emotional antidote for American society whose world seems to be characterized by revolution, war and violence. In his early work[17] Parsons was concerned less with historical trends and more with creating a general theory of society in which the various components could be analytically distinguished. But rapidly the cards have been shuffled to produce a series of societal types beginning with the Australian aborigines and moving through the Ptolemaic Egyptians, the Moguls, Manchu China, Feudal Europe to 'modern' society, the ultimate product of which reads suspiciously like the U.S.A.[18] Unfortunately for the theory it is difficult to distinguish a classification from an explanatory theory of stages. In 1964 Parsons wrote an essay called *Evolutionary Universals in Society*,[19] but the fact that comparative sociology had become dominated by evolutionary considerations had already been demonstrated in the majority of American studies concerned with development. Evolutionary theories had marked research both in relation to historical material and the study of modern non-industrial societies.

The basic concepts used by sociologists in examining historical data are openly borrowed from biological theories of organic evolution. In particular they have been concerned with the extent to which societies are capable of adapting to change and how they themselves induce change. The crucial topics here are whether units like religion, politics, economics, the family and their sub-categories became specialized. How labour was divided into many distinct tasks, or how politics involved the development of law courts, civil servants, professional experts and so on. Following from this it has become important to see how the social systems manage to maintain cohesion in spite of changes in structures. Finally, some sociologists have been interested in what kinds of values and codes the various systems produce at all levels to cope with the changes. Historically, therefore, there has been a dual task. Societies are classified according to the extent to which particular institutions, jobs and patterns of behaviour are specialized. From this a ranking of world societies is arrived at moving from the primitive to the modern. In individual cases the object is to specify the evolution of particular stages. If this has done violence to the nuances of particular historical periods, it has produced some interesting research or reinterpretation of research. The analysis of Social Change in the early industrial revolution has itself been revolutionized. The study of Chinese peasant communities has become central to any discussion of the 1948 revolution and monographs on the development of Puritanism and Capitalism have added to historical perspectives on religion and economic action. More frequently, however, history has been ransacked for examples that provide evidence of particular sets of classifications, with little respect for the total social and cultural context involved.[20]

Much more serious has been the effect on the study of contemporary non-industrial countries. For what is attempted here is a study of societies in the process of becoming 'modern' or 'industrial' or at least 'developed', each of these concepts joining the long line of evolutionary jargon. If the modern society is one in which activities are highly specialized, the central social and political organizations flexible and adaptive, then the non-industrial society can only be analysed in so far as it is either progressing towards this state or failing to measure up to it. Political institutions, education, religion and economic behaviour can therefore all be analysed in terms of degrees of modernity.[21] The fact that most of the leaders of the non-industrial societies are in some measure also committed to entering the modern world provides comforting living evidence of the utility of the evolutionary framework. In terms of the general model good change can only be in the direction of modernity:

revolutions, coups, millennial sects, trade unions, even sport can be classified according to the particular symptoms of modernity or traditionalism displayed. Sociological analysis is thus made remarkably easy. 'History' provides a model of what has to be done to succeed: it is necessary simply to plot the course for the new states. As with Walt Rostow's ideology of the stages of Economic Growth,[22] sociology is producing its counterpart on Social Growth. Even the Soviet Union, so long ignored in the models, has attained a measure of respectability in the 1960s. A sociologist has recently made efforts to demonstrate that Russia, too, can be fitted into the general framework.[23] If the task of sociologists is to plot the road to modernity, Russia is almost too perfect a case. Recent contacts with Soviet sociologists have indicated that they are not uninterested in the existence of a set of theories that legitimize social structures in terms of both evolutionary and equilibrium analysis.

And yet for all its ideological implications, the rediscovery of evolutionary perspectives has had its advantages in providing tools for the re-examination of the organization of contemporary societies.[24] In part this comes from the concern with how societies become industrial and urbanized, which provides a convenient framework for gathering a vast amount of material on different societies. In part by exposing the liberal fallacy of democratic forms of government, it directs our attention to the social foundations on which institutions are based. The stress on functionalism in much contemporary sociological theory is at least a way of directing our attention to the underlying *purposes* of institutions as opposed to their *ostensible* aims. As a large amount of evolutionary sociology is directed towards the actual uses to which the institutions are put we are today a bit nearer that stage when we will see our societies for what they are than for what they try to appear.

But as I have suggested, in doing this sociology has helped to create a new mythology of what we are becoming. By emphasizing the structural changes necessary for modern societies sociology seems to be postulating a similar course as inevitable for all countries. It is true, of course, that all societies are changing (but they always have done) and that changes introduced by industry, urbanization and commerce will have far-reaching consequences for their social structures. What is not clear is what kinds of societies will emerge as a result of these changes. It is obvious that not all countries will become industrial and probable that many will never become prosperous in any way that is comparable with existing industrial societies. It is also likely that some societies—such as Britain or Belgium—which were once prosperous and entrepreneurial will attain a colonial or dependant status and may even lose such prosperity as they have. In the range of sociological literature on modernization there is very little about decadence, and yet the contemporary world abounds with societies which have 'fallen' from a once powerful state to being quaint relics of former greatness.[25] Modern Spain or Austria provide excellent examples. Even within the definition of development, there are some modern societies, such as Argentina, which appear doomed to stagnation,[26] and many societies which, though modern in the sense of having developed industry and commerce, retain remarkably archaic social structures. Italy or France both contain within them large areas where the occupations, community organizations and attitudes have greater similarity with some developing countries than industrial ones. The causes of these variations may be structural in part, they may be cultural in the sense of having to do with traditions and values which attempt to or are unable to adapt to new pressures, or they may be due to factors entirely outside the control of the societies themselves. Britain ceased to be an empire more because other societies became more powerful than because she became corrupt and less efficient. Indeed she may have been more corrupt and less efficient when she was at the height of her power than when she was in decline.[27] The present urge to modernization in Britain therefore represents less an attempt to bring British society up to date than the stamp of decline, the final mark of colonial status. From this point of view the American evolutionists may be right: America *is* modernity as far as lesser societies like Britain are concerned, but it is a modernity which is very much affected by the imperial relationship. When Rome colonized Greece or Israel no historian discussed the conquest in terms of modernization of traditional structures: indeed they tended to argue that Rome destroyed something that was culturally superior. Therefore one records with some sympathy the apocalyptic utterances of an anthropologist viewing the transformation of Mexico:

until today the community of cultivators has retained its capacity to turn in upon itself and to maintain its integrity in the face of doubt and disaster—until today and perhaps not much longer, because the modern world is engaged in severing once and for all the ties which bind people into local unity, in committing them to complete participation in the Great Society. This is a one-way street, along which there is no return.[28]

But perhaps this, too, is to take the modernizers too seriously. The transformation may not entail the dramatic and cataclysmic introduction of the Great Society, but something neither modern nor traditional.

> Thou has neither youth nor age
> But as it were an afterdinner sleep
> Dreaming of both.

In a recent study on the *Social Origins of Dictatorship and Democracy*[29] the American social historian, Barrington Moore, shows how the coming of industrial society has had *many* routes and *many* end products. Some societies became industrial because of a combination of internal factors which led to the emergence of powerful élites committed to commercial and industrial change. In other societies, the pressure from outside challenged the power of existing landed gentry and military élites; in others the two pressures combined to provide an effective threat to the established social order. But in all cases the real problem lay in the original base for industrialization. In some cases a long commercial past preceded industrialization: in others very feudal systems were transformed overnight. The consequences for the future development of the society are incalculable, because what was transmitted to the new society was a whole tradition of behaviour. It is this tradition, this sense of the influence of the past on the present that is absent from much sociology. By emphasizing the structures, sociology has often failed to illuminate the real differences. If sometimes the result was Communism, sometimes a Parliamentary system, or sometimes Fascism, we can never know why unless we do a lot more comparative history.

Of course this exaggerates, but it helps to underline my point

SOCIOLOGY AND CULTURE

that there is no one type of modern society, no finite end to the sociobiological process. We can certainly not judge the end product by *per capita* income, or electricity consumption, or indices of democracy, or the extent to which work skills are sub-divided into myriads of components, or the number of Inter-Continental Ballistic Missiles. The attempt to measure development by the acquisition of facilities or the differentiation of structures is bound to produce a set of meaningless categories, where the graphs cross and recross each other with dexterity and each equation introduces a different solution.

But the attempt of sociologists to find total explanations for society and change is itself a consequence of their academic relationships and the expectations of a grudging but demanding public. This public has come in some measure to expect sociologists to provide answers. But the questions posed are not only the specific ones of what to do about delinquency or education or race relations, but the more fundamental ones of The Human Condition. It is one of the tragedies of sociologists that whereas their daily research is on the pedestrian run-of-the-mill policy questions, they feel compelled to use this data to provide the lodestone for the deep truths that they feel sociology must contain. But most of the policy questions are already culturally fixed – they are questions of the here and now, of the societies in which the sociologists find themselves and of the immediate problems of administration. On the basis of these, sociologists construct their grand theories. In the United States the theories are more ambitious because the policy questions that sociologists are asked to research into cover a wider field. Above all America is an imperial nation and sociologists are even more a cultural appendage of this imperialism than anthropologists were in Britain in the nineteenth and early twentieth centuries. A recent book has shown how American sociologists were persuaded by the State Department to collaborate in an expensive research project designed to show how revolution in Latin America could be contained.[30] In Britain as the Empire recedes into history the policy questions are narrower, restricted more to domestic problems: education, industry, race relations and town planning.

The argument against evolutionary theories is not so much that they are concerned with progress or sequences of change or development but that they purport to offer total interpretations of human behaviour. The past century has seen a large number of attempts to construct total theories: Marx, Freud, Jung, Spengler, Parsons. In all of these cases the exercise has produced many new insights; but in each of them the main contribution has been less towards creating a system of knowledge and more towards illuminating particular aspects of social change. Their contributions add up in part to increased total knowledge, but none of them represent an effective or viable *system* of knowledge. But their disciples, over-impressed by the pretensions to science and devoid of the same imagination as their masters, reduce the magic formula to pedestrian imitation of scientific method, create a cult and perpetuate a mythology. For them Wittgenstein's castigation of philosophers is apposite:

> Philosophers constantly see the method of science before their eyes, and are irresistibly tempted to ask and answer questions in the way science does. This tendency is the real source of metaphysics, and leads the philosopher into complete darkness.[31]

But of the theory builders already mentioned, Parsons and the acolyte systems theorists stand out alone as the legitimizers of their particular society. Hitherto whereas social scientists have been presumptuous enough to create total theories they have done so in the belief that somewhere, somehow there might exist the better society. With Marx somewhere in the communal past and future things might be different: the present could be analysed as transitional between these two millennia. With Freud the discovery of self and the mastery of consciousness provided a critical perspective to view contemporary society; and even with the nineteenth-century evolutionists questions about the past at least led to its discovery. But with Parsons, as with Hegel, all history moves towards the eternal present in which what matters is the organization and the mechanics of maintaining the balance between all sections of the society. In this kind of analysis the key to development is contained in the instruments of organization: what happens to men is entirely a consequence of this. Sociology becomes the handmaid of the technical culture.

III Sociology and British Culture

One of the lessons arising out of this exploration of the history of recent sociology is that its academic fashions are largely dictated by social and political contexts and that its most impressive work is developed because of political-power pressures. Karl Mannheim may have been right when he distinguished between 'ideology' (the backward looking legitimation of power) and 'utopia' (the forward looking innovations of a struggling class), but what is equally clear is that different forms of ideology and utopia arise out of particular groups in ruling and oppressed classes, though at the same time all groups initially share certain ideological assumptions. In Britain the common currency of all social research is its empiricism. The ruling élite legitimized their power during the early part of this century by encouraging research which pointed out the differences of the inferior peoples being dominated. When the empire dissolved, these anthropologists–as a downwardly-mobile élite–had three options available: they contributed to 'developmental' studies (for international rather than national agencies), they switched their interests to domestic sociology, or they continued their traditional research but in an increasingly quietistic way (anthropology becomes philosophical, reflective and religious). The example is very close to the demotion of the *noblesse de robe* by Louis XIV, so imaginatively analysed by the French Marxist sociologist Lucien Goldmann.[32] But while the anthropologists have their own particular problems, the expanding sociology departments have become increasingly responsive to the pressures of the domestic political scene–the Fabians may have willingly aided official policies but today the sociology departments have become more directly subject to government policy. Most research is financed by government agencies–the Social Science Research Council, the Department of Education and Science, the Home Office, the Ministry of Social Security, the Ministry of Overseas Development, and a few foundations with committees which overlap with the S.S.R.C. It is therefore not surprising that much research is concerned with 'policy' questions–educational selection, industrial relations, social welfare, crime and recently town planning.[33] The odds are that the spawning of new departments will simply generate more 'service' research for the government. In spite of their attempts at remaining impartial the S.S.R.C. and the research foundations are unlikely to be able to resist a tendency which affects the recruitment of university staff. However brave the picture presented by sociology, its imagination does not extend much beyond social stratification and its various correlations. The problem is, of course, largely related to the social structure into which sociological research is injected. The power politics of social science inhibit real curiosity and invention. Whatever happened in the past, future chairs in sociology will not be gained by imagination and learning but by the capacity to collect data within a framework which has become acceptable to the lumpen-intelligentsia of the university departments. For we can be sure that as the structure operates at present, its values will remain those of policy-orientation and empiricism. Sociologists will accept – without self-consciousness – their part in the dominant culture.

Is this inevitable? Is a sociology doomed to answering questions posed by the D.E.S., the O.M.D., and Richard Crossman's paternalist circus the only road ahead? Methodologically it probably is – as British anthropology and American sociology have demonstrated, the tools of analysis are most fully developed when they are part of a ruling power complex. This was surely Trotski's point. The technology of culture is bound to develop most rapidly in close relationship with the political and economic élite: we would have no nuclear energy without the close relationship between warfare, the state and industrial capital. But besides this – and this is also Trotski's point – the alternatives are spelt out partly by those who share in the manufacture of this technology, and partly by those who represent opposing forces. For Trotski the cultural revolution will come when the proletariat learns the technical culture, assimilates the criticisms of the dissident intellectuals, and *then* begins to create its own art. It is worth spelling out the possibilities for sociology in this context.

Most of what I have called the technical culture of sociology involves methodology (the way of collecting data and assessing its relevance) and the theoretical framework which spells out the interconnections between different elements in society. In other words, this is the way things get done. Some of this would clearly survive whatever the ideological premises of the sociology; but some of it is purely ideological. The problem is to determine which is which. There seems only one solution: to assess what are the implications for *action* on which a theory is based. In other words, how are the premises and conclusions of the sociology related to what the sociologist thinks *ought* to be done. This is, of course, an extremely complex problem which cannot be discussed at length here, but in passing it should be noted that it involves some classification of action systems and these in turn are related to the social contexts within which the sociology is developed. If we distinguish crudely between sociological variants of Mannheim's 'ideology' and 'utopia' it is clear that the possible range of sociology within each is quite vast. But I think that it is equally clear that if we do this a remarkable amount of sociological methodology and theory will be seen to stand irrespective of the ideological preconceptions. But there is a further point. Much of what is seen as ideological may in fact represent the legitimizing of a particular *type* of society, which is in fact a concrete, historical stage: for example the distinction between French and American sociology is not simply a distinction between different ideologies but between different kinds of society, in fact less and more highly developed societies. One further problem therefore is to distinguish between these elements which represent technical responses to particular socio-economic levels and those which represent legitimizing ideologies of a particular status quo. A less developed country may therefore depend for its technical, sociological culture on more developed ones, though holding theoretical paradigms and ideological premises which are different. The international impact a less dominant sociology makes depends largely on its assimilation of the technical culture which it refashions according to its own paradigms and ideologies. This is what gives Polish and Hungarian sociology their impressive quality. Unlike the British sociologists they had actually assimilated the technical culture and transcended it with new theoretical perspectives. Stanlislav Ossowski, Zygmunt Bauman, Andrzej Malewski and Georg Lukács have produced more significant sociology than any Englishman living or dead. (Karl Mannheim has to be excepted as a refugee whose best work was done before he came here. Significantly enough his work has had little impact on British sociology.) On the other hand the ideology of a dominant sociology will largely be in terms of its superior methodology: method becomes ideology. This was true of anthropology in Imperial England and remains true of American sociology today. The danger for an inferior sociology is that it will consider the acquisition of method as being the whole point of sociological competence: this seems now to be the case in Scandinavia where the development of theory is largely within the terms set by the dominant technical culture (i.e. the U.S.A.). For satellite countries like Britain sociology can *either* be a simple appendage of the technical culture of the U.S.A. (sophisticated methodology), *or* it can remain a no-man's-land between cultures, itself representing nothing but impotence (as it is at present), *or* it can acquire the sociological technology as an aid to refashioning or creating a sociological culture. This latter is the more challenging task and the more urgent.

There is one feature of British society which has, to date, prevented such a development. The ramifications of the educational institutions and the dominant culture-styles have emphasized both the necessity of technical particularism ('empiricism') and the dubiousness of posing theoretical interrelations. For various historical reasons[34] the major changes in British social structure and styles of living (such as the industrial revolution and two world wars) have not seriously affected this tradition. The academic power structure as well as the legitimizing symbols of society have militated against an alternative dominant culture. We have had no successful communist party, the Catholic church is as 'empirical' as the Anglican and such radical movements as have emerged have been consigned to the ranks of the sectarians. Sociology has fitted in uncomfortably, but predictably. Most of it is empirical and untheoretical and that which has attempted to provide a consistent theoretical alternative has been treated as maverick and sectarian. Even legitimizing theory has not fared too well.[35]

What then is the point of considering alternatives? For two reasons. If we are serious that sociology should represent more than attributes of a technical and legitimizing culture, it is important that the debate should continue, even if the odds against success seem high. But more strategically it is clear that the dominant culture is now in flux – for the first time since the

Norman Conquest, Britain is being subjected to foreign domination – the ruling culture can never be the same again. Further, in spite of the predilections of the academic élite, the recipients of education (the students) are *for the first time* seriously questioning the basis of pedagogy and the ideology of knowledge. There is no guarantee that these processes will produce a major reorientation in culture – or in any one direction – but the situation is unique and challenging enough to be considered seriously.

The new culture, however, can only be constructed by first examining the avenues of escape from the dominant one. These relate in part to the structural features of English culture – the under-pinnings of values and styles by institutional forms – and in part to signs of the liberation of thought itself. This second is of course itself due to structural features – on however small a scale – but what is significant about cultural change is that the small-scale liberations are related in some measure to large-scale structural changes. The small-scale escapes have always been there: what seems true today is that the structures are changing too, and the activities of students in this country (whatever may be true elsewhere) are directly related to these structural changes. What are they? Paradoxically they seem to be in diametrically opposed directions. On the one hand the government has set up, or is in the process of setting up, higher educational institutions which are directly related to vocations: the new national polytechnics and technical universities are nothing if not this. On the other hand, the structure of pedagogy is changing both in relation to the flexibility of curricula and the authority relations within Universities (logically one change involves the other). Within the colleges and institutes of education changes are slowly moving in the same direction as the universities: curricula are becoming more 'open' and old hierarchies are being broken down. Interestingly (and I put it no higher than that) both the polytechnic and the university reforms are responses to the same demands: that education should be relevant to future careers and be not purely concerned with 'disciplines' (though in technology it is easier to show that 'disciplines' have more direct relationship to jobs). Although the danger exists that this revolution will simply usher in the age of randomly-selected options (on the Sussex model) the possibility for having really *integrated* curricula is here for the first time: the colleges of education are perhaps the best openings for this because their job-orientation is education itself which might just produce curricula which are concerned with culture. It hardly needs to be said that this would be the real educational revolution.

For sociologists this revolution should prove to be their only means of salvation. At last it should be possible—at the level of teaching—to have real debates with such potentially revolutionary subjects as electronics, biology, physics, quantum mechanics, literature, social history and art. To date the real bearers of dissenting culture have been in literature, and, to a lesser extent, social history—the debate on what a radical sociology must be, necessarily has to begin here. There is no British sociologist of comparable radical depth to Raymond Williams,[36] or Edward Thompson[37] but *their* failings are those of a lack of radical sociology, just as their strengths are those of a radical literary tradition passing from the seventeenth to the nineteenth century through the Puritan Divines, Milton, Swift, Coleridge, Arnold, Morris, Ruskin and Hardy. In the twentieth century we have only to compare the scholarship of the literary critical debate round *Scrutiny* or, in social history, *Past and Present*, with any sociological equivalent (and that is difficult to find) to realize how dead British sociology has been. There have been no catalysts in British sociology, no intellectual events to compare with Marx and Max Weber in Germany, Lévi-Strauss and Durkheim in France or Parsons in the U.S.A. (Our only monument is Radcliffe-Brown: and that tradition has been transcended by Lévi-Strauss.) In all of these foreign cases the major characteristics of great sociology have been the ability to transcend 'discipline' (though inevitably each genius has produced his entourage of disciplinary hacks) and to pioneer new directions in the understanding of human problems. This greatness did not come from contributions to the technical apparatus of the social sciences (though they were all well learned in it) but from the imaginative apprehending of cultural moments. The same is true of other social sciences: Smith, Mill, Keynes in Economics; Jacobson, Chomsky in linguistics; Freud, Piaget in psychology. But any British sociologist who consciously tries to be a Weber or a Parsons at this moment in time is bound to fail: the traditions of the discipline and the research and pedagogical structures are too constricting and castrating. But the signs of change are

SOCIOLOGY AND CULTURE

there—in some new institutions and the reorganizations of some old ones—and indications of what is intellectually possible came from a few research sources: Basil Bernstein's work on sociolinguistics[38] and school curricula, Tom Burns's on industrial innovation[39] and organization, David Lockwood's on White Collar Workers,[40] David Martin's,[41] Brian Wilson's[42] and Alasdair MacIntyre's[43] on English Religion, Nigel Harris on the Ideology of Conservatism,[44] John Rex and Robert Moore's on Race Relations.[45] There is at last one serious British introduction to sociological theory.[46] These small seeds give hope, but they *are* small and might not flourish if pedagogy and research do not provide a fertile ground. The plethora of small sociology departments teaching bad social administration with little research money are matched by large departments concerned with their professional reputations and acquiring the technical culture of the U.S.A. It is this wasteland that could prevent a sociological culture from developing.

NOTES

[1] See Donald G. MacRae, *Ideology and Society* (Heinemann, 1961), Ch. 2, for an outline of Sociology in Britain which puts the eighteenth-century Scottish writers Adam Ferguson and John Millar in this preeminent position. See also discussions of Millar and Ferguson in two short pieces by William Millar, *Sociology*, Vol. 1, No. 2, 1967, pp. 197-8 and 201-5.

[2] T. H. Marshall, *Sociology at the Cross Roads* (Heinemann, 1963), p. 15.

[3] Karl Mannheim, *Ideology and Utopia* (Routledge 1960), esp. Chs. 2 and 3, and Leon Trotski, *Literature and Revolution* (Russell and Russell, 1957).

[4] Trotski, op. cit, p. 226-7.

[5] See Thomas Kuhn, *Structure of Scientific Revolutions* (Univ. of Chicago Press, 1962), for a discussion of paradigms and scientific development. This book is useful as a general thesis, though some of its particular cases are very debatable.

[6] For general analysis which attempts to locate these processes, but using a basically individualistic framework, see Peter Berger and Thomas Luckman, *Social Construction of Reality* (Allen Lane, 1967).

[7] For summary essays see Donald G. MacRae, op. cit., esp. Chs. 2 and 3.

[8] How important this change has been and how powerful the anthropological tradition must remain is well indicated by the six monographs published recently by the Association of Social Anthropologists, Tavistock

Publications 1964-8 (Vols 1-4 are edited by Michael Banton, Vol. 5 by Edmund Leach, and Vol. 6 by Raymond Firth).

[9] See especially the work of W. M. Williams and Raymond Firth and the A. S. A. Monograph 4, ed. M. Banton, *The Social Anthropology of Complex Societies* (Tavistock, 1967).

[10] Tom Lupton, *On the Shop Floor* (Pergamon Press, 1963); Mary Douglas, *Purity and Danger* (Routledge and Kegan Paul, 1967).

[11] Edmund Leach, *A Runaway World* (BBC Publications, 1968).

[12] Peter Worsley, *The Present as Anthropology* (Prentice-Hall).

[13] For classic examples see R. M. Titmuss, *Essays on the Welfare State* (Allen and Unwin, 1958) and *Income Distribution and Social Change* (Allen and Unwin, 1962); J. Floud, A. H. Halsey and F. M. Martin, *Social Class and Educational Opportunity* (Heinemann, 1956); P. Townsend and B. Abel Smith, *The Poor and the Poorest* (L.S.E. Monograph, 1966); and for a thoughtful reconsideration, T. H. Marshall, *Sociology at the Crossroads* (Heinemann, 1963).

[14] For discussion see R. Aron: *Main Currents in Sociological Theory* (2 Volumes) (Weidenfeld and Nicolson, 1966 and 1968), and T. Parsons, *The Structure of Social Action* (Free Press 1937).

[15] K. Popper: *The Poverty of Historicism* (R and KP, 1958).

[16] See, for example, B. Hoselitz and W. E. Moore (eds), *Industrialisation and Society* (UNESCO, 1962); M. Levy, *Modernisation and the Structure of Societies*, 1966: D. E. Apter, *The Politics of Modernisation* (Chicago, 1966).

[17] See, for example, *The Social System* (R and KP, 1951).

[18] See T. Parsons, *Societies - Comparative and Evolutionary Perspectives* (Prentice-Hall, 1966).

[19] In *American Sociological Review*, June 1964.

[20] The material referred to in this paragraph is vast, but see N. J. Smelser, *Social Change in the Industrial Revolution* (R and KP, 1962); M. J. Levy, 'Contrasting factors in the Modernisation of China and Japan', in S. Kuznets *et al.*, (eds) *Economic Growth: Brazil, India and Japan* (Duke U.P., 1955); C. Kerr, *et al.*, *Industrialism and Industrial Man* (Heinemann, 1960); R. N. Bellah, *Tokugawa Religion* (Free Press, 1957).

[21] For examples see G. Almond and J. S. Coleman (eds), *The Politics of the Developing Areas* (Princeton U.P., 1960); S. N. Eisenstadt, *Modernisation-Protest and Change* (Prentice-Hall, 1966); E. A. Shils, *Political Development in the New States* (Mouton, the Hague, 1962); W. E. Moore and A. S. Feldman (eds), *Labor Commitment and Social Change*, (Social Science Research Council (New York), 1960); M. F. Millikan and D. L. M. Blackmer (eds), *The Emergent Nations* (Little, Brown, 1961).

[22] W. W. Rostow, *The Stages of Economic Growth - a non-Communist Manifesto* (Cambridge U.P., 1960).

[23] J. P. Nettl: *The Soviet Achievement* (Thames and Hudson, 1967).

[24] For summaries of trends see Robert M. Marsh, *Comparative Sociology*

(Harcourt, Brace and World, 1967), and R. Merritt and S. Rokkan, *Comparing Nations* (Yale U.P., 1966).

[25] But see S. Huntington, 'Political Development and Decay', *World Politics*, 17, 1964/5, pp. 386–430.

[26] For a personal and idiosyncratic view of Latin American stagnation see Stanislav Andreski, *Parasitism and Subversion* (Weidenfeld and Nicolson, 1967); and for Latin American viewpoints, Claudio Veliz (ed), *Obstacles to Change in Latin America* (O.U.P., 1966).

[27] See, for example, R. Wraith, *Corruption in Developing Countries*, (Methuen, 1963).

[28] Eric R. Wolf, *Sons of the Shaking Earth* (Univ. of Chicago Press, 1960).

[29] Barrington Moore, Jr., *Social Origins of Dictatorship and Democracy* (Allen Lane, The Penguin Press, 1967).

[30] I. L. Horowitz, *The Rise and Fall of Project Camelot* (MIT Press, 1968).

[31] L.Wittgenstein, *The Blue and the Brown Books* (Blackwell, 1958).

[32] See L. Goldmann: *The Hidden God* (Routledge, 1965), for a discussion of philosophy, religion and literature in the context of this change in seventeenth-century France.

[33] For indications of what the money is spent on see the S.S.R.C. *Newsletter* published three times a year and including details of research allocations.

[34] See Perry Anderson, 'Origins of the Present Crisis' in Anderson and Robin Blackburn (eds), *Towards Socialism* (Collins, 1965), for an attempt to account for this. But see also Barrington Moore, Jr., *Social Origins of Dictatorship and Democracy* (Allen Lane, 1967), Chapter One, for the historical-structural underpinning of this analysis.

[35] For a critical analysis of British élite culture, see Perry Anderson: 'Components of the National Culture', *New Left Review*, 50, 1968.

[36] Raymond Williams, *Culture and Society* (Chatto and Windus, 1958), and *The Long Revolution* (Chatto and Windus, 1961).

[37] E. P. Thompson, *The Making of the English Working Class* (Gollancz, 1963). It is important to note that both the above writers developed their creative energies from teaching extra-mural classes: that is, research was a direct result of flexible, 'open' pedagogy. Commitment largely involved the class and was not something independent of it. For this reason structural university changes and curriculum flexibility are essential for any radical sociology to develop.

[38] See, e.g. B. Bernstein, 'Language & Social Class', *B.J.S.* 1959, II; and 'A socio-linguistic approach to social learning', in J. Gould (ed), *Social Science Survey* (Penguin, 1965).

[39] T. Burns, and G. M. Stalker, *The Management of Innovation* (Tavistock, 1966).

[40] D. Lockwood, *The Blackcoated Worker* (Allen and Unwin, 1958).

[41] D. Martin, *A Sociology of English Religion* (Heinemann, 1966).

168 LITERATURE AND ENVIRONMENT

[42] Bryan Wilson, *Sects and Society* (Heinemann, 1966).
[43] Alasdair MacIntyre, *Secularization and Moral Change* (Oxford, 1966).
[44] Nigel Harris, *Conservatism: The State and Society*, unpublished Ph.D. thesis (Univ. of London, 1963). A summary appears as Ch. IV in N. Harris, *Beliefs in Society* (Watts, 1968).
[45] J. Rex and R. Moore: *Race, Community and Conflict* (Oxford U.P., 1966).
[46] P. Cohen, *Modern Social Theory* (Heinemann, 1968).

READING LIST

A. HISTORY OF SOCIOLOGICAL THOUGHT

R. Aron: *Main Currents in Sociological Thought*, 2 Vols., (Weidenfeld and Nicolson).

B. INTRODUCTORY PERSPECTIVES

P. Berger: *Invitation to Sociology* (Pelican Books).
S. Cotgrove: *The Science of Society* (Allen and Unwin).
J. Beattie: *Other Cultures* (Routledge).
P. Cohen: *Modern Social Theory* (Heinemann).
Henri Lefebvre: *Sociology of Marx* (Allen Lane).

C. HISTORY AND SOCIOLOGY

T. Parsons: *Societies: Evolutionary and Comparative Perspectives* (Prentice-Hall).
M. Weber: *General Economic History* (Prentice-Hall).
K. Marx: *Pre-Capitalist Economic Factors* (Lawrence and Wishart).

D. SOCIOLOGY AND CULTURE

J. Henry: *Culture Against Man* (Tavistock).
V. Lanternari: *Religions of the Oppressed* (Mentor).
H. Marcuse: *One-Dimensional Man* (Sphere).
C. Lèvi-Strauss: *Totemism* (Merlin Press).
T. Kuhn: *The Structure of Scientific Revolutions* (University of Chicago Press).
E. Goffman: *The Presentation of Self in Everyday Life* (Doubleday).
T. Brameld: *The Remaking of a Culture* (John Wiley).
H. Becker: *Outsiders* (Collier-Macmillan).
A. MacIntyre: *A Short History of Ethics* (Routledge).

E. SOCIOLOGY AND PUBLIC POLICY

P. Marris and Martin Rein: *Dilemmas of Social Reform* (Routledge).
Herbert J. Gans: *People and Plans* (Basic Books).

SOCIOLOGY AND CULTURE

John Rex and Robert Moore: *Race, Community and Conflict* (O.U.P.).

F. SOCIOLOGY AND INDUSTRY
R. Blauner: *Alienation and Freedom* (University of Chicago Press).
S. Parker and others: *Sociology of Industry* (Allen and Unwin).
T. Burns and G. M. Stalker: *The Management of Innovation* (Tavistock).

G. THE TECHNICAL CULTURE OF SOCIOLOGY
K. A. Yeomans: *Statistics for the Social Scientist*, 2 vols. (Penguin).
Richard S. Rudner: *Philosophy of Social Science* (Prentice-Hall).
Carl G. Hempel: *Philosophy of Natural Science* (Prentice-Hall).

N.B. This list does not attempt to cover all the possible approaches to sociology, nor even all the most fashionable. Sections A, B, C, and G cover what I feel is a fair cross-section, while D, E, F are very personal choices. Some of the fashionable approaches are, of course, contained in the footnotes to my essay. As far as possible I have kept to paperbacks but occasionally it has been impossible to find a cheap edition which provides adequate representation for what I mean, but sometimes I have used a paperback edition in preference to a superior book available only in hardback.

7

Political Theory

DAVID McLELLAN

POLITICS is, or should be, about what it is to be human. For men are not isolated beings whose nature can be described apart from the society in which they live. Their very individuality has come to them through society. Experience that is wholly private is impossible: all experience—even the most intimate—comes to us through the social reality of which we are a part. Thus the notion of a private language (as Wittgenstein showed conclusively) is nonsensical.

This needs emphasizing for it is often said—by those too lazy to reflect on themselves and their fellow men—that 'politics is a dirty game' or 'I'm not politically minded'. Not to be politically minded is not to have an interest in one's own society and, ultimately, not to have an interest in oneself. For politics is not solely about the way institutions work, the means of acquiring and preserving power, the impersonal techniques of government. Fact can never be entirely separated from value, and the ambition of many writers on politics to make it into a purely descriptive science with the consequent prestige associated with neutrality and objectivity, has proved a chimaera. Behind every description there lies a point of view. More important, however, such an attempt to narrow the definition of politics is extremely dangerous. It carries with it the conclusion that the most intimate values and beliefs of individuals belong to a 'private' world separate from the 'public' world of politics in which, it is implied, they have no place. Politics thus becomes a specialized profession in which only the opinions of 'experts' have any weight. Hence a growing gap—more and more felt in recent years in this country and others—between what most people experience as important to themselves and the increasingly irrelevant and mystifying manœuvres of the public world.

In fact this divorce between the two worlds is itself a specifically political ideology designed to exclude from the political process all those who do not possess an expert opinion; and, by the same token, to remove political discussion from the sphere of values—where all men start equal—to that of techniques—where professionalism can reign supreme. And since techniques are easier to deal with than values, those wielding them can afford the added luxury of not having to think too much.

By the end of the 1950s it became fashionable to talk of 'the exhaustion of political ideas' and 'the end of ideology'. At least in the Western World the differences dividing parties of the left and right seemed to be getting less and changes of government only involved a slight change of emphasis on the amount of economic planning and welfare. One of the most widely read of American political scientists, S. M. Lipset, said at the end of the 1950s:

... the fundamental problems of the industrial revolution have been solved: the workers have achieved industrial and political citizenship, the Conservatives have accepted the Welfare State, and the democratic Left has recognized that an increase in overall state power carries with it more dangers to freedom than solutions for economic problems. This very triumph of the democratic social revolution in the West ends domestic politics for those intellectuals who must have ideologies or utopias to motivate them to political action.

However, the following decade has given the lie to this (in my opinion) pessimistic view and has seen the growth of very varied political ideologies, particularly among dissident groups in the Western World and in the Third World who are not content with contemporary society and have begun to act politically to alter it. Literacy in political theory consists (at least) in having a knowledge of the most influential of contemporary political ideologies—Marxism. However, like Christianity before it and like any widespread system of ideas, Marxism means many things to many men. This chapter is therefore designed to give a brief survey of some books on Marx himself and then to describe the various contemporary applications of his ideas.

The problem confronting most thinkers in the first half of the nineteenth century, and Marx in particular, was the failure of the progressive principles of the previous century to cure basic social evils. These principles are to be found in the French Revolutionary constitutions of 1791 and 1793 and in the Constitution of the United States. The liberty, fraternity and equality of all men were proclaimed; men were free to worship as they pleased, to dispose of property as they wished and to pursue their own ideas of happiness. However, as the nineteenth century progressed, it became clear that only certain sections of the population were in a position to benefit from these freedoms, namely those with the economic resources. Marx saw that the rights of man remained, for the majority of the population, purely theoretical: he considered that the problem of a just distribution of society's wealth could only come about through changes in the socio-economic basis of society. Unless this happened, talk of 'rights' would remain irrelevant: Marx would have seen the point of the remark that even the grill room of the Ritz was 'open' to everyone, or, conversely, that the law recognized the right of millionaire and tramp alike to sleep under the bridges of the Seine.

Marx himself summed up the kernel of his theory as follows:

> In the social production of their life, men enter into definite relations that are indispensable and independent of their will, relations of production which correspond to a definite stage of development of their material productive forces. The sum total of these relations of production constitutes the economic structure of society, the real foundation, on which rises a legal and political superstructure and to which correspond definite forms of social consciousness. The mode of production of material life conditions the social, political and intellectual life process in general. It is not the consciousness of men that determines their being, but, on the contrary, their social being that determines their consciousness. At a certain stage of their development, the material productive forces of society come in conflict with the existing relations of production, or—what is but a legal expression for the same thing—with the property relations within which they have been at work hitherto. From forms of development of the productive forces these relations turn into their fetters. Then begins an epoch of social revolution. With the change of the economic foundation the entire immense superstructure is more or less rapidly transformed.

This is one of the rare passages where Marx codified his basic ideas. The difficulty in trying to grasp Marx is that many of his important writings were either unfinished or unpublished in his lifetime; hence the importance of consulting good selections from his (vast) work. The best of these is *Karl Marx, Selected Writings in Sociology and Social Philosophy*, edited by T. B. Bottomore and M. Rubel. There is also a more personal selection by David Caute *The Essential Writings of Karl Marx*. Reliable commentaries on Marx are surprisingly hard to come by, partly because many of his writings have only been published comparatively recently, and partly because commentaries tend to be slanted by a political bias. No comparatively recent figure can have so many false legends attached to him: that Marx died at his desk, that he had a happy marriage, that he failed seriously to envisage a revolution in Russia, that he called his doctrine dialectical materialism or even historical materialism—all these popular imaginings are quite unfounded. One of the best general books on Marx himself is Shlomo Avineri's *The Social and Political Thought of Karl Marx*; still the best introduction is Isaiah Berlin's eminently readable *Karl Marx: His Life and Environment*. The rediscovery of Marx's early writings has led some commentators (wrongly) to exalt the 'humanist' young Marx at the expense of the 'rigid' mature Marx. An extreme example would be Erich Fromm's *Marx's Concept of Man*. Two books on the formation of Marx's thought are *The Young Hegelians and Karl Marx* and *Marx Before Marxism*. The various schools of Marxist thought up to and including Lenin are well covered in George Lichtheim's *Marxism. A Historical and Critical Study*.

So much for the foundations. By the turn of the century, however, and increasingly thereafter, three factors were making for a change in the interpretation of Marxism. Firstly, as far as the more developed countries were concerned, Marx's idea of the progressive pauperization of the proletariat and its necessary evolution to a realization of its revolutionary role, had been rendered obsolete. The creation of labour unions and the growth of reformism demonstrated that, far from aiding a proletarian revolution, the economic infra-structure of society made for the progressive integration of the working classes in the existing social order (though Marx's other major analysis, that of man as an alienated being dominated by the products of his own creation acquired an importance far greater than Marx had imagined). Secondly, it became clear that there was indeed an important 'pauperization' taking place, but that it was between the rich minority of nations and the poor majority. This led to theories of imperialism (that Marx himself had only vaguely sketched) and the growing influence of Marxism in the countries of the Third World. Their problems, however, being very varied, so were the 'Marxist' solutions that were proposed. Thirdly, with the adoption of Marxism as the official ideology of Soviet Russia and her satellites, it was no longer the exclusive ideology of the under-dog: instead of being a revolutionary theory, it could be, and was, used to defend the *status quo*.

Looking, then, at the different parts of the world where Marxism is now a political influence, the most striking fact is that 'Marxism' no longer exists: there is virtually no common factor in the different systems and movements that claim to draw their inspiration from Marx.

In Western Europe, there are two main streams of Marxist thought: the first is contained in the Communist Parties and particularly those of France and Italy, where the existence of pluralist democracies has led the Party (at least tacitly) to abandon such theses as the one party state and violence as a means of achieving power. It seems that the Communist Parties of Western Europe are on the way to adopting the position and ideology of the European social democrat parties in the early years of this century. The first clear example of this tendency was contained in the 'Testament' of Palmiro Togliatti, Secretary of the Italian Communist Party, published after his death in August 1964; it was continued in the protests of the French and Italian Communist Parties at the Russian invasion of Czechoslovakia in the August of 1968. Nevertheless, this tendency is not very far advanced and the original thought of Western Marxists is in fields peripheral to politics, such as the literary criticism of writers like Lukacs or Goldmann or the reinterpretations of Marx in Lefebvre's *Dialectical Materialism* and *Sociology of Marx*. A sign of this loosening of dogma has been the growing popularity of a Christian-Marxist dialogue. For the English scene, those interested can read *Dialogue of Christianity and Marxism*, edited by James Klugman, or *What Kind of Revolution? A*

Christian–Communist Dialogue, edited by James Klugman and Paul Oestreicher, though the dialogue in this country is extremely abstract when compared with continental Europe where the tradition of clericalism makes it more relevant. The basic issues here are best explored in Terry Eagleton's *New Left Church* and *Slant Manifesto*.

Equally inspired by Marx, though in a tradition that comes via Mao Tse-tung or Marcuse, is the student movement. Beginning in California in 1964, it achieved its greatest impact so far in France in the summer of 1968. The distance between the ideas of the sclerotic, and, in the most important sense, conservative Communist Party and the mass of the students was brought out in the events of May–June on which one of the best accounts is *A French Revolution 1968* by Patrick Seale and Maureen McConville. An obviously more partisan account by one of the leading participants is Daniel Cohn-Bendit's *Obsolete Communism: The Left Wing Alternative*. On the student movement in Britain *Student Power* edited by Robin Blackburn and Alexander Cockburn, should be consulted, though it contains many shrill generalizations unworthy of anyone aspiring to the title of student. A world-wide perspective is contained in *New Revolutionaries* edited by Tariq Ali. The general theoretical background to these ideas comes from the early Marx and has been taken up and strikingly analysed by writers such as Marcuse and Lukacs. Marx's analysis aims at showing that in a commodity society the products of men's labour acquire a material power *vis-à-vis* their producers and that thereby the relations between persons appear as relations between things. This fetishism imposes a passive character on men's attitudes to life and on the behaviour of individuals subjected to economic laws of a market that becomes like a quasi-natural power.

A contemporary version of these ideas will be found in the much publicized *One Dimensional Man* of Herbert Marcuse, extremely difficult to read for a book said to have sold more copies than the Little Red Book itself. Here Marcuse describes modern industrial society as as structure in which the individual is totally manipulated by material rewards and information management. Life is one dimensional since real dissent or protests are no longer possible. The establishment must be provoked if the myth of freedom and tolerance are to be shattered and a revolution begun. The only group that can resist manipulation are the students. Marcuse thus advocates the creation of an international vanguard of students, who in turn can make the workers aware of their oppression by the system and allow them to escape. Then together the workers and students can destroy the system and erect a new one in its place.

Many of these themes have been taken up by intellectuals in Eastern Europe. For these, and particularly those in Czechoslovakia, Poland and Yugoslavia, the early writings of Marx have acquired a great importance. After Khrushchev's denunciation of Stalin in 1956, the humanist attitudes of the young Marx were used as a basis for opposition to remaining Stalinist elements in Eastern Europe, much as the New Testament was used by the Reformers to oppose the Catholic Church. In Czechoslovakia the 'human face of socialism' that the country's leaders were trying to achieve in 1968 prior to the Russian invasion, and particularly the '2,000 words' manifesto, is very close to Marx's early works. On this topic, see Zeman's *Prague Spring*. In Poland the discussion began in 1959 with the publication of Kolakowski's article 'Karl Marx and the Classical Definition of Truth', since republished with other articles in his book *Beyond Marxism*. This article drew a sharp distinction between the theories of knowledge of the young Marx on the one hand and those of Engels and Lenin on the other, and implied that Marx was not a dialectical materialist at all in Engels's and Lenin's sense. Kolakowski's views were taken up by Adam Schaff, a member of the Central Committee of the Polish Communist Party, and expanded into an inquiry into the reasons for socialism's inability to overcome human alienation. In Yugoslavia since 1966 a large degree of decentralization and social self-government has been achieved. A Leninist type of party has been abolished and they even talk of their goal as being a 'no party state'. Yugoslav 'critical socialism' recognizes that conflict is inherent in every society, even a socialist one, turns its criticism even against Marxist doctrines, and tries to put a premium on human freedom and self-government. In general the developments of Marxist thought current in Eastern Europe comprise the following four points: that there are problems of ethics and philosophy that transcend classes; that even under socialism men are liable to experience alienations that are in no way lessened by the promise of a distant realm of freedom from alienation, and that the study of Marx has little to offer on this question; that the false consciousness inherent in official Marxism is a partial cause of such alienation; and that scientific and technological developments have created new forms of alienation that are in some ways more oppressive to contemporary man than the alienation of labour that was central to Marx's own thought. These new currents are well discussed in Richard de George's *The New Marxism*.

In the Soviet Union, to quote Mr Khrushchev, 'we are getting richer, and when a person has more to eat, he gets more democratic'. From the point of view of contemporary political theory, however, Russia is a barren land. Those interested in the 1917 revolution should consult E. H. Carr's massive and scholarly *History*. An outline of Lenin's contribution to Marxist theory can be found in Carew Hunt's *Theory and Practice of Communism*, though the anti-communist bias makes the book not always a reliable one. Lenin believed that the bourgeois-democratic and the proletarian revolution could be telescoped into one; he allotted to the dictatorship of the proletariat a more permanent role than had been conceived by Marx; he popularized the idea of imperialism as the highest stage of capitalism; and, most importantly, he conceived of the Party as the 'vanguard of the proletariat', a small, secret, highly disciplined organization guiding the proletariat both before and after the revolution. For further information see Adam Ulam's *Lenin and the Bolsheviks*. On Russia between the wars, Isaac Deutscher's biographies of Stalin and Trotski are the best reading. In post-war Russia the basic document is Khrushchev's speech to the 20th Congress of the Communist Party of the Soviet Union which first revealed to the Communist world at large that Stalin had been a god with feet of clay. This can be found *in extenso* in Wright Mills's *The Marxists*, the best of the many collections of documents to illustrate the evolution of Marxist thought. The effect on Russian life of Khrushchev's revelations is dealt with in Edward Crankshaw's *Khrushchev's Russia*.

China, by contrast to Russia, is a country where political theory seems to play an almost abnormal role. The Chinese revolution was different from the Russian in that firstly it was a peasant revolution and secondly it was successful only through a prolonged military struggle. The first factor led to the importance of co-operative forms of agricultural development (in contradistinction to Russia where the peasants were starved); there was also no proletariat in the Marxist sense which explains Mao's remark about the Chinese people's being poor and blank. The second factor led to a quite un-Marxist emphasis on personal effort and struggle being decisive elements and also, the war being a guerrilla one, to a close attention to maintaining the good will of the local population. From this evolved what has come to be known as the 'mass-line' doctrine particularly associated with Mao Tse-tung. This says that all power comes from the people; that all decisions have their origin in the people and must ultimately be ratified by them (whence the mass meetings and demonstrations); that there is latent in the masses a boundless power waiting to be released (whence the Great Leap Forward); that officialdom must be constantly called into question to prevent the growth of hierarchies and preserve revolutionary momentum.

Most of these elements are present in the recent Cultural Revolution which, as a reviewer in the *Times Literary Supplement* has said, is 'well on the way to becoming all things to all men; an inspiration to discontented French students, a resurgence of the Yellow Peril to Russian leaders, and the long awaited self-destructive climax of Communist rule to the anti-Communists'. The Cultural Revolution is best understood as the latest episode in the struggle between two different schools inside China: the first led by Mao Tse-tung and believing in the mass line, the second, of whom the most representative figure is Liu Shao-chi, branded 'the Chinese Khrushchev', who wishes to instal a more organized and traditional form of economic planning and development. The first would seem to be a strategy appropriate to the achievement of power, the second to the government of a country after a revolution: China's instabilities spring, in large part, from a conflict between the two. The first two or three years after the inauguration of the Chinese People's Republic in 1949 were occupied in settling down. Then the first five-year plan was inaugurated. At the end of this, the 'mass line' broke through with Mao's Hundred Flowers' Speech and the Great Leap Forward. This proved so disastrous economically (largely due to exceptionally poor harvests) that Mao resigned from presidency of the party, and in 1961 a second five-year plan was introduced. The end of this saw once again a return, in the Cultural Revolution, of Mao's 'mass line'. Obviously, given that our present knowledge of the Cultural Revolution campaign is still very slight and that the outcome is uncertain, many different interpretations of the origin and events of the campaign are possible. A fair assessment of the evidence at present available is contained in Gray's and Cavendish's *Chinese Communism in Crisis*, the first four chapters of which contain a stimulating and well-written introduction to recent Chinese history. A smaller and more accessible account is Joan Robinson's *The Cultural Revolution in China*. There is an excellent biography of Mao Tse-tung by Stuart Schram, who shows how Mao's views were formed by his guerrilla experiences among the peasants and the Long March to Yenan.

Among the voluminous works of Mao Tse-tung, the Little Red Book with its plastic cover is very easy to get hold of. Before smirking at the mention of 'Mao Tse-tung's thought' it should be remembered that most of the contents are severely practical and simple instructions whose inculcation is largely designed to bring the mass of Chinese peasantry from the illiteracy of the Middle Ages to the twentieth century. The most commonly read selections from Mao are the three short articles entitled 'Serve the People', 'In Memory of Norman Bethune', and 'The Foolish Old Man Who Removed the Mountains'. The first two are studied as a counter to selfishness, the *bête-noire* of Chinese Communism. In the first, a funeral oration, Mao tries to make sense of a rather silly death died in 1944 by a common soldier who was killed when a charcoal burning kiln collapsed. In the second, Mao praises the selflessness of a Canadian doctor who came to China in 1938, worked among the wounded at the front and died eventually of septicaemia. The last of the 'Three Old Faithfuls', as they are commonly known, is about an old man who got thoroughly fed up with the presence of two mountains outside his front door. Whenever he wanted to go away anywhere, he had to walk all the way round these mountains. Finally, he decided to remove them, and enlisted his family to help. A neighbour came by and laughed at him. 'You've got one foot in the grave,' he said, 'and you start a great labour like that. When do you imagine you'll finish it?' The 'foolish' old man explained: 'I won't see the end of it. But my sons and grandsons, and their sons and grandsons, will continue the work. It will be done in the end.' To understand contemporary China it is essential to read these simple documents, for they are being studied and absorbed daily by millions of Chinese.

China and the Chinese brand of Marxism (if it can be called that) is at the present time the chief inspiration to countries of the Third World. To understand revolutionary currents in developing countries, where racial and economic factors are intertwined, to understand what it is like to be a black man in a white man's world, two books might be read in conjunction: Malcolm X's *Autobiography* and Franz Fanon's semi-autobiographical *The Wretched of the Earth*. Follow them up with the, no doubt over simplified, but terrible book *The Race War* by Ronald Segal, that documents in four hundred pages the most striking fact of our world:

> At no other period in history have there been such enormous differences in power as exist at present between the few and the many of mankind . . . The middle classes of the white industrial states enjoy a comfort and–barring war–a security, a command over their environment that in the past the most magnificent of princes lacked, while hundreds of millions of peasants in the rest of the world live as they have always done, menaced constantly by hunger, disease, and unseasonable death. Pharaoh or Caesar would have coveted air conditioning, the modern lavatory, the aeroplane and the motor-car; their subjects would have found little to covet in the way that multitudes of Asians, Africans and Latin Americans still scratch a precarious survival from the obstinate earth.

In Africa, there are no important movements that are specifically Marxist: Sekou Touré's Senegal is really no more than social democratic, and Senghor's Marxism in his book *On African Socialism* is the humanism of the young Marx. For further information see Friedland and Rosberg's *African Socialism*.

In Latin America, on the other hand, there is a very vigorous Marxist movement that draws its inspiration from Cuba, influences most of the South American continent and is the third main stream in the Communist world beside the Soviet Union and China.

The story of the Cuban Revolution and the subsequent activities of Cuban guerrillas is an absorbing one in itself, quite apart from any political considerations. The book to read here Guevara's *Reminiscenses of the Cuban Revolutionary War*. Guevara was converted to Marxism in 1954 after seeing Arbenz's reforming government in Guatemala being put down by the C.I.A. His *Reminiscenses* describe the conquest of Cuba by twelve men who, little more than walking corpses, survived the landing from Mexico and went on to topple the regime in a guerrilla war anticipating the tactics that have become so familiar in Viet Nam. Victory was, however, achieved without widespread revolutionary consciousness among the people – the guerrilla movement had a pronounced middle-class basis. The result is that workers and peasants exercise little control in Cuba over their work situations, and the administration is firmly in the hands of the Party bureaucracy. But of all Communist revolutions, the Cuban does seem the one whose practice is most akin to Marx's ideas: since 1959 there had indeed been a drop in the standard of living, but an attempt has been made to create a society where money is no longer king. Books, teaching, lodgings, medical services and the telephone are all free. Castro acts on the principal that 'To give a material incentive to a man so that he shall fulfill his duty is to buy his conscience'. The result is a society without prostitutes or beggars, but a society that some observers find rather boring. The Cuban Revolution is well set in context by Ramon Ruiz's *Cuba: The Making of a Revolution*. Hugh Matthews has written a reliable and readable *Castro: A Political Biography*.

Ruiz's book does, however, tend to show that Cuba is untypical of Latin America and to explain why the guerrilla movement has so far failed in Bolivia, where Guevara was killed in October 1967 following an eleven month's campaign. The reason for this failure seems to have been the lack of support received from the peasants; the open hostility of the Bolivian Communist Party (vividly illustrated by the fact that Tania, one of the guerrillas killed with Guevara, was an East German double agent keeping an eye on Che for the Soviet K.G.B.); and thirdly the U.S. intensive training of the Bolivian Army. This information can be deciphered from *The Complete Bolivian Diaries of Che Guevara and Other Captured Documents*, edited by Daniel

James. This (American) version is fuller than the Cuban version entitled simply *Bolivian Diary*. The theoretical basis of the guerrilla struggle has been brilliantly discussed by Regis Debray, the young French Marxist now released from a thirty year prison sentence in Bolivia, in his book *Revolution in the Revolution?* Debray–in opposition to a Marxism of Russian obedience– asserts that 'the revolution is formed in the struggle itself' and argues that guerrillas can create the 'objective conditions' for successful revolution by a military struggle taking place in the countryside and *sierra*. A sympathetic critique of Debray's ideas, and particularly of his elevation of military factors over political and his romantic emphasis on sheer will-power, can be found in *Regis Debray and the Latin American Revolution*, edited by Leo Huberman and Paul Sweezey.

These, then, are the main currents in present day Marxist thought. The best short introduction to the evolution and eventual splitting up of the Communist world is Hudson's *Fifty Years of Communism*. But the golden rule in the study of Marxism, even more than most other political theories, is, if possible, to read the texts themselves; if not, to read commentaries that are favourable; and only then to read criticism–for criticism almost invariably tends to distort its subject-matter.

Political theory is the language in which we discuss how men should live together, in society. And since living together in society is the normal human condition, when we talk about politics we are talking about what it means to be a man, to be alive. Political theory should never forget this. It would do well to take as its motto Regis Debray's moving speech at the end of his trial, reprinted at the beginning of Tariq Ali's *New Revolurionaries*:

Revolutionary war is not a question of individuals facing individuals–everyone has a family, parents, sons, loved ones, a childhood. They are but mere representatives of two irreconcilable orders. These acts of war are the fruits of social, economic and moral antagonisms, existing independently of the will of the actors and preceding them. No one has created these antagonisms, and no one can take them away, but they should indeed be surmounted and settled. Naturally, the tragedy is that we do not kill objects, numbers, instruments, but, precisely, on both sides, irreplaceable individuals, essentially innocent, unique for those who have loved, bred, esteemed them. This is the tragedy of history, of any history of any revolution. It is not individuals who are placed face to face in these battles but class interests and ideas; but those who fall in them, those who die, are persons, are men. We cannot avoid this contradiction, escape from this pain.

READING LIST

H. Acton: *The Illusion of the Epoch* (Cohen).
T. Ali: *New Revolutionaries* (Peter Owen).
S. Avineri: *The Social and Political Thought of Karl Marx* (C.U.P.).
I. Berlin: *Karl Marx* (O.U.P.).
R. Blackburn and A. Cockburn, eds.: *Student Power* (Penguin).
R. Carew-Hunt: *The Theory and Practice of Communism* (Bles).
E. Carr: *History of the Bolshevik Revolution* (Macmillan).
D. Caute: *Communism and the French Intellectuals* (Andre Deutsch).
L. G. Churchward: *Contemporary Soviet Government* (Routledge).
D. Cohn-Bendit: *Obsolete Communism: The Left Wing Alternative* (Andre Deutsch).
E. Crankshaw: *Khrushchev's Russia* (Penguin).
A. Cunningham, et al.: *Slant Manifesto*
R. Debray: 'Revolution in the Revolution', *Monthly Review*, London, 1968.
M. Drachkovitch: *Marxism in the Modern World* (Stanford University Press). *Marxist Ideology in the Contemporary World* (Praeger).
T. Eagleton: *New Left Church* (Sheed and Ward).
F. Fanon: *The Wretched of the Earth* (MacGibbon and Kee).
W. Friedland and C. Rosberg: *African Socialism* (Stanford University Press).
E. Fromm: *The Marxist Concept of Man* (Routledge).
J. Gray and P. Cavendish: *Chinese Communism in Crisis* (Pall Mall).
E. Guevara: *Reminiscences of the Cuban Revolutionary War* (Allen and Unwin). *The Complete Bolivian Diary of the Che Guevara and Other Captured Documents* (Allen and Unwin).
L. Huberman and P. Sweezey eds.: 'Regis Debray and the Latin American Revolution', *Monthly Review*, London, 1968.
G. Hudson: *Fifty Years of Communism* (C. A. Watts).
L. Labedz, ed.: *Revisionism* (Allen and Unwin).
H. Lefebvre: *Dialectical Materialism* (Cape). *The Sociology of Marx* (Allen Lane).

G. Lichtheim: *The Origins of Socialism* (Weidenfeld and Nicolson).

N. Lobkowicz: *Marx and the Western World* (University of Notre Dame).

Malcolm X: *Autobiography*, ed. Haley (Penguin).

S. Schram ed.: *Quotations from Chairman Mao Tse-tung* (Pall Mall).

Mao Tse-tung: *Selected Works* (Pall Mall).

H. Marcuse: *One Dimensional Man* (Century Books).

K. Marx: *Selected Writings in Sociology and Sociol Philosophy* (C. A. Watts). *Essential Writings*, ed. D. Caute (MacGibbon and Kee). *The Early Texts*, ed. D. McLellan (O.U.P.).

D. Matthews: *Castro: A Political Biography* (Allen Lane).

D. McLellan: *The Young Hegelians and Karl Marx* (Macmillan). *Marx Before Marxism* (Macmillan).

J. Robinson: *The Cultural Revolution in China* (Penguin).

R. Ruiz: *Cuba: The Making of a Revolution*.

S. Schram: *Mao Tse-tung* (Allen Lane).

P. Seale and M. McConville: *French Revolution 1968* (Heinemann).

R. Segal: *The Race War* (Cape).

L. S. Senghor: *On African Socialism* (Pall Mall).

A. Ulam: *Lenin and the Bolsheviks* (Sheed and Ward).

D. Watt, et al.: *A History of the World in the Twentieth Century* (Hodder and Stoughton).

R. Williams ed.: *The May Day Manifesto* (Penguin).

8

Economics

ALAN BUDD

ECONOMISTS usually give one or more of three reasons for their original interest in the subject. The first reason is curiosity about certain aspects of the world. Why are some people, and countries, richer than others? Why do prices keep going up? How does the international monetary system work? The second is a desire to use knowledge of the economic system to achieve a particular objective. The aim may be selfish; for example, a wish to make a fortune on the Stock Exchange: it may be unselfish: for example, a desire to improve the standard of life of people in underdeveloped countries. The third reason for studying economics is based on the belief that a particular kind of society is evil, and that its economic system causes it to be evil. Thus, to remove the evil, the economic system must be changed. Although these distinctions are not watertight, the three reasons are related to the three roles the economist can play. The first is the economist as scientist, the second is the economist as engineer, and the third is the economist as social critic. I shall discuss these in turn, and summarize what economists are doing in each case, examining some of the practical and philosophical difficulties that result.

I. THE ECONOMIST AS SCIENTIST

One guide to the present state of economics is provided by the contents of what is taught to first year undergraduates. There must by now be several hundred introductory text-books. A glance at them reveals a high degree of consensus, at least in the West, about the fundamentals of the subject. The order of presentation may change, the diagrams will have different colours, but perhaps ninety per cent of each text will consist of theories and results which are common to all of them. There will not even be much difference between a text-book published ten years ago and one published today. Most text-books divide economics into two parts. The first is concerned with individual decisions and actions in buying and selling, and the second is concerned with national totals such as the level of employment, the size of national income or the level of prices. Much of the first part, which is described as Price Theory or Micro-economics (the two titles are not precisely equivalent), is based on theoretical results which were established in the nineteenth century and are sometimes known as neo-classical economics; the second part, which is usually known as Macro-economics, was developed in the 1930s and is usually associated with the work of J. M. Keynes. The student may be puzzled that there is no apparent connection between the two parts of the subject, and much effort is consequently devoted to examining whether the theories underlying them are consistent with each other or not. However, there are good precedents in science for retaining apparently inconsistent theories, provided that they perform usefully in their respective spheres.

Economics is concerned with a particular part of human behaviour. It must contend with two serious difficulties before behaviour can be explained scientifically. Human behaviour is thought to be unpredictable and subject to random whims, follies and foibles. Secondly, in general, controlled experiments on humans are impossible or morally unacceptable. Neither difficulty is insuperable. Social life depends upon a considerable amount of regularity and predictability in human behaviour. Think how often in the course of every day we rely on people behaving in the way we expect them to. We hand over money and get a bus ticket in exchange; the bus goes to the destination indicated on the front; everyone else arrives at the place of work at their usual time; the building has been unlocked and cleaned, and so *ad infinitum*. Our expectations of others are not always fulfilled; it may be impossible to explain and predict all human behaviour, but in economics it is usually sufficient if we can predict how seventy or eighty per cent of the people will behave in a particular situation.

The inability to use controlled laboratory experiments is not peculiar to economics, but is true, for example, of meteorology and parts of astronomy. In each subject it is possible to devise alternatives. The most important alternative used in economics is the branch of study known as econometrics. Very roughly, this treats the past as a series of economic experiments in which economic theories may be tested retrospectively. Difficulties remain, for the significance of *controlled* experiments is that they allow the scientist to examine the effects of changes in one variable, for example, heat, on the situation, while holding everything else constant. The economist may want to examine the effects of changes in taxes on purchasing behaviour. But the government usually introduces a 'package deal' which changes taxes and a number of other things, for example, hire purchase regulations, at the same time. Econometrics has developed techniques which can cope with this difficulty.

These two problems—that human actions are not completely predictable and the inability to conduct experiments—make economics difficult but they do not make it impossible. The economist as scientist seeks to explain and predict economic activity. The science has developed, firstly by abstracting simple assumptions about behaviour from the total range of attitudes, emotions and motives involved in economic activities, and secondly, by producing deductive theories based on a limited number of these simple assumptions. In micro-economics, the first abstraction is the emphasis on scarcity. There is a gap between people's wants and the resources available to satisfy them. A household can spend its income on clothes, food or holidays; but it cannot have as much as it likes of each. Society can use labour and materials to build hospitals or luxury hotels; but it cannot have an unlimited supply of either. Scarcity implies choices between alternatives, and micro-economics is the study of the way in which individuals and firms make these choices. The decisions and choices are explained by two further general principles or further simplifications of behaviour—utility maximization for individuals and households, and profit maximization for firms.

The concept of utility maximization can be paraphrased by saying that people do what makes them happiest. Professor Joan Robinson has called utility 'a metaphysical concept of impregnable circularity' and the crude paraphrase just given would suggest that her criticism is fair. Since we have no sure way of knowing whether people are happy or not, we cannot check directly whether the principle of utility maximization is true or false. However, economics makes a number of specific assertions about what makes people happy. For example, the Theory of Demand assumes that the utility an individual derives from goods depends only on the quantity that he owns or acquires, it does not depend on the quantity that other people possess. Both envy and altruism are ignored. The theory also assumes that individuals know in advance what utility they will derive from a good.

On the basis of these two assumptions–utility maximization and profit maximization–an economic theory has been developed to explain and make predictions about the behaviour of individuals in a free market. An elementary guide to its main results can be found, for example, in Samuelson's *Economics. An Introductory Analysis* or Lipsey's *Introduction to Positive Economics*, which are the best-selling University text-books in the United States and Britain respectively. A free market means, approximately, that people are free to buy and sell whatever they wish. Since a large part of the British economy is a free market in this sense, we may therefore ask whether the results of Price Theory are correct; do they describe reality? This is an extremely difficult question to answer. Certainly Price Theory provides a satisfactory explanation for many everyday phenomena. It explains, for example, why a loaf of bread costs about one shilling and a television set costs about £70, and not vice versa. It explains, why, in general, shops are neither full of goods they are unable to sell, nor are there long queues for some commodities. Where there are shortages, for example, in certain types of housing, this can often be explained by government interference in the pricing system. (The government has taken the just decision that rents should be controlled. But it relies on the private sector to provide much of the housing, and the rents may be too low for enough housing to be provided to meet the demand for it. The private sector will not provide housing unless it is profitable for it to do so.) Price Theory also explains, though rather imperfectly, the differences between people's incomes.

However, doubts remain; over a large area of economic behaviour, we simply do not know whether the theories are correct or not. These doubts are due to the gap in economics between theoretical developments and the process of collecting data, which may be used to support or refute the theories. In part, the shortage of data is unavoidable. Economists generally rely on the government to collect data for them. Not surprisingly, the government collects data for its own purposes, which may not coincide with the economists' interests. In many cases the data are either not available or are available in a form which does not correspond to the economists' categories. In part, the lack of well-established empirical results is due to fashion. In economics, as in most subjects, theoretical work has greater prestige than experimental and applied work. In the physical sciences a strong selective process operates to ensure that this prestige is justified. The selective process is created by the findings of the experimentalists. New theories must either be consistent with well-established empirical results, or, if there are no relevant results, there is an immediate search for ways of establishing them. This process frequently involves immense skill and ingenuity. In economics, unfortunately, facts do not press so hard upon theories, and the result is the peculiarly English vice of armchair empiricizing, in which conclusions are based on assertions about facts rather than on facts themselves. This results in the survival of a mass of theories (and theorists) which would have to be abandoned under the hard light of evidence.

As an empirical science, economics has to avoid the two extremes of empty theorizing on the one hand, and aimless fact-gathering on the other. In the past, it has not always succeeded, but the situation is now improving. Many of the advances of the post-war years have been in the development of techniques, particularly econometric techniques, and the fruits of these will become increasingly apparent. More data is becoming available, and computers can now be used to reduce the effort of processing it. In the United States, where considerably more effort is devoted to empirical work, impressive results are being achieved. The same results should be possible in this country, though this will require an increased supply of applied economists who are skilled both in economic theory and in statistical techniques.

The empirical results that have been established about economic life suggest that micro-economics is more successful in making predictions about groups than about individuals. For example, theory may suggest that after a tax cut, all firms will increase their production. In practice, this is correct for the total of all firms' production, but it is not true of all the individual firms. The same result occurs with predictions about consumers. Two fields of study are concerned with this problem. The first is the Economics of Uncertainty, which takes specific account of the fact that men's decisions are influenced by uncertainty about the future. The second is concerned with the actions of firms, and considers not only the importance of uncertainty, but also the fact that firms are organizations which are likely to have a far more complicated set of goals than simply to make as much profit as possible. Both these studies are already yielding valuable results. For some time they will continue to co-exist with the conventional 'neo-classical' theories (which are themselves subject to continuous development and improvement). The science of economics aims to provide a set of consistent theories which will explain all the phenomena which fall within its domain, but the goal is still far away.

The attempt of economics to establish itself as a science has led to a number of moral and philosophical objections to the discipline. Many of these are included in the general accusation that economics is materialist. A further objection is that, in its claims to make predictions, economics is denying free will. Not all economists make this claim; for example, Professor Jewkes:

... there is a danger that economics, to its own discrediting, will be directed towards the discovery of pots of gold at the end of rainbows. One glaring example of this is the implication in much planning that economists can or will be able to predict the economic future. Perhaps no economist really believes this but some have been slow to disclaim such supernatural powers.

(*New Ordeal by Planning*)

(In this, as in many other matters, Professor Jewkes must be said to be in a minority.) Whatever the meaning of free-will, it is difficult to see how its existence or non-existence is related to predictability. If free-will implies the possibility of choice, economics is perfectly consistent with it. It takes the wishes and motives of individuals as given, and tries to predict how they will behave when faced with certain alternatives. Success in these predictions does not deny free-will, nor does failure support it. Often the objection that economics denies free-will is part of the practical objection mentioned earlier, that human behaviour is erratic. Erratic behaviour does not prove free-will (many inanimate objects behave erratically), and as far as predictability is concerned, it is often possible to predict the behaviour of groups even when it is not possible to predict the behaviour of individual members.

A more coherent criticism of economics is its emphasis on material pleasure and self-interest in human actions. Jevons, who played a major role in the development of the subject, described economics as the mechanics of self-interest. It is true that Price Theory is based on the assumption of selfish behaviour on the part of consumers and firms. This assumption is used because in the sphere of actions with which they are usually concerned, economists have found that self-interest provides a useful explanation. In general, people buy goods because they want them, not because they feel sorry for the shopkeeper. People work because they want the pay, not because they want to help their employer. Firms sell goods because it is profitable, not because they want to improve the quality of life. No one suggests that such motives dominate all human actions. For example, within the economic sphere, Price Theory does not explain the way in which goods are shared within a family. The accusation of materialism must imply firstly that motives of self-interest are undesirable, and secondly that economists are in some way responsible for the support and extension of these motives to many areas of life.

There are economists who have great skill in extending the ideas of economic theory to areas where it might appear to have no relevance. A leading example is Professor H. G. Johnson who, for example, has explained the troubles at the London School of Economics in terms of the low pay and inefficient promotion structure of the lecturers and in terms of the high ground rents in central London. This type of exercise, though, is merely seeking to explain what happens, it is not changing people's motives. Part of the accusation of materialism is that economists try to turn everything into a commodity to which they then attach a price. This exercise applies equally to flowers which have survived since the ice-age, a landscape view about to be destroyed by pylons, the convenience of sitting down in a train, or even life (for the purpose of valuing road safety expenditure).

It is true that economists do this. A branch of economics called Cost-Benefit Analysis has been developed for the purpose of trying to evaluate choices in cases such as the problem of siting an airfield. The techniques are used, not to emphasize material effects, but to try to take into account all the effects of a project rather than just the narrowly commercial ones. Many cost-benefit analysts are concerned to support human values, such as the need for peace and quiet, against encroaching commercialization.

There is one sense in which it is fair to accuse economists of having increased materialism. It is undeniable that economic matters have played an increasingly important part in national politics. The emphasis in party politics is on material prosperity. When Mr Macmillan said 'You've never had it so good', the Labour Party did not reply by questioning the importance of material well-being, it merely made counterclaims about its own ability to increase national output. Policy will be discussed in more detail in the next section; but if we try to explain the change in the emphasis, a plausible explanation can be given in terms of our increased ability to achieve economic goals. People do not strive to have what they know they cannot get; economic policy only becomes a matter for the government when it thinks that it is possible to do something about it. The economist's role in this seems to have been neutral; but increased knowledge has changed our preferences and the economists provided the increased knowledge. It is not clear what the economist could have done about this in the past, or can do about it now.

The role of the economic expert is both powerful and congenial; he can both influence policies and yet avoid the acrimony of having his values challenged and his interests revealed. But such detachment from the consequences of one's actions is good neither for the economist nor for society. The painful lesson learnt by the physicists after Hiroshima was that it was not enough to make new discoveries; the academic profession must try to ensure that they are used rightly. The processes of consultation and argument with non-scientists that this involves are not only uncongenial to the theorist, but entail that he must define his own values about how he works. To an academic who pleads that making moral choices of this kind is not his job, it can only be retorted that no one else thinks it is their job either. Our civilization suffers in too many ways from the grossly unreflective use of increasing knowledge. Can we use our new discoveries without repeatedly being overtaken by the fate of the sorcerer's apprentice?

II. THE ECONOMIST AS ENGINEER

Engineering is the application of science to social ends. The engineer takes scientific laws as given and uses them for a particular purpose. For example, the civil engineer can use his knowledge of physics and materials to construct a bridge to meet a given set of requirements such as expected loads, etc. Anyone who uses a hammer, or wears clothes, is adapting physical laws to his own use. In economics, engineering can occur at all levels. The businessman uses his knowledge of market behaviour and of production conditions to increase his profits. The most publicized use of economic engineering is at the national level, where economics is used to achieve policy objectives such as full employment. Many of the practical difficulties of economic engineering are illustrated in national economic policy, and I shall discuss them here because economic policy has become so important a part of government. (An excellent guide to recent British experience is given in R. E. Caves, *Britain's Economic Prospects*.)

In this country, there are four main objectives of economic policy—full employment, avoidance of inflation, faster economic growth, and a solution to the balance of payments problem. Each objective illustrates the process by which the development of science first allows us to understand a phenomenon so that consequently we can intervene to alter the course of events. The best example of this is employment policy. Before the Second World War, capitalist economies were characterized by an alternation of booms—periods of full employment, business optimism and rapid economic expansion—and slumps—periods of unemployment, business depression and economic stagnation. The slumps were periods of appalling social misery, with the particular quality that families suffered a dramatic fall from previous standards of living. In the ten years following the Great Wall Street Crash of 1929, the level of unemployment in the United States only once fell below eight million. In 1933, about one in four of the labour force was out of work. In England, although the pre-war slump was less severe, it was serious enough; in the worst year, over twenty-two per cent of the labour force was unemployed.

Governments either regarded this process as beyond their control, or adopted hesitant, and usually incorrect, measures to correct it. In England, the credit for understanding the causes of slumps has been given to Keynes. Although it is easy to find precedents for his ideas, both in England and in Sweden, Keynes's importance was due to the powerful influence that he exerted both at the governmental and the academic level. He is certainly responsible for the acceptance, by all post-war British governments, of a particular range of policies designed to avoid high levels of unemployment. Keynes's theories are now part of the received economic wisdom, and an account of them can be found in the two text-books mentioned. Another introductory guide for laymen is given in J. Pen, *Modern Economics*. (This 'modern economics' was developed in the thirties. In the United States, Keynesian policies are still known as the 'New Economics'. This reflects the slow and reluctant acceptance of interventionist policies in that country.)

The two stages, the understanding of the causes of slumps and the adoption of policies to avoid them, occurred in quick succession. The scientific theory on which Keynesian policies are based is founded on a number of simple assumptions about the way in which people spend incomes and about how businessmen decide how much machinery and capital goods to buy. In Keynesian policies, no attempt is made to change this behaviour, any more than an engineer tried to change the law of gravity. The government introduces a particular measure, for example it reduces taxes, in the belief that, as the theory predicts, people will spend more and thus employment will increase. Compared with pre-war experience, governments have had considerable success in maintaining full employment. Apart from the exceptional conditions of the winter of 1947, when much of industry stopped because of a fuel shortage, unemployment has rarely risen above three per cent. Nowadays, unemployment levels much above two per cent are regarded as high, and are usually the result of deliberate government policy.

There has been considerably less success with the other three objectives. The interesting question is to what extent this is due to failure by economists to understand the processes involved, or to the refusals of governments to adopt the proposals suggested to them. Certainly part of the blame must fall on economists. The tired joke about economic advisers, that if you have four economists in a room together they will provide five different proposals, contains enough truth to make us uneasy. The main reason is the shortage of data; but there is also a need for more adequate economic theories, especially to explain economic growth and inflation. Economic growth is an extremely fashionable subject in economics, but the theories that have been developed are not, in general, designed to solve the problems involved in making a country's income grow faster.

An important exercise in the study of growth is currently being conducted at Cambridge. It explores the implications of accelerating the rate of growth using the technique of *input-output analysis*. This technique is simple to grasp intuitively, but difficult to apply in practice. It recognizes the importance of the interdependence of different sectors of the economy. For example, the steel industry uses electricity and the electricity industry uses steel; both industries use coal and the coal industry uses both electricity and steel. The types of problem that input-output techniques try to solve are as follows. Since the war, national output has grown at the rate of about two-and-a-half per cent a year. The government may wish to study the implications of accelerating the rate of growth to four per cent. We assume that it decides at the outset what proportion of output is to be allocated to the government, and allows the allocation of the rest to be determined by consumers' preferences, i.e. the market. Past experience tells us that as a country's income increases, its pattern of demand changes; for example, it spends relatively more on entertainments, cars, luxury foods and domestic appliances, and relatively less on cheap foods and clothing. The economist will make a prediction of what the pattern of demand will be in, say, ten years' time. The question is, how much will sectors such as steel and electricity have to grow to meet this demand? Input-output analysis attempts to provide the answer. Some sectors will have to grow at considerably more than four per cent a year. Others will shrink.

There are considerable technical difficulties involved, but a table can be produced showing what the output of each sector must be if the growth target is to be achieved. Economic engineering is involved in ensuring that the individual sectors produce the required amount of output. What form this engineering takes depends partly on political preferences and partly on technical possibilities. The government may be averse to direct intervention, since economic plans are associated with totalitarian regimes. It is sometimes believed that the mere publication of the table, by removing uncertainty and showing what is required, produces the desired pattern of output. This appears to be the philosophy behind the ill-fated first economic plan in England. In its Introduction, Mr George Brown stated:

It is not a Plan to tell us all what to do and when and how. That wouldn't be acceptable to a nation like ours. But it does show us what is necessary and possible. What is available to do it with. Where the weaknesses are. What degree of change is required.

A possible result of the growth exercise is the demonstration that a given growth rate is not possible. This is the most sensible interpretation of the famous 'man-power gap' in the National Plan. It was an admission that the proposed growth rate was not feasible. A brilliant guide to the logic and philosophy of the Cambridge project is given by its director, Professor Stone in *The Model and Its Environment: A Progress Report*. (It becomes more difficult as it goes on, but no one, however inexpert or non-mathematical, should need to give up before page 24.)

In the control of inflation (rapidly rising wages and prices), there has been far less theoretical development, and very little empirical evidence has been collected which would enable us to choose between rival theories. At the moment a combination of two policies is being used. The first can be described as the Unemployment Policy, and the second is the Prices and Incomes Policy. The first is attributed to Professor Paish and aims to control wage increases by maintaining a margin of unemployment. The economic law which is relied on here is the observed tendency for wages to rise more rapidly when there is full employment. If this is combined with an observed tendency for price rises to be associated with wage increases, it seems plausible that a deliberate policy to maintain a margin of unemployment will be successful in preventing prices from rising. But we lack a satisfactory theory to explain the connection between full employment and rapid wage increases. It is possible that a second factor apart from the level of employment is operating and that a deliberate policy to maintain unemployment will fail to slow down wage increases.

Possibly because it too has doubts about the effectiveness of the Paish doctrine, the government has also used a Prices and Incomes Policy. Clearly if the government can, by law, prevent or control wage and price increases, it can, by definition, control inflation. In this policy the Unemployment Policy plays an additional, supporting, role. It is believed that it is easier to impose wage restraint on Trades Unions when there is unemployment. The Incomes Policy is thus more likely to succeed if it is accompanied by the Unemployment Policy.

The final policy's aim, to solve the balance of payments problem, has dominated post-war British economic policy. The successive balance of payments crises, and the measures used to cure them, have certainly been a contributory factor in our slow rate of economic growth. In trying to solve these crises there have again been a number of proposals based on economic theories which are asserted with some confidence, but which have not been proven. One example concerns the relationship between exports and the level of home demand. Some economists assert that when firms cannot sell goods at home, they will be more inclined to try to sell them abroad; others assert that unless there is buoyant home demand, average costs of production will rise and it will not be possible to sell abroad. Neither side has provided a coherent theory to support their view, and little convincing evidence has been provided. The most important feature of the balance of payments, as far as economists are concerned, is that the government has had the wrong priorities, and I now turn to this general problem.

It is sometimes suggested that the role of the economist in policy must be very restricted. Policy aims, it is said, are decided by politicians, and the role of the economist is simply to advise how best to achieve these aims. This is an excessively naïve view of the relationship between ends and means, and also ignores the importance of having information about the economy before deciding upon an economic policy. A major problem of economic policy is that the four basic aims that I have described conflict with each other. The achievement of full employment probably conflicts with the prevention of inflation. The prevention of inflation probably conflicts with the achievement of economic growth. The particular way which the government has chosen to solve the balance of payments problem conflicted both with full employment and economic growth. Even if the ultimate choice is left to politicians, the economist must indicate what the possibilities are. He must show what effects the control of inflation will have, for example, on the rate of economic growth. Ideally, he will present a series of alternatives. For example (using imaginary figures), the government may be presented with the following choices:

(i) two per cent unemployment, three per cent rate of growth, four per cent rate of inflation.

(ii) four per cent unemployment, two per cent rate of growth, one per cent rate of inflation.

(iii) three per cent unemployment, four per cent rate of growth, six per cent rate of inflation.

Each possibility has advantages, the government can choose the one it likes most.

I believe that the economist's responsibility goes beyond the presentation of these technical possibilities. Why is inflation thought harmful? Why is economic growth thought good? In each case, the government presumably has some idea of the economic and social consequences of these processes. It tends to be rather mysterious about these; it is therefore doubly important for economists to investigate and analyse them. These problems are discussed in M. Lipton, *Assessing Economic Performance*. One case in which economists have, wrongly, not attempted to question policy is in the balance of payments problem. From 1949 to 1967, economic policy was based on a desire to preserve a particular exchange rate between the pound and the dollar. In the end devaluation was thought necessary, and it was hailed as national disaster and a defeat. Dramatic phrases, such as bankruptcy and Dunkirk spirit, were widely used. The costs of preserving a particular exchange rate in terms of lost opportunities for economic growth were enormous; what were the benefits? Somehow it was regarded as unpatriotic to mention the possibility of devaluation, and rational discussion on exactly why it

ECONOMICS

was so harmful never happened. Here there was a clear case in which a policy objective should have been questioned.

Another policy objective which has been attacked is that of economic growth. The main attack is by E. J. Mishan, *The Costs of Economic Growth*. His main argument is that the obsession with economic growth has focused attention on one particular index of growth, namely the Gross National Product, which is a very poor measure of what we mean by the standard of life. His particular target is the motor-car. There is a vicious spiral in which, at the same time, driving becomes more and more of a miserable ordeal, and public transport becomes more costly and inefficient because no one uses it any more. There are many cases in which we are running hard to stay in the same spot, because we have to devote more and more effort to coping with the congestion and mess caused by our technological advances. Yet the effort devoted to clearing congestion is all counted as part of Gross National Production, so the rising costs of motoring appear as economic growth. Lipton has defended growth as an objective:

> Whatever a nation's goals—more help for the poor countries of the world, stronger defences, a larger public sector, a larger share of output for underprivileged persons at home—they can be most easily achieved by providing more resources through the growth of available output her head.
>
> It (growth) is not a materialistic goal. It covers the increase of resources of all types, including those devoted to the better training of painters and violinists, the support of scientific research and poets, and the improvement of scientific productivity so as to increase leisure time.

The dispute between the two in their assessment of the worth of economic growth could be resolved if a more satisfactory measure of output could be provided. Nobody believes that the Gross National Product measures happiness. We do not believe that the Americans are twice as happy as us, nor that we are twenty times as happy as the Burmese (though these are the ratios of our respective outputs per head); and it is wrong to measure our progress solely by this very crude indicator.

This discussion of economic engineering has been limited to

British experience. What is probably the most important role for the economic engineer currently—the attempt to improve the standard of life of the two thirds of the world's population who live in the so-called 'underdeveloped countries'—must be omitted in this brief review. A useful introduction to the problem is given in J. Bhagwati *The Economics of Underdeveloped Countries*. In these countries, as in advanced economies, we still need to develop useful scientific theories on which engineering can be based. The extent to which theories, which have been developed for advanced capitalist countries, can be used in underdeveloped economies (which have a different political, family and social structure, and, often, a different attitude to work and the accumulation of wealth) is disputed. There is a full discussion of this problem in Volume I of Professor G. Myrdal's *Asian Drama*.

When the economist acts as engineer, i.e. when he is called in to analyse a situation and provide a remedy or improvements, he can fail in two ways. He may not have the theoretical tools to analyse the situations, or economics may not yet have developed them. Desperate needs do not always produce remedies, and though he may very much want to cure inflation or improve the situation of poor countries, he may not understand their causes sufficiently to do so. Another, common failure is a moral one. If the economist allows himself to be used purely as an engineer, he may be helping to perpetuate a society he despises; if he works within a set of priorities such as 'don't redistribute or offend overseas creditors' he may fail to cure a situation because he does not challenge it. With the rapidly developing and increasingly difficult range of techniques the economist must master, it is difficult to remember that an economist must also be able to see implicit assumptions and the conventional wisdom for what they are. To be a good economist, one must analyse and criticize, as well as apply techniques.

III. The Economist as Social Critic

Many people would deny the economist this role. Or, rather, they would allow the economist to criticize society but would deny that economics played any part in his criticisms. Their argument is that economics as a science is neutral; it provides description and explanation but it provides no basis for judgement. Without attempting for the moment to decide whether this is true, we can begin the discussion by examining the work of a man who was both an economist and a social critic, and who clearly believed that there was a close connection between the two. The man is Karl Marx.

It is a brave man who attempts to summarize Marxist thought even if the summary is limited to Marxist economics. A start can be made by establishing what part of Marxist economics is scientific, as opposed to evaluative. Marx gives us a theory of the history of society. His fundamental assumption was that society organizes itself into the system that is most efficient for the production of output at each stage. Since techniques and products change, the required system also changes. Feudalism is succeeded by Bourgeois society and this in turn is followed by Communism. Each type of society is most efficient for the current state of technology. This process is inevitable. One can accelerate the process or prepare for the consequences but it cannot be postponed indefinitely. Bourgeois society involves capitalist production characterized by the private ownership of capital by a class of entrepreneurs. It collapses because it cannot avoid ever-worsening trade crises. In predicting these trade crises, Marx provided a theory of the trade cycle which had much in common with Keynes's theories.

If the worst that could be said of capitalism was that it is inefficient and subject to crises; and if it is now apparently possible to avoid the crises, there seems little reason to condemn it. The inefficiency can, at any rate, be remedied by minor changes. Marx was, however, concerned with more than crises and inefficiency. He was outraged by what he regarded as the complete immorality of capitalist production. A passionate sense of injustice recognized the appalling living and working conditions of the nineteenth-century workers. Just as Marx used his economic theory to explain trade crises, so he used his economic theory to explain the contrast between the poverty of the workers and the wealth of their employers. Further, he predicted that under the capitalist system, the earnings of workers would rarely rise above subsistence level.

The link between Marx's economics and his criticism of society is clear. He developed a theory which related the determination of wages to the system of ownership. Unless the private ownership of capital were abolished, wages would stay low despite the benevolence of individual capitalists.

He also sought to show that these low wages represented an exploitation of labour. Exploitation implies that someone is being deprived of what is justly due to them. Marx considered that profits rightly belonged to the labourers because their labour had created them. 'Profits are unpaid wages.' His demonstration proceeded by showing that labour was the sole producer of value. This was a conclusion derived from his theory of price (the so-called Labour Theory of Value) which showed that goods exchanged according to the labour embodied in them. That is, if one good takes three man-hours to produce and the other takes six man-hours, the second good will cost twice as much as the first. If labour is the sole producer of value, what role is played by capital, i.e. machinery? Marx includes in the value of a good the labour previously embodied in any machinery used, when that machinery was made. Thus it is still labour that is the sole producer of value. What role is played by the capitalist, whose only function is that he owns the capital? Since the whole of exchange value can be explained by labour, Marx concludes that the capitalist makes no contribution to value. Thus by keeping profits for himself, he is exploiting labour. It is not difficult to see that in this case there is a flaw in the argument. Even if the Labour Theory of Value is correct, it does not lead us to any conclusions about whether capitalists exploit labourers unless we define exploitation in a narrow, and morally unimportant, sense. An explanation of prices (and wages are one type of price) tells us nothing about the just level of wages. We may or may not believe that capitalists are worthless to the community; but we cannot expect a theory of price to tell us what income they deserve.

This seems to be an elementary error; but it is just as frequently made by a mistaken interpretation of Bourgeois economics (by Bourgeois economics, I mean the agreed body of thought current in the West). Bourgeois economics provides an alternative theory of prices to that of Marx, based, as we have said, on utility and profit maximization. Bourgeois economics explains why commodities do not exchange exactly in proportion to the amount of labour required to construct them. It also introduces a new scarce factor – waiting – which is paid a reward.

But it does not justify the distribution of income between workers and capitalists. In a market economy it may be necessary to pay a rate of interest to encourage lending; but the resulting incomes will depend on the initial distribution of wealth, which may be regarded as wholly unjust. (In Britain, five per cent of the population receives ninety-two per cent of the property income.)

A similar misunderstanding of bourgeois economics is often encountered in the theory of wages. The theory explains why people with scarce and desired talents are paid high salaries, but does not justify them. (One confusing factor is that these payments are usually called 'earnings'.) In an ideal market system (ideal in the sense that a long set of conditions is met) wages and salaries reflect the values that society placed upon particular labour services. But the scarcity of particular types of labour is largely a matter of innate or social and education advantages. The desirable aspect of the market system is its success in allocating these scarce skills efficiently; but the payments required to bring about this allocation are not necessarily those that bring about an equitable distribution of income. To illustrate this distinction, we can imagine a system in which all labour services are owned by the state, although all production is conducted by private enterprise. Firms thus have to buy labour services from the state, and by competing with each other will, let us suppose, bring about roughly the pattern of wage and salary payments which we observe at the moment. These payments will not, however, determine people's incomes. The state will only need to pay salaries that are adequate to compensate people for the effort or unpleasantness involved in different jobs. This, I assert with some confidence, will result in a considerable reduction in the highest salaries. This will permit an increase in the salaries paid to the lowest paid workers. The main difficulty of this scheme is matching the supply of different types of labour to the demand. However, these difficulties can be exaggerated. Most people's view of the labour market is that the most pleasant jobs are also the most highly paid. It is the persistence of this situation that suggests that effort accounts for only a small part of the differences in incomes.

I initially referred to the claim that economic science is neutral with respect to judgements on society. I showed that

Marx used economics in both a legitimate and an illegitimate way as a social criticism. According to his theories, the private ownership of capital in bourgeois society was unable to cope with the increasing complexities of industrial production. It would inevitably be replaced, though the process could be accelerated. His conclusions followed from his theory of trade cycles and economic growth. His second legitimate use of economics was to show the link between the miseries of working life and the prevalent system of production and ownership. If his theories are correct, it is clear what must be done if such miseries are to be removed. It was, however, illegitimate to try to prove that workers are exploited. Marxist economics does not prove this, any more than bourgeois economics proves the opposite.

Bourgeois economics can also be used in legitimate ways to criticize society. It can elucidate the links between economic activities and undesirable features of society and suggest how they can be removed. This is an extension of the economic engineering discussed in the previous section. Here again economics cannot claim any expertise about deciding what is undesirable, but it can explain what is happening. Mishan's book is an example of this type of criticism from within the traditional system of economics. A more radical set of proposals is given by Professor J. E. Meade in *Efficiency, Equality and the Ownership of Property*. Professor Meade emphasizes the distinction that I discussed earlier between the two functions of wages and salaries—as allocators of labour and as determinants of income. He predicts a future in which a larger and larger proportion of the national income goes to owners of property, and in which wages may in fact fall below their present level. Meade's solution is to redistribute property. The main difficulty about this exercise is that his basic premise about the growing importance of property income may be false—there is no evidence that it has started to happen yet in the United States. Meanwhile, efforts to bring about a more equitable distribution of income will have to rely on a redistribution of earned income and on a widening of opportunities for entry to the highest paid jobs.

One important criticism that can be made of bourgeois economics is that it is apparently but not really neutral as an analysis of society. It is suggested that its structure implicitly supports the economic system that it describes. In other words, it is part of capitalist ideology. To quote *The Communist Manifesto*:

What else does the history of ideas prove, than that intellectual production changes its character in proportion as material production is changed? The ruling ideas of each age have ever been the ideas of its ruling class.

Some evidence that this is so can be derived from the way in which bourgeois economics has been used to extol the virtues of capitalism. Individualism is an assumption of bourgeois economics. The Theory of Price is based on a picture of the separate and autonomous individual, guided by prices and his utility function, making choices from among all available goods in such a way that he maximizes his utility. This exercise of free choice is seen as one of the virtues of the market economy. Professor Jewkes has described the results of economic freedom in these terms:

In fact the prizes are the ultimate prizes: room for the mind freely to follow its own courses; room for society to enrich itself by the encouragement of diversity and the tolerance of eccentricity; room for the growth of dignity in human relations, Everything, indeed, that is bound up with the uniqueness of personality and with the Christian ethic.

This quotation is taken from *New Ordeal by Planning* which is, as its title suggests, an attack on central economic planning. In another passage, Jewkes praises the institution of property:

Property is the means by which the individual creates independence for himself against the powers of the State and the powers of organised opinion in the community.

Professor Jewkes is exceptional, among professional economists, in holding these views so strongly; but they are often held in a milder form. Two rather different beliefs are involved. The first is the belief that the very activity of exercising choice and making individual decisions in economic affairs is good. It is far better spiritually than having one's decisions made for one and being told what to do. The second belief is that the market system allocates resources in an efficient way. Roughly speaking, this means that labour and other factors of production are employed where society values their services most. The goods that are produced are those that consumers want. This is naturally assumed to be most desirable.

An important part of both views is the belief in the importance of the individual. The market system not only allows him to exercise his choice, but also ensures that the economic system operates in an efficient way to reflect and help him satisfy his choice. This second result occurs even though everyone is only concerned with their own interest.

Two well-known quotations from Adam Smith's *Wealth of Nations* express this view.

> It is not from the benevolence of the butcher, the brewer, or the baker, that we expect our dinner, but from their regard to their own self-interest, and we never talk to them of our necessities but of their advantages.

> He is in this as in many other cases led by an invisible hand to promote an end which was no part of his intention. By pursuing his own interest he frequently promotes that of the society more effectually than when he really intends to promote it.

A belief in the importance of individual choice seems to be unquestionable in a culture permeated by liberal and protestant views such as our own. It can be regarded as a natural extension of the idea of individual freedom. But surely if we are to attach importance to choice, we must also ask what determines choice. The individual is a product of society. His preferences are influenced and created by his upbringing, his education, his friends, the paper he reads and the television programmes he watches. Bourgeois economics by contrast, envisages a picture in which the individual arrives at the market place with a set of preferences and a knowledge of all possible commodities. The only thing he learns from the market is a list of prices. His tastes are independent of economic activity. Economic activity is affected by men's ideas, but not vice versa. This picture is not supported by other branches of social science. Over a wide range, our tastes are determined by our economic role in society. This is evident from the differences in tastes in food, furnishing and entertainment between the working class and the upper middle class. Can it really be true that by some miracle of selective breeding, only the upper middle class likes the taste of avocado pears? or opera? It is legitimate for economics to take tastes as given in studying a particular range of economic activity, but it cannot then claim to draw any conclusions about the way in which particular institutions support or encourage individualism.

It is true that the market system permits free choice (subject of course to one's income) but if we are to evaluate the effects of a particular economic system, we want to know how it affects the quality of life of those who belong to it. Bourgeois economics is not exactly neutral with respect to these questions; rather it begins by making assumptions that support the economic system it describes. It is not surprising that the conclusions seem also to support the economic system. An example of this can be given by the study of labour. Marx condemned the effects of factory working, whilst recognizing its supreme efficiency and productivity.

> Owing to the extensive use of machinery and to division of labour, the work of the proletarian has lost all individual character, and, consequently, all charm for the workman. He becomes an appendage of the machine, and it is only the most simple, most monotonous and most easily acquired knack, that is required of him.
>
> *(Communist Manifesto)*

Bourgeois economics makes no comment on the mental state of the worker but confines itself to explaining his wage. Again it is neutral. But again this neutrality is misleading. The Theory of Wages assumes that the worker has exercised his free choice (subject of course to his abilities and market constraints) about where he works and how long he works. He thus maximizes his utility. Even if we believed in this freedom of choice, what determines his abilities? Bourgeois economics does not ask; it takes his abilities as given. It treats labour as yet another commodity whose price is to be determined by the market. Marx recognized this, but condemned it;

These labourers, who must sell themselves piecemeal, are a commodity, like every other article of commerce, and are consequently exposed to all the vicissitudes of competition, to all the fluctuations of the market.

(Communist Manifesto)

It is perhaps unfair to blame economics for failing to do something which it does not claim to do. Economics has, rightly, attempted to be neutral and to use a language that is free from emotive and political overtones. To a large extent, in spite of the difficulties, economics has succeeded in the attempt. But part of the cost of this process has been a switch away from the type of problem that concerned Marx towards apparently neutral questions about costs and prices. It is usually a mistake to try to reverse this process using the concepts of bourgeois economics because they imply the very points that we want to question. These questions–about the relationship between the economic system and the social and political structure it supports–are ones that economists should be especially qualified to answer; but unfortunately, through a narrow and historically imposed idea of the scope of the subject, and the pursuit of technical sophistication, they have chosen to ignore them.

Professor J. K. Galbraith is the major economist in the West (apart from the identifiable Marxist economists) to consistently attack conventional views. In *The Affluent Society* he draws attention to the inability of capitalist economies to organize themselves efficiently for the benefit of all their members. In *The New Industrial State* he emphasizes the growing importance of the large corporation, which may be as powerful, economically and politically, as a government department, but which is not subject to democratic control. Professor Galbraith is something of an embarrassment to economists, since he is probably one of the most famous economists in the English-speaking world, whilst remaining intellectually dismissed by much of the profession. *The New Industrial State* was reviewed with remarkable venom in *The Times Literary Supplement* of November 23rd, 1967. A more moderate, though critical, review by Professor J. E. Meade appeared in the *Economic Journal* of June 1968. Both reviews reveal empirical errors in Galbraith's work, but a nagging doubt remains that much of the criticisms of Galbraith by economists

ECONOMICS

arise because he works within an unconventional framework. It might be preferable to try to use his framework to extend economics into areas which are undoubtedly important, even if, at the moment, we cannot accept Galbraith's conclusions.

Economics may be a materialist science; but unless we halve or quarter our existing population, break down our extreme specialization and division of labour, and return to a series of small-scale, largely self-supporting, traditional communities at a low level of subsistence, we cannot live without it. Economic decisions will continue to be made about factories versus hospitals versus tractors; wage-levels and profit-levels will go on being determined. We can try to understand the causes and results of what happens, to try to judge it and control it, or we can simply suffer the results of a laissez-faire system. We can send men round the moon, but we cannot house many of them sufficiently or pay them enough. The economic facts of life cannot be ignored; by trying to understand them, we can control and use them.

READING LIST

Economics is by now a highly developed subject and little of its advanced work can be understood by the layman. This difficulty is increased by its necessary use of technical language and mathematics. A general reading list must therefore be limited to elementary text-books or to 'literary' works which are not necessarily representative of the subject (or of their authors). The adventurous who have access to a University library should look at *Econometrica* to see the heights to which theoretical economics can rise. The best introductory book is Donaldson's.

There is no equivalent of *New Scientist* to provide simplified versions of current work in economics. Despite its title, *The Economist* contains little economics in any of the senses I have described. *New Society* has tended to ignore economics. There is also very little application of economics in newspaper discussions of government policy, though its relevance is obvious. This may be due to a commendable reluctance by economists to give glib answers to complicated problems, but unfortunately discussion of economic matters is consequently left to people who are even less well qualified.

J. Bahagwati: *The Economics of Underdeveloped Countries* (Weidenfeld and Nicolson).

R. E. Caves, et al.: *Britain's Economic Prospects* (Allen and Unwin).

P. Donaldson: *Guide to the British Economy* (Penguin).

J. K. Galbraith: *The Affluent Society* (Penguin). *The New Industrial Estate* (Hamish Hamilton).

See 'Dominie's Economy'; (Review of J. K. Galbraith, *The New Industrial Estate*), *The Times Lit. Supplement*, 23rd Nov., 1967.

J. Jewkes: *The New Ordeal by Planning* (Macmillan).

H. G. Johnson: *The Economic Approach to Social Questions* (Weidenfeld and Nicolson).

R. G. Lipsey: *An Introduction to Positive Economics* (Weidenfeld and Nicolson).

M. Lipton: *Assessing Economic Performance* (Staples Press).

K. Marx: *Communist Manifesto* (Foreign Languages Publishing House).

J. E. Meade: *Efficiency, Equality and the Ownership of Property* (Allen and Unwin). 'Is "The New Industrial Estate" Inevitable?', *Economic Journal*, LXXVIII. June 1968.

E. J. Mishan: *The Costs of Economic Growth* (Staples Press).

G. Myrdal: *Asian Drama* 3 Vols. (Penguin).

J. Robinson: *Economic Philosophy* (Penguin).

P. A. Samuelson: *Economics. An Introductory Analysis* (McGraw-Hill).

R. Stone: *A Programme for Growth. 5 The Model in its Environment* (Chapman and Hall).

9

Work and the Intellectual
FRED INGLIS

WHAT are the preconditions for a living culture? One may seem to ask such a question out of a desperate personal sense of homelessness, and the question may easily be taken as an invitation to set out on one of those familiar, necessary, sometimes exhilarating, mostly dispiriting comminations of contemporary England which one finds in the weeklies and on television. And certainly some attempt at diagnosis, and some at stricture too, is called for if we are at all to understand where we are now and what idea of the future we possess. For any sufficient and creative idea of the future carries with it a living sense of the meaning of the past and of the action possible in the present. To know what to do now involves knowing what you really want, which is notoriously the hardest thing in the world to know, and involves further the prior explanation of how you came to be where you are in the first place. No one, then, who is alive in the present can be freed from history; it is a main business of living to understand the controls of history, and the possibilities for choice. A sombre view of the future is not necessarily passive or fatalist, and the point of intellectual activity is not to remain alive to talk to other intellectuals.

For it is of the intellectual that we ask the opening question, what are the preconditions for a living culture? And before we can ask *him* anything, we must know who he is. These past years it has been hard to know where to find him. In the universities and establishments of sixth form or further education no doubt, but which of the thousands of people there? 'Intellectual' has been a word set over against the traditional virtues of the *bien-pensant* middle-class Englishman for many years, those hard-headed, soft-middled virtues of 'practicality', 'service', 'competition', 'self-reliance' and 'individualism'. In the wealthiest days of nineteenth-century England, the national intelligentsia had a key place in the formation[1] of a national ideology and this, tangled in the brutality, illusions, and hypocrisies of gigantic investment in a vast empire, military and commercial, had its own strength and moral dignity. But at the same time there divided from the main body of the intelligentsia that famous line of radical dissenters which runs from the early makers of the English Working Class[2] Hazlitt and Cobbett, through William Morris, Sidgwick and Ruskin in the 1880s to F. R. Leavis and George Orwell in England of the past thirty years. It is a long line of many ranks and it has taught its members—who may be found in many places of education—a certain style and vocabulary. It is symptomatic, however, of the deep English aversion to a recognizable style of thought and speech, especially when it may be formulable as a theory to work from, that the members of the line who try to push on, to keep open communication with the future, live a sectarian life in society and that society is largely innocent of any radical influence from the dissenters upon the great issues of contemporary life.

The isolation of the dissenting intellectual in his sect has tended to produce one of two results. In the first, he learns the style and the theodicy too well and living it becomes a matter of keeping to the liturgy in the company of the devout; in such recitation, the circle of communication is closed; society encapsulates the foreign body but does not digest it nor cast it up. The recognition of this insulation produces the second and much more attractive alternative, in which the dissenting intellectual in order to connect with his society lowers his sights from an ideal order and tolerates the consequent lack of focus upon the 'central and truly human' things[3] because unblameably the conversation with others on shared human matters is essential to him. He does not withhold criticism, but he mutes his radical dissent, for that is not how others feel. The consequent stance which reconciles the intolerable—say, *Pick of the Pops*, *Woman's Own*, motor-car talk, bungaloid growth, high fashion and cosmetics, babylore—for the sake of human dialogue is exceedingly difficult and probably impossible to hold. Yet the conversation must remain open, if the intellectuals are to find and nourish the points of new growth, to cherish and strengthen the images of a wholesome and thriving culture such as define our vision of utopia.

WORK AND THE INTELLECTUAL

It is important to add here that a haughty inversion of fashionable pop-talk is no satisfactory alternative. A high intellectual style which perhaps self-consciously counterposes itself against the pop world may be as often as not merely stylishness: the assured conversion of Renaissance paintings, and plainchant on Hi-fi, of Georgian terrace-houses and château-bottled claret, into the easily won signals of power, wealth and status. In the life I parody there is no sense that it can, in its own fullness, brace and poise itself against the denseness of social living and of history, against the weight and substance of another subject held over against its own. The intellectuality and its relation with culture is without roots. Its inner motion is driven by other sources of energy, classically located by R. H. Tawney in this passage:

The rejection of the idea of purpose involves another consequence which everyone laments, but which no one can prevent, except by abandoning the belief that the free exercise of rights is the main interest of society and the discharge of obligations a secondary and incidental consequence which may be left to take care of itself. It is that social life is turned into a scene of fierce antagonisms, and that a considerable part of the industry is carried on in the intervals of a disguised social war. The idea that industrial peace can be secured merely by the exercise of tact and forbearance is based on the idea that there is a fundamental identity of interest between the different groups engaged in it, which is occasionally interrupted by regrettable misunderstandings. Both the one idea and the other are an illusion. The disputes which matter are not caused by a misunderstanding of identity of interests, but by a better understanding of diversity of interests. Though a formal declaration of war is an episode, the conditions which issue in a declaration of war are permanent; and what makes them permanent is the conception of industry which also makes inequality and functionless incomes permanent. It is the denial that industry has any end or purpose other than the satisfaction of those engaged in it.

That motive produces industrial warfare, not as a regrettable incident, but as an inevitable result. It produces industrial war, because its teaching is that each individual or group has a right to what they can get, and denies that there is any principle, other than the mechanism of the market, which determines what they ought to get. For, since the income available for distribution is limited, and since, therefore, when certain limits have been passed, what one group gains another group must lose, it is evident that if the relative incomes of different groups are not to be determined by their functions, there is no method other than mutual self-assertion which is left to determine them. Self-interest, indeed, may cause them to refrain from using their full strength to enforce their claims, and, in so far as this happens, peace is secured in industry, as men have attempted to secure it in international affairs, by a balance of power. But the maintenance of such a peace is contingent upon the estimate of the parties to it that they have more to lose than to gain by an overt struggle, and is not the result of their acceptance of any standard of remuneration as an equitable settlement of their claims. Hence it is precarious, insincere and short. It is without finality, because there can be no finality in the mere addition of increments of income, any more than in the gratification of any other desire for material goods. When demands are conceded the old struggle recommences upon a new level, and will always recommence as long as men seek to end it merely by increasing remuneration, not by finding a principle upon which all remuneration, whether large or small, should be based.[4]

Tawney first wrote his indictment in 1921. It is a measure of the motionlessness of English society that his analysis still holds so true fifty years on. The analysis locates the inner drives of English society and the logic which realizes the drives in economic behaviour[5] and it implies a model which explains the failure of English society to effect structural change. For the social drives which turn relentlessly about an axis of individual rights are morally circular:

So the perversion of nationalism is imperialism, as the perversion of individualism is industrialism. And the perversion comes, not through any flaw or vice in human nature, but by the force of the idea, because the principle is defective and reveals its defects as it reveals its power. For it asserts that the rights of nations and individuals are absolute, which is false, instead of asserting that they are absolute in their own sphere, but that their sphere itself is contingent upon the part which they play in the community of nations and individuals, which is true. Thus it constrains them to a career of indefinite expansion, in which they devour continents and oceans, attempt to attain infinity by the addition to themselves of all that is finite.[6]

The symptom of this abiding truth is the obsession of governments with short-term credits—and Tawney has previously had cutting things to say about the degrading worship of productivity—which evidences makers of policy at a loss for social purpose and meaning. No one asks the old question of the social democrat, 'productivity for what?' because no answer is currently possible. The debased individualism which is presently the source of our rotary motion permits no point of insertion for such a question. But the circle of our present references is under very heavy pressure from outside. We have become aware that we are, nationally, participating in a crisis of identity[7] brought about by the pressure of these external and uncontrollable forces. There can be no doubt that the forces will fracture and break inward the present structure of things. After the infinite postponements by timorous vote-catching, change will come. Either we can predict and partly control its course, or we shall be bound to the vacancy and rigidity of the present system magnified to a global hemisphere. Of course it won't at all do to talk so blithely of 'we' as though it were easy to write to an audience of good men and true who took one's meaning and shared one's view of the world. It is an old heresy, as the quotation from Tawney makes clear, and to understand the completely other state of our social, and therefore moral and political disagreement is to understand a central part of our history and its crisis. For our morality[8] where it is generally shared can offer no answer to the central questions of our lives: who am I? What does my life mean? What are the lives of others worth to me? Do I recognize an impersonal destiny or is my life a matter of my private interests? We—and here the pronoun is a truthful and not a rhetorical one—share no answers to these questions and possess no common vocabulary nor style in which to discuss them. All we can share are what are chauvinistically thought of as the English virtues, which have their uses but are also uniquely successful in setting up a barricade for the protection of the hordes of the Philistines against social change and also, as I have argued, in closing the circle of thought and action to critical dissent. Such virtues are 'co-operativeness, fairness and fairplay, tolerance, a gift for compromise, a practical approach to problems', scepticism about abstract theories.[9] Whatever one's opinion of such qualities (and it is clear that they can easily encourage a state of mindless stupefaction), they cannot define the moral purpose and terminus of a civilization. Their special status none the less ensures that claims to moral or political absolutism cannot be made in England with any conviction, and this discovery returns us to our first difficulty, which is to know how to resist, with whatever expectation of local failure, the demon of Tawney's Industrialism, and its grotesque offspring, the giant of international capitalist imperialism. The enormous power of imperialism is the product (in terms of simple ideology) of the unharnessed free enterprise released across Europe by the individualist ethic. It isn't only demonologists who find that colossal power in its hidden omnipresence across so much of the world inhuman and destructive. Mr McLellan's quotation from Segal on p. 180 states the case with piercing brevity. Nor is it enough to rejoin, in the tones of individualism, that these peoples are 'underdeveloped' and we are (happily) members of the 'advanced' industrial nations, nor even that we shall help them along the road to advancement. As has been bitterly said 'Charity begins at $9\frac{1}{2}$ per cent'. It is no doubt true that a colossal number of emergent nations would crumple inwards if Western capital were withdrawn; but it is also true that the Western investment in these countries is misunderstood by itself as an act of munificence, while in reality bringing those countries under an economic subjugation as total in its different way as the oldstyle colonialism of *Heart of Darkness*. The controls are revealed with an unselfaware ingenuousness which would be laughable if it weren't revolting, in this quotation from the *New York Times*:

India's Drift from Socialism to Pragmatism. There are signs of change. The Government has granted easy terms to private foreign investors in the fertilizer industry, is thinking about decontrolling several more industries and is ready to liberalize import policy if it gets sufficient foreign aid . . . Much of what is happening now is a result of steady pressure from the United States and the International Bank for Reconstruction and Development, which for the last year have been urging a substantial freeing of the Indian economy and a greater scope for private enterprise. The United States pressure, in particular, has been highly effective here because the United States provides by far the largest part of the foreign exchange needed to finance India's development and keep the wheels of industry turning. Call them 'strings', call the 'conditions' or whatever one likes, India has little choice now but to agree to many of the terms that the United States, through the World Bank, is putting on its aid. For India simply has nowhere else to turn.[10]

Western capital has organized into client-status 59 per cent of the underdeveloped world, or 1·56 thousand million people.[11] Of these 500,000 children had been killed in Vietnam by January 1969[12] to justify that configuration of beliefs upheld by Wall Street, Zurich, Bonn and the City of London which issues in such liturgy as 'I believe in the sanctity of the individual against the state', or these amiable pieties:

I hold a number of beliefs that have been repudiated by many of the liveliest intellects of our time. I believe that order is better than anarchy, creation better than destruction; I prefer gentleness to violence and forgiveness to vendetta. On the whole I think that learning is preferable to ignorance and I am sure that human sympathy is better than ideology.[13]

Which intellects? one wonders. It's the trick of rhythm which purports to retrieve the declaration from truism – 'On the whole I think... and I am sure...' Nobody in his right mind could say that these mild and mournful platitudes *cause* the clash of powers, but it is in the name of their version of unimpeachable positives like order and creation and human sympathy that the U.S.A. launches its counter-insurgency enterprises such as the Bay of Pigs invasion or Project Camelot[14] or that, more parochially, the 'unofficial' strikers in England are publicly traduced for ransoming a country in which, as Mr Budd points out on p. 203 5 per cent of the population receives 92 per cent of the income from private property, and in which 7·5 million people live in poverty – 1·25 million of whom are children, a total which has doubled since 1954.[15] A belief in 'order rather than anarchy' turns out to mean a preference for things as they are rather than things as they might be. But it is only possible to prefer things as they are within a society whose permitted ambit of knowledge does not include the sort of statistics I quote nor an analysis of modern neo-imperialism which recognizes the hegemony exercised by Western capital. At the moment, world spending on armaments equals the whole income of two thousand million people in the 'underdeveloped countries'. It is predicted that by 1980 60 per cent of the world's business will be in the hands of 200 giant combines, most of them American.[16] In such a situation 'aid' to the developing countries becomes derisory in moral terms not only because it is pitiably disproportionate to human need but also because those countries can only gain critically limited access to the tariff-protected capitalist markets which are in their turn striving for unlimited growth. Not only this. The investments (to drop the canting term 'aid') tie those countries to sudden projects which have often no relation to social or ecological conditions and, like some of the Japanese plant in Kenya, are an insult to local need. It is the imperialist interests which control such industrialization and these operate increasingly to make huge numbers of people in the exploited countries redundant if the interest rates are to be kept up. All that prevents these economies becoming a process of leisurely but accelerating starvation is the refusal of the colonies to accept their sentence. There is then–in Peru, Bolivia, Ecuador, Brazil, Angola, the Congo, Laos, South-West Africa, Nicaragua, the Dominican Republic, Panama, and elsewhere–a variety of armed and efficient or unarmed and sporadic revolutionary movements. The twist to the spiral is violently turned by the great powers deploying their vast force against the insurgents. The Gross Global Product swells under the costs of the butchery and growth rates hold up. The supreme type of this process is Vietnam, and as the logic of things is at the moment, there can only be more Vietnams ahead. In the present terms, the only events that may break the insane spiral are either world revolution with Marxist China as the arsenal for the proletariat, or the completion of American and Russian drives for mutual world monopoly. The human alternative is to get clear of capitalism, and so to organize (as is perfectly possible) modern technology that economic life serves human need, and then with the new techniques offered by electronics, communication systems, atomic energy and minute but intensive heavy industry plant it will be at least imaginable to live in small, free, and self-subsistent communities.[17]

Arguments such as these are simply not thinkable without a good deal of commonplace work in our society at the moment. It is eloquent of that mindlessness in our sociology and social theory which Mr Davies criticizes in his essay that this is so. For it is not difficult to gain access to this information nor to understand these arguments. The trouble is, our own imperialist past and mortgaged present so bind us to a terror of insurgency that we share American anxiety and rapaciousness wherever subversion occurs. We do not see that a present state of affairs may ruin and destroy people much more surely than insurrection, nor that seeing this way rather than that is controlled by what we accept as part of our knowledge. Our notions of what a fact is and what facts we are prepared to learn, control our moral view of the world. It's at this point that I would fetch out into the open the questions implicit throughout my remarks so far: Who are the intellectuals and what are they for? Which of their members betray them? What ought to be the distinctive nature of their study and, subsequently, the recognizable hallmark of their thought? What, in the teeth of the power-élite and–Mr Williams's point–its control of the 'facts' we know–can they do? Where can they with honour stand?

Noam Chomsky has written: 'It is the responsibility of intellectuals to speak the truth and to expose lies.'[18] Well, one can certainly begin there, and it is much more than a footnote to say that Chomsky himself, the greatest and most original linguist in the world, sets a magnificent example as a highly specialized intellectual finding himself unable to endorse the conventional divisions between his studies and his citizenship and indeed driven to refute such divisions as a treasonous denial of the intellectual's function.

Intellectuals are in a position to expose the lies of governments, to analyse actions according to their causes and motives and often hidden intentions. In the Western World, at least, they have the power that comes from political liberty, from access to information and freedom of expression. For a privileged minority, Western democracy provides the leisure, the facilities, and the training to seek the truth lying hidden behind the veil of distortion and misrepresentation, ideology and class interest, through which the events of current history are presented to us.[19]

The questions raised by Chomsky's theories of transformation grammar penetrate deep into problems of philosophic meaning, of environmental influence, of the structure of the human mind and its growth, and they thus prompt speculation across a wide terrain. Maybe the range and density of associations in these ideas excite political connections in a way other studies do not. Yet one can think of contingent areas like cybernetics or the biochemistry of the brain which fail to call out from their practitioners the passion and courage Chomsky has shown in his stand on behalf of intellectual integrity.

It is such a signal presence which drastically emphasizes the absence of any but a handful of others making such an effort in this country or in the U.S.A.—though the Vietnamese War has concentrated American efforts.[20] There is a tendency increasing even in centres of outstanding contention and easy, unfettered argument across a long front of ideas (such as sixth forms) to accept and harden the long habituation to specialisms and to make any venture outside one's private territory timorous and provisional. Keats saw the tendency earliest:

> Each of the moderns like an Elector of Hanover governs his petty state, and knows how many straws are swept daily from the Causeways in all his dominions and has a continual itching that all the Housewives should have their coppers well scoured: the ancients were Emperors of vast Provinces. they had only heard of the remote ones and scarcely cared to visit them.[2]

I am not asking for loose, unverified and ritual generalization. Any proposals for the adequate training of an intellectual's conscience would be precisely aimed at making such remarks unmakable. But the only alternative is not timidity. The marshalling and control of evidence by which Chomsky in his series of essays indicts the conceit, self-righteousness and duplicity of so many American social scientists is the *kind* of enterprise, informed by the *kind* of intelligence and moral passion which ought to be the moral centre and spring to action of any intellectual at any time. He speaks out with the mature anger of a man who has not let his vision of heroism and generosity go out of focus and for whom the bitterness of this judgement is the obverse of a gladness which in the present can find no expression.

We are hardly the first power in history to combine material interests, great technological capacity and an utter disregard for the suffering and misery of the lower orders. The long tradition of naïveté and self-righteousness that disfigures our intellectual history, however, must serve as a warning to the Third World, if such a warning is needed, as to how our protestations of sincerity and benign intent are to be interpreted.[22]

Chomsky and the small but increasing number of scholars who have rallied to his standards refute by their example the now notorious theory that there is 'an end to ideology' amongst Western intellectuals.[23] The theory sets out a map of the modern state in which social security and welfare provisions have bridled free enterprise and made brutal exploitation impossible and which by a mixed and uncontentious adjustment of economies and interest groups makes for a stable class system and a sufficiency of social mobility. The implicit model is static, or as Mr Davies points out in his essay, gently Fabian: society finds equilibrium in the maintenance and reconciliation of predictable tensions in a fixed number of dimensions. Social engineering is a matter of tensions control in the interests of 'fair-play' 'compromise' and the platitudes of secondary virtues with no historical reference. A reasonably mobile, safe, unresentful society with a national average wage of £23–12–6[24] can't be too bad a place to live these days; this is the sort of thing most people carry around as a theory of their society, and something like it is implicit in many more sophisticated analyses, even the apocalyptic ones. I am not going to slight the gains in domestic comfort: to do so is to insult not only the work of great reformers, from Francis Place to Aneurin Bevan, but also the misery lived through by the millions they worked for.

None the less, the welfare state as the Western World knows

it, is hollow at the centre. What drives it is that acquisitive individualism whose motion is circular because competitive and which centrifugally throws people outwards from any lived centre of reference. Capitalism resists at any price social controls over internal production decisions because the only usable criterion is profitability, which then becomes the source of productive energy and strips the essential decisions of any social reference. To say it again: productivity for what? What do we do with profit? How shall we apportion reward? According to need, or as now, according to investment or contribution?

The intellectual fails to answer these questions as he should, because his own work is so deeply coloured by the mechanics of capitalism and conceptions of welfare. One finds within every humane discipline in higher education an unusually close-knit set of relationships and a unified language. But the cohesion which should be possible and decisive to the inner life of such groups is crucially wanting. The groups lack any idea of collaboration with other such groups, and even more fatally, lack any image of what such a community is like. They have not counted what they share because they find themselves at home in the prestige, the lucrative busywork, the parochialism, and the intriguing for promotion. Consequently they only act in concert when they feel their parochial interests threatened: they vote together—for a rise in salary. There are subtractions to make from this critique: the point missed by many student dissenters is that their teachers are much more sympathetic to the claim of idealism than anybody else. Man for man, they are likely to be more liberal-minded, more international, more pacific, more tolerant and politically conscious than most other prestigious officials. To pull away the carpet from under their feet is rather like, as Bernard Williams has put it, 'being unkind to your father not because he's as nasty as the others but because he's the one who's at home and gets upset'.[25] The nub of the argument lies in my description—'more liberal, more tolerant' and so on. What is missing is not so much 'commitment' (a word open to many abuses) as an idea of function—and such an idea can only be a product of an image of community. The collective action of teachers, primary, secondary or tertiary, is prompted generally by cash. The only social measure of a person is by monthly cheque. The professional bodies work in complementary ways to close the circle of action (and thought is action) against radical contraversion. Run your eye down the agendas for national conferences in academic studies; the subjects are turned inwards upon the ahistorical problems of technique and method. A great number of books for schools or further education published in the Humanities are the necessities on the one hand of economic growth in publishing and on the other of careers whose internal vacancy is defined by book making. The knowledge industry begins to work within capitalism like any other industry. And the currency of the industry has only a very restricted use-value (few 'A' level students relate their pass in History or English to their understanding of society and themselves) but sizeable exchange-value; e.g. a degree will purchase a given salary.

The origins of this dismal commercialism lie, as I have said, in the acquisitive ethic. One cannot get round Weber's picture of our history.[26] And the individualism which subtends the ethic ratifies a special kind of social thinking, a certain sociology of knowledge. For the individualist ethic has long been linked in fundamental ways[27] with the empirical scientists. Consequently, observable phenomena ('facts') take on atomic life independent of the circumstances which produced them. A fact is one thing and an interpretation is another, and a value judgement is a third which you bring up to the fact and attach to it like a ticket. Since only facts (so conceived) are independent of people, then, the attitude goes, we must devise a way of observing the facts which insulates them from the dangerous and heady air of values. Hence the hard-mouthed cant of the social sciences as 'value-free' and the concomitant delusion that scientism in the study of humanity will solve the problems of technocratic engineering and get all these embarrassing slogans about social injustice and democracy out of the way. What the social scientists and educationists fail to see is that the isolation of *any* phenomenon from the movement of life involves a selective judgement of some sort, often a very rigorous one, and to pretend that this is not so is simply to delude oneself. In humane studies, the delusion is positively dangerous, because the 'value-free' investigator raises no questions about the value of what he studies nor about the system of values which, in order not to take in problems of value, he has to take for granted. Consequently, he can only endorse that system. Yet that system is inextricably part of what he studies. To ignore it is therefore to be guilty of moral and intellectual evasiveness or triviality. It is the minimal charge to bring against a great heap of work in the social sciences and in the humanities. If, however, the students and teachers of the humanities lay no claims to being 'value-free' their only alternative is to insist on a jealous individualism – 'the response, right or wrong' at the cost of misunderstanding the common pursuit of true judgement. This defensiveness issues inevitably in an extraordinary timorousness outside the particular discipline. We either offer a diffident generalization, and then withdraw shyly, or we launch into after-dinner assertion. What authentic social insight is possible?

It may be said that where moral philosophy is displaced from where it belongs, the moral spirit will shift its centre to whichever human ground is argued over with the fullest, most passionate intelligence of the time. At a crucial stage in the intellectual history of England during this century that ground became literature and the intelligence literary–critical. Literary criticism found a language in which to raise matters of life and death, and to raise them with dignity and conviction. There are signs that things are changing. The long pathology of English history[28] which concealed itself in a neurotic reverence for empiricism and specialization anywhere between grave-counting to numismatics seems to be coming to an end. The best English historians have outgrown the constitutionalists and started to construct a theory of historical movement which will account for rather more than the acts of Parliament, jacked-up biographies, and nursery diplomacy which is still the worms-'A'-level view of history. The men who have built this frame have worked in collaboration and not privately. Piece by piece they have constructed a frame of reference whose shape can be seen emerging in the pages of *Past and Present*.[29] As a result, although the halls of the Historical Association are still thronged by the Whigs, it is now possible to speak respectfully of a group of English historians whose work faces and responds to fundamental questions of social ebb and surge. Things are hardly so hopeful in adjacent areas: the absence of political theory and sociology from most 'A'-level courses is evidence of the English conspiracy of silence about radical or comprehensive theories which emasculates those studies in Universities and colleges of education. The same sciolism in school work develops into the blankness of the psychology or philosophy courses at the further levels. The study of psychology offers a supreme example of self-approving inertia. A mass of evidence bulks in one place but has no movement and no meaning. The animal-watchers of English psychology, in a masquerade of bluff empiricism, have rejected any interpretative system by which to order and discharge their facts. The English habit is still, at this time of day, to feel that there's something fishy about all this subconscious stuff, and that the whole explanatory structure of Freudian psychology is an arbitrary (because unprovable) hallucination. Meanwhile conventional wisdom believes unquestioningly in a theory of economic motive driven by the crude impulses of incentives and competition because the theory fits the vulgar demands of shopkeeping common sense.

Yet the changes in historical studies are a start and a symptom, and the work cleared by the pioneers of English studies has left the next colonizers with a language—a grammar and a vocabulary—which can engage with large indigestible matter and recalcitrant detail in such a way as to organize and relate both. Even though the instantly corrective tendency of English intellectual life to restore the equilibrium by insulating any integrative movement as a new specialism came into busy play, English studies remain the impulse towards the building of a common centre of reference. But it is enormously to the point that a similar impulse towards convergence and collaboration marks such diverse studies as social anthropology and linguistics. It is here, again, that Noam Chomsky's astonishing originality has connected the structures of the brain, of computer output, of human language and the relation of all these algebras to the sense we make of our speech and our society and our lives. One can make too much of this. Chomsky himself has rejected scornfully[30] any science fiction idea of a universal computer language. There can be no question of a comfortable euphoria drawing all studies together for the best of all possible reasons. So the questions are still: what is the function of an intellectual? What marks his thought? Where does he belong? And in answer to such questions, who would not respond to such a rallying statement as this one:

We have not to debate whether it is to produce specialists or the 'educated man' that the university should exist. Its essential function involves the production of both–though to say 'the educated man' is perhaps misleading. The problem is to produce specialists who are in touch with a humane centre and to produce a centre for them to be in touch with; but this centre is not best conceived as a standard 'educated man'. There will be 'educated men' with various stresses, various tendencies towards specialization . . . How to produce the 'educated man'–the man of humane culture who is equipped to be intelligent and responsible about the problems of contemporary civilization–this is a truly urgent study, but a study that apart from an adequate preoccupation with the Idea of a university is likely to end in despair. If the universities make it possible to hope for something of education, that is because their function, fully performed, comprises so much more than any talk of education–or of research and scholarship–can suggest. The full performance of their inclusive functions involves the performances of many functions.[31]

Any such concern with the idea of a University is now, it is clear, going to comprehend many institutions outside the university and discard several within it. The centre looked for is more than just a meeting place–though it needs to be at least *that*–it is 'a focus of humane consciousness'; that is, and quite consciously, it signifies a place, a group of people and a programme of work which intend to discover, concentrate and cherish those forces in a society which press towards its finest achievements. Such a pressure, properly harnessed, of force directs itself towards the destruction of anything which impedes its way. The work can only push outwards from a centre of reference which controls (in Leavis's later phrase) a 'disciplined and mature preoccupation with value', a preoccupation which in turn makes possible the sanctions and pieties of a living community. For we must start somewhere in the making of a civilization, and it is only by the right and laconic use of such a phrase that we are likely to get anything done at all. 'A sense of community', and 'a making of images': these are the cloudy and elusive concepts we are trying to come at. That community must, if it is to mean anything, have found its distinctive strength, its 'central, its truly human point of view'.

If such work is to mean anything, then 'community' must lose its connotations of doleful social welfare on the one hand and monasticism on the other. Any adequate notion of an intellectual centre involves a going reciprocal relationship with the world, and this will alter according to the 'various stresses, various tendencies towards specialization' which are proper and necessary. The emphases of a literary critic will not be like those of a student of music, nor those of either like those of a social anthropologist. But in each case, the shared centrality which we look for will make a common information and correlation possible. The necessary thinking cannot be at all exonerated from lonely and aloof enterprise—I am not recommending any easy collectivity—and such enterprise will generate contradictions of an immovable kind. Even so, it ought to be possible to work with a sound sense of all that is omitted and with a sense, too, of the overwhelming difficulties which, if the work is to be done at all, we sort and direct into some sort of controllable though richly diverse interplay of currents. Each of the possible specialisms—and I would intend here that such a description apply as directly to the best kind of work in each—should be able to know what manifestations of the qualities adduced here would show up in the specialized work:

> In such a piece of work it would be preeminently the unacademic virtues that would be demanded and tested: a pioneering spirit; the courage of enormous incompleteness; the determination to complete the best possible chart with the inevitably patchy and sketchy knowledge that is all one's opportunities permit one to acquire; the judgement and intuition to select drastically yet delicately and make a little go a long way; the ability to skip and to scamp with wisdom and conscience.[32]

These qualities, that is, are called to the service of that 'mature and disciplined preoccupation with value' which can only live in a sustained and tense relationship with concrete actuality. This is the 'practicality' of that practical literary criticism which has sponsored some of the decisive moves, in England at any rate, towards a full and mature weighing of life in the present, and the present as the intersection of past and future. The paradox of this 'practicality' which is at first glance the much-hugged slogan of the philistine Englishman, is that it commits the practical man to a strenuous and difficult search for values which can only live in actuality but which transcend the actual and give off a vivid and beneficent light, as a result of which we can say, 'There! That's the constellation one can steer by; theirs is the direction we can point to.' The practical man becomes theoretician. Arnold starts off the definition needed:

> . . . perverse as it seems to say so I sometimes find myself wishing when dealing with these matters of poetical criticism, that my ignorance were even greater than it is. To handle these matters properly there is needed a poise so perfect that the least overweight in any direction tends to destroy the balance. Temper destroys it, a crotchet destroys it, even erudition may destroy it. To press to the sense of the thing itself with which one is dealing, not to go off on some collateral issue about the thing, is the hardest matter in the world. The 'thing itself' with which one is here dealing—the critical perception of poetical truth—is of all things the most volatile, elusive, and evanescent; by even pressing too impetuously after it, one runs the risk of losing it. The critic of poetry should have the finest tact, the nicest moderation, the most free, flexible and elastic spirit imaginable . . .[33]

The well-disposed and patient reader may get very impatient here, as who should say, 'yes, yes, it's all very difficult, but how do I do this special thinking? An answer of *some* kind must be possible.' The point of the Arnold quotation is that doing the thinking isn't necessarily linked to huge amounts of annotation, reading, data-collecting (as the cant goes) and so forth. For

> I suspect that what literary critics call a 'social insight'—the sense that such and such a gesture is 'significant'—is the result of the writer *holding in his imagination* an enormous amount of material, of 'facts' about society. I believe that he holds this material *in a kind of suspension*, and that it is at the moment of his finding a unifying image— a single gesture or a large theme—that we say he has had a 'significant' insight . . . sustained imaginative perception of any depth into a society only looks like a sudden gift; it takes off from saturation in experience.[34]

The nature of the thinking then is not the result of something dogged and cumulative. Absolutely, it is not the conventional academicism which in its patient laboriousness can only serve to endorse specialism; indeed that work is its own tautology, for minute description without a grasp on the larger values can only spawn more such descriptions. Nor can the perception of social reality ever be merely descriptive; for we are incorrigibly linked to the perception of value in all our thinking. It becomes degenerate not when it abandons valuation, for that is impossible, but when it releases itself from the challenging and solid bracing of itself against the presence of values. In loosing that tension, the moral sense slackens its hold on concrete life and the moral vision implicit in the language of that life. You cannot evacuate language of its moral history and to suppose you can serves only to endorse a debile because inert morality. And electric contact with problems of valuation generates (the metaphor holds up) a source of energy. The right ascription of value commits the valuer to an active relation with his society. His living becomes a source of its change. Leavis gives us the valuing experience with all the density, exhilaration, and sturdy seriousness which it calls out, in this famous passage:

> No doubt (as I have admitted) a philosophic training might possibly–ideally would–make a critic surer and more penetrating in the perception of significance and relation and in the judgement of value. But it is to be noted that the improvement we ask for is of the critic, the critic as critic, and to count on it would be to count on the attainment of an arduous ideal. It would be reasonable to fear–to fear blunting of edge, blurring of focus and muddled misdirection of attention; consequences of queering one discipline with the habits of another. The business of the literary critic is to attain a peculiar completeness of response and to observe a peculiarly strict relevance in developing his response into commentary; he must be on his guard against abstracting improperly from what is in front of him and against any premature or irrelevant generalizing–of it or from it. His first concern is to enter into possession of the given poem (let us say) in its concrete fulness, and his constant concern is never to lose his completeness of possession, but rather to increase it. In making value-judgements (and judgements as to significance), implicitly or explicitly, he does so out of that completeness of possession and with that fulness of response. He doesn't ask, 'How does this accord with these specifications of goodness in poetry?'; he aims to make

fully conscious and articulate the immediate sense of value that 'places' the poem.

Of course, the process of 'making fully conscious and articulate' is a process of relating and organizing, and the 'immediate sense of value' should, as the critic matures with experience, represent a growing stability of organization (the problem is to combine stability with growth). What, on testing and re-testing and wider experience, turn out to be my more constant preferences, what the relative permanencies in my response, and what structure begins to assert itself in the field of poetry with which I am familiar? What map or chart of English poetry as a whole represents my utmost consistency and most inclusive coherence of response.[35]

Such writing has the brimming plenitude of a great poem; it becomes its own meaning, and something of the kind must always be true in the creation of the concepts which we live by. For unless at this late hour you manage to be some kind of Platonist, it is timely to remember Heisenberg's words—made, indeed, about that notoriously theoretical and provisional science, nuclear physics—

Natural Science does not simply describe and explain nature; it is part of the interplay between nature and ourselves; it describes nature as exposed to our method of questioning.[36]

The world we know is in part the product of how we know it. Max Weber describes the method of social science by a kind of dialectic in which concept collides with concept and issues in a new and mobile picture of reality.

For none of those systems of ideas, which are absolutely indispensable in the understanding of those segments of reality which are meaningful at a particular moment, can exhaust its infinite richness. They are all attempts, on the basis of the present state of our knowledge and the available conceptual patterns, to bring order into the chaos of those facts which we have drawn into the field circumscribed by our *interest*. The intellectual apparatus which the past has developed through the analysis, or more truthfully, the analytical rearrangement of the immediately given reality, and through the latter's integration by concepts which correspond to the state of its knowledge and the focus of its interest, is in constant tension with the new knowledge which we can and *desire* to wrest from reality. The progress of cultural science occurs through this conflict. Its result is the perpetual reconstruction of those concepts through which we seek to comprehend reality. The history of the social sciences is and remains a continuous process passing from the attempt to order reality analytically through the construction of concepts–the dissolution of the analytical constructs so constructed through the expansion and shift of the scientific horizon–and the reformulation anew of concepts on the foundations thus transformed.[37]

To understand this is, in Alasdair MacIntyre's words, to see that 'History is neither a prison nor a museum, nor is it a set of materials for self-congratulation'[38] and the reminder implies a colossal range of mistakes made in the name of various blindnesses in our intellectual work, made, moreover, in the name of intellectual work in the primary school right through to the university. For our studies are never self-validating. To think strenuously about art or social science or philosophy or cybernetics or TV or anything else, is to think about life, and so to think is to search out a rare personal adequacy, to cultivate an incorruptible responsibility to individual experience as the product of a given history and a totality of human relations which may indeed misshape itself as something ugly but which, for the sake of the race, the individual is to create as full and good a thing as possible. Something of the kind is the function of creative art and this I take Dr Betsky to mean when he writes of American novelists in his essay as contributing to 'a sense of (their own) community'. Mr Capey finds any such personal adequacy dismally lacking in his review of English novelists. If the novelists fail us, in the provision of images to live by, what are the alternative sources, and where are they to be found? In beginning an answer, I might complete the intellectual ambit by setting beside the last quotations from Leavis this further one from Max Weber:

. . . when the possibility of attaining a proposed end appears to exist, we can determine (naturally within the limits of our existing knowledge) the consequences which the application of the means to be used will produce in addition to the eventual attainment of the proposed end, as a result of the interdependence of all events. We can then provide the acting person with the ability to weigh and compare the undesirable as over against the desirable consequences of his action. Thus, we can answer the question: what will the attainment of a desired end 'cost' in terms of the predictable loss of other values? Since, in the vast majority of cases, every goal that is striven for does 'cost' or can 'cost' something in this sense, the weighing of the goal in terms of the incidental consequences of the action which realizes it cannot be omitted from the deliberation of persons who act with a sense of responsibility. One of the most important functions of the *technical criticism* which we have been discussing thus far is to make this sort of analysis possible. To apply the results of this analysis in the making of a decision, however, is not a task which science can undertake; it is rather the task of the acting, willing person; he weighs and chooses from among the values according to his own conscience and his personal view of the world. Science can make him realize that all action and naturally, according to the circumstances, inaction imply in their consequences the espousal of certain values–and herewith–what is today so willingly overlooked–the rejection of certain others. The act of choice itself is his own responsibility.[39]

The various answers to our question, what concepts and images of life do we need? come from all over the place. Saying so, it should now be possible to define the characteristic products of the intellectual, trained in the delicacy, the large and ready play of the mind over its material, the vivid consciousness of moral perception, the pressures of invisible history, which I have glanced over. Further, we should be able to see an honourable role for the intellectual as well as to map one version out of many of the terrain he might break open for himself. Finally, and in the teeth of things as they are, I shall offer a provisional strategy for the establishment of an adequate centre and the work which many men are now attempting.

'Definition'; 'strategy'–the temptation to declare slogans for political action is overwhelming, and indeed I cannot see that it is naïve to say, straight out, that a sufficient intellectualism must carry with it subscription to socialism. It is not just because D. H. Lawrence refutes the statement that he should have his say here, but

As far as anything *matters*, I have always been very much alone, and regretted it. But I can't belong to clubs, or societies, or Freemasons, or any other damn thing. So if there is with you, an activity I *can* belong to, I shall thank my stars. But of course I shall be wary beyond words, of committing myself.[40]

Commitment may be very cheaply purchased, and to be wary can look so repelling. And the multiplicity of choice bewilders one so; what shall we belong to, and why? Lawrence, again:

Men are free when they belong to a living, organic, believing community, active in fulfilling some unfulfilled, perhaps unrealized purpose.[41]

Well, for the time being, the purposes are likely to remain unfulfilled but they are also sure to be realized and conscious. At a very basic level, there is no escape from certain specific responsibilities and some pieces of information. Famine, slaughter, the pillage of Africa and Asia by the big combines, the arms and interstellar races: within a brief time-scale there can be no doubt whose side we are on in any struggle about these horrors. The common intellectual action can begin there. Beyond that point the action may break down into a series of guerrilla skirmishes against much of mass culture, pop music, advertising, spec. building, without any generalled policy. But as a course for action, these sporadic gunfights won't do. We need a sense of human and extra-human responsibility and direction of the kind great creative artists capture and concentrate. So any adequate training involves a full and strong response to contemporary artistic responsibility—we have, for example, Benjamin Britten, Henry Moore, F. R. Leavis, *The Buildings of England* to turn to. We have not yet assimilated the utterly radical challenges to our unexamined individualism held out in recent history by (let us say) D. H. Lawrence, Le Corbusier, Leon Trotsky, Ludwig Wittgenstein or Melanie Klein. An adequate education (for this is what we are discussing) will shape a feeling for experience which can take account of these challenges and can come at a living language to realize the inner and outer forces we have all to reconcile. We can't know everything; we **must retain 'the courage of enormous incompleteness' and in** that drastic and delicate partiality, be able to see and value the life around us.

Who are the most vivid members of any given people? . . . a Negro just released from a Utah prison trying for the life of him to find out, with all the dangerous sense of nuance a delicately experienced man has, how to get from this corner to the restaurant in the next block without becoming too precise in the eyes and noses of the indigenous loafer—whether he be businessman or town bully or cop, and the prisoner never has to sort the differences.[42]

To see life and value like this is to begin to know what full life in the present—and life as the continuity of a living culture—might mean. At first sight, the answers to the writer's question might look merely surprising, or they might look simply as if he's on the renegade side against the bully, as who is not? But the writer is a poet—Edward Dorn; I discuss his work elsewhere in this volume. Earlier in the book quoted here, Dorn visits an American Indian, one hundred and two years of age, living in a shanty on a reservation. His account of that visit suggests a model for the human responsiveness to relation and value that I am talking about. Dorn knows who he is and who his people are and he knows too and much more rarely what conscientiously anxious clichés in feelings do *not* come into the reckoning. The result is writing of exceptional tact and purity. Dorn faces unfalteringly the claims of history and finds in himself a courage adequate to the immense task of so re-ordering them that the experience is a source of new and flaring life. He is not mere object to the claims of the past; he tenses himself against them and deflects them towards new, unirrigated resources. What he says is difficult; some of it is obscure, as new things will be. But he says it beautifully, with an ease, an unforced grace which must be the property of intellectuals if they are to push on from the war against rapacity to building a civilization which may be, quite without complacent irony, a brave new world.

Mr Dorsey sat on the edge of the bed with his feet on the floor, a piece of cotton over his thighs. He looked up at me with clear eyes, the eyes of the ancient, bright, but the shine from behind a milky covering, a tough overlay almost a protection formed by the years.

Brightened only by a sudden cognition which in turn seemed a completely self-determined generosity. Very old animals have such coats over the eyes, a privacy impenetrable from the outside. He made a shaking motion with his finger, trembling in space, toward a chair. The room itself was overpowering. I was struck right off and singularly by his beauty, the sense of the power of his presence I later remembered I felt immediately, but I also saw myself as a curious paleface. My attention was suddenly arrested – this man was a great deal more than old. I was looking at the scene, and at myself, in a mirror, seeing the looking. The chair was covered with spilled water and bits of debris from his eating. I sat down on it, and without, I told myself, thinking to prove anything. It was difficult to do it. I felt crossed by an embarrassed confusion: what and who I was compressed all at once into one consideration, again I watched myself as I might think of a god watching, and there was in me at the same moment the hopelessly practical hesitation to soil my seat and the public willingness to do so – followed by a self-censure for having thought of it in either sense. The point in any case for me was moral. I must sit in this man's refuse.[43]

Dorn commits himself with a brief qualm to an endeavour to reach the religious meaning of the meeting – and the difficulty, as always, is to *meet* whoever it is who is there before us.

The place was intensely neglected, I gradually saw, and not just filthy as it looked to be at first glance. It was simply the remains of a life, and one must not forget a century is a difficult space of time for a man gone to the utter end. There was a safe, or cupboard, in the corner. It had some things in it, back of the glass. The light too dim to tell what. There were two beds. His wife, nearly as old and even frailer than he, went every now and then to his ear and spoke in the whispered endings and stopped throat tones of the Shoshonean speaker. He made low, nodding, assentive replies. She should have died, by the rules of our biology, thirty years ago. But it was evident that she would stay on, the weaker of the two, until he smelled the summary message in his nostrils, then she would be free. Once in a while she went to the edge of her bed and curled up on her side to rest. A discontinuous sound came from her throat. A chant she barely said. Her final spark was deeply internal, wrapped in the unending wrinkles; silent, nearly departed, she lived to administer his last service. And trying the sense of their relationship with my own subjectivity, at that moment it seemed to me here was the contrary of my own Western notion that one goes through the portal of death alone to greet some large blank which hopefully might be an extension of a 'personality', whether that be God or oneself as a continued state. Thus wrapped in the service of their ritual antiquity, they formed an effective edge of the real, an area of existence both life and death, neither morbid nor quite quick. A substantial prayer of flesh, plasma, spirit, all one fluid. And so, if this all sounds religion, I hope it does in no orthodox sense, more *religare*–to tie back: the nearly absolute briefness of ceremony, its power an intense spark, renewable as each time it reconstitutes the entirety of creation, the *Every Thing*. I did not for one instant look upon that qualified vitality as mystic. This man and woman were the most profoundly beautiful ancestors I've witnessed go before me. He is the spirit that lies at the bottom, where we have our feet. The feet which step between the domains, the visible sign, the real evidence of the coming event, and which one can see on the Humboldt fragments from Mexico, or on a linguistic map where this man's low, incantatory verbs spill down across the plateau and basin, between the mountains into the final plexus of the great Uto-Aztecan image of the world he sings in his daughter tongue. My point is that one can hardly think to be merely in Idaho, or Nevada, and that his beauty is that simple one would not treat it as anything special, not more Indian than man, still as much the flower as the fruit.'[44]

The struggle is between the momentous experience and the uncomfortable feeling that he, Dorn, was thinking about it. 'Should we be there. There was in me an oppressive thrill over the idea of my own presence. I thought of it as a ruptured cord in the consciousness, a strong confusion of the signals of my culture ... I must say I thought of my government's relationship to this man, I felt I would "realize" him somewhere in the cache of all *my own* sentience' (Dorn's italics). Finally, after strained failures of communication, they share a packet of cigarettes which makes for a relieved departure.

I had a great desire to be off, to not take any more, or give any more, to let the spiritual fact be the function of its instant and not an exposure, not a continuum. A Heathenism, of course, entirely of my own origin. For I will say it, at the risk of blunder: it is impossible for myself and my people to offer themselves in any but the standard senses. The minute there are human implications we back off. It was painful to go back, and at the screen door redo the unlatching, see again the room, take his hand again, reconsider the social and economic configurations that rise inevitably like specters in the eye of an enlightened Western mentality; not to do all that was then a problem, the cross-telling in the busy circuits of the mind in the oppressive heat for which we are the fuel. None of that. Not why did those pasty doctors at the agency hospital not come and bathe the man at least, of course not to clean him because that was certainly none of their business, his cleanliness was established far beyond what their pop-ritual of medical deodorization could manage, but to cool him? That *seemed* reasonable. But was it? It was I who objected to the heat and stillness of the air. Not him. It was his place, his home, that *was* where he was, his own chamber, own rectification.[45]

This vivid prose should make it clear that the conscience and identity which would be the natural product of a thriving culture and which we must construct out of the bits and pieces of our education is no easily political thing. Such a politics is the result, certainly, of specialism and also of reciprocal contact with a 'centre of reference'. But through and beyond these connections, conscience and identity grow, alter, and replenish themselves in tension with sorting the claims of actuality. For we are each of us the intersection of many 'specialisms' and peculiarities. To know one set of contingencies without laying claim to absolutism is to chance, in Dorn's words, saying 'I will say it, at the risk of blunder'. We must say what we can. One such way of saying is suggested by this book. To begin with a language is to begin with a literature. The study of literature moves imperceptibly into politics, economics, anthropology and sociology, to measuring the weight of a place. It might lead to many other disciplines; the configurations are various and in process. One might start and end with anthropology. Perhaps the most dense, rich interpenetration of techniques and values pushes at the back of a good architect. At any rate, he can serve as a touchstone. For he needs to reconcile the disparate claims of cash, class, geography, morality and human truth. However short-lived his buildings, he is putting together a monument to what his age believes to be possible in terms of human and natural ecology. Conscious or not, *any* building is a moral statement, a plenteous or impoverished image of its civilization and a lesson in its rhetoric. The function of an intellectual education should be to make this moving remark of Lewis Mumford's not only a truism for oneself, but teachable to a community:

> If planners were conscious of the phases of life, they would not be so blank about the need of late adolescence for places of secluded beauty, accentuating and expanding, and yet tempering their erotic needs; and enriching with happy visual images, their erotic rewards.[46]

There can be no future in rallying cries to a single standard. We shall not make one centre of the necessary kind which could serve many different groups. Nor is this the place to set out a programme of the work it might accomplish. I do not even wish to write out a curriculum. But there is an educational moment to be captured. Britain is still a country in which, in spite of the gross inequalities of wealth and property, discussion of national values is publicly supportable. As I have said, the changes at work now may bind our society much more brutally to the dominion of capital and power-élites. The mass purchase of American intellectuals by the government which Chomsky indemnifies suggests that the sell-out in the U.S.A. is near total. What we have the chance of doing in Britain now is designing an educational system of knowledge which, while opening avenues of necessary specialisms, carries within itself an honourable vision of collective and individual action and of intellectual integrity. It must not be tied, as now, to the exchange-value of certificates and the commodity-value of knowledge. (The only alternative bond we admit is to the ethic of individual fulfilment – nineteenth-century liberalism – which correlates so finally with income.) There must be an educational system which bodies forth a full and thriving culture and this must be in living contact with its society. Until the essential economic adjustments – one hundred per cent death duty, universally nationalized labour, restriction of maximum private income, nationalizing the City of London, disappearance of private landlords and so forth–the contact can only start. But until the training of teachers and the composition of curricula have found more dignified meanings our education will be, as largely now, a metaphor of social hierarchy (streaming) and the wage spiral (class orders and exams).

It is not juvenile to expect something better. Teachers are transmitters and generators of culture. Some of them can fight clear of mundanity and pull back from the tight hierarchical structure of educational status. Even in the chloroforming philistinism of our schools and colleges of technology, men and women of goodwill and common purpose keep up the English language. Then the idea of a university is that it shall make the essential discoveries, and more vitally, maintain in creative renewal the continuity and consciousness of a society. The Colleges of Education mediate between the two institutions, school and university. The complex, mighty life of a national education is the source of a nation's moral and intellectual energy and this will in a secularized world be true long after the disappearance of conventional nationhood. Only an effort in our educational life will give meaning to the faceless, directionless gods of productivity. Such an effort is barely in motion today and yet we have, without posturing or bogus urgency, a historical moment to capture which will not always be in our grasp. The men and women who work in education live out the tension between theory and practice (that arid and favourite English dichotomy), between culture and society, between vision and action. Such intersection is rare in a highly specialized society. It provides the point of new departure. The men and women who live it through are in their manifold ways the sources of social energy. The accidents of a social moment throw them into close contact; most teachers have access to leisure, collaboration, ample information, security. Doors open to them in mass communications. Only the sociology of their ignorance prevents the seizure and retention of a radical social power. Teachers of all kinds, tertiary, secondary and primary, betray their responsibility by living a half-life in the present. Their class keeps the moral memory of the race and is the organizer of social knowledge. Yet they–we–live apart and in stupor. It may be painful to live in hopes of too much, but it is merely contemptible to live in hopes of too little.

NOTES

[1] Noel Annan: 'The Intellectual Aristocracy' in *Studies in Social History: A Tribute to G. M. Trevelyan*, J. H. Plumb, ed. (London, 1955).

[2] The line is classically drawn by Raymond Williams in *Culture and Society 1780–1950* (Chatto and Windus, 1958, also Penguin), and E. P. Thompson, *The Making of the English Working Class* (Gollancz, 1963, also Penguin).

[3] Arnold's phrase in *Culture and Anarchy* (1896).

[4] *The Acquisitive Society* (Bell 1921, Collins 1961), pp. 40–1.

[5] The logical relations between belief and action are set out by Alasdair MacIntyre, 'A Mistake about causality in Social Science' in *Philosophy, Politics and Society*, 2nd series, Laslett P. and Runciman W. G., eds. (Blackwell, 1962).

[6] Tawney, op. cit., p. 47.

[7] Valuably anatomized by Perry Anderson in 'The Origins of the Present Crisis', *New Left Review* 23.

[8] The succeeding account I largely summarize from Alasdair MacIntyre, *Secularization and Moral Change* (Oxford, 1967).

[9] MacIntyre, op. cit., p. 24.

[10] *New York Times*, 28 April 1966, quoted by Noam Chomsky, 'The Responsibility of Intellectuals', in *The Dissenting Acadamy*, T. Roszak, ed. (Pantheon, New York, 1967) (Chatto & Windus, 1969).

[11] See Peter Worsley, *The Third World*, (Weidenfeld and Nicolson, rev. edition 1968).

[12] *Children in Vietnam*, occasional publication (London, March 1969).

[13] Kenneth Clark, *Listener*, 27 February 1969.

[14] For a full account see I. L. Horowitz, 'The Life and Death of Project Camelot', *Trans-Action*, 3, 5, November–December 1965.

[15] For these and more detailed figures see Ministry of Social Security, *The Circumstances of Families*, (H.M.S.O., 1967) and B. Abel-Smith's and P. Townsend's *The Poor and the Poorest, Occasional Papers on Social Administration 17* (Bell, 1965).

[16] P. Baran and P. Sweezy: *Monopoly Capital: An Essay on the American Economic and Social Order* (Penguin, 1968).

[17] I accept the possibilities outlined by Lewis Herber, *Contemporary Issues*, 39, 1960.

[18] Chomsky, in *The Dissenting Academy*, previously cited, p. 256.

[19] Chomsky, op. cit., p. 255.

[20] The astonishing coalition of heterodox factions which finally came together in the famous march on the Pentagon in October 1967 is richly

retold by Norman Mailer in his properly best-selling *The Armies of the Night* (Weidenfeld and Nicolson 1968).

[21] To J. H. Reynolds, 3 February 1818.
[22] Chomsky, op. cit., p. 262.
[23] See Daniel Bell, *The End of Ideology* (Collier-Macmillan, 1961).
[24] *Employment and Productivity Gazette*, July 1970.
[25] Annual Oration at Birkbeck College (London, 1968).
[26] In *The Protestant Ethic and the Spirit of Capitalism*, 1st English translation, London 1930.
[27] First, though controversially, demonstrated by Christopher Hill, *The Intellectual Origins of the English Revolution* (Oxford, 1965).
[28] The title of an interesting though very partial essay by G. Stedman-Jones in *New Left Review*, 46.
[29] *Past and Present: a journal of historical studies*, Corpus Christi College, Oxford, quarterly.
[30] Noam Chomsky, 'The Menace of Liberal Scholarship', *New York Review of Books*, 2 January, 1969.
[31] F. R. Leavis, *Education and the University* (Chatto and Windus, 1943), pp. 28–30.
[32] Leavis, op., cit., p. 32.
[33] Matthew Arnold, *On Translating Homer: Last Words*, 1862.
[34] Richard Hoggart, *The Literary Imagination and the Study of Society*, Occasional Paper 3, Centre for Contemporary Cultural Studies, University of Birmingham 1967, pp. 5–8 (author's italics).
[35] F. R. Leavis, 'Criticism and Philosophy', *The Common Pursuit* (Chatto and Windus 1952), pp. 212–14.
[36] L. Heisenberg, *Physics and Philosophy*, (Allen and Unwin 1959), p. 69.
[37] Max Weber, *The Methodology of the Social Sciences* (The Free Press, New York, 1949), p. 105.
[38] Alasdair MacIntyre, *A Short History of Ethics* (Routledge, 1967), p. 4.
[39] Max Weber, *Methodology*, op. cit., p. 53.
[40] To Rolf Gardiner, Thursday, July 1926.
[41] *Studies in Classic American Literature*, p. 12.
[42] Edward Dorn, *The Shoshoneans*, with photographs by Leroy Lucas (William Morrow, New York, 1966), p. 83. I first heard about this book through a fine review by Richard Gooder in *The Cambridge Quarterly*, 3, 1, Winter 1967/8.
[43] Dorn, op. cit., p. 11.
[44] Dorn, op. cit., pp. 12–13.
[45] Dorn, op. cit., pp. 14–15.
[46] Lewis Mumford, *The Urban Prospect* (Secker and Warburg), p. 32.

10

Home Thoughts from Home: Landscape and Society

ANDOR GOMME

ACROSS the garden from where I write, there is a field of oats that look as if they will ripen, if at all, dangerously late. A mile or so away the dumpy hills of north Staffordshire begin, and the stubborn, curiously individual outliers of the Pottery towns begin with them. From here I can only see the edge of one, which at this distance looks like a compact little hilltop community. If I walk fifty yards to the other end of the garden, there is no doubting the kind of landscape we live in: from there I can see the ungainly expanse of Kidsgrove, a nineteenth-century growth which would be entirely featureless if the land formation itself did not force some character on to it; smoke from a smeltery is often hanging or blowing across the sky. But from here, if I carefully ignore the factory chimneys that poke out of a dip to the right, it is almost like being in the country. Last year our oatfield had cattle in it; then suddenly it was up for sale, and we held our breaths for a few weeks. It seemed a 'natural' for any spec-builder. Then a tractor and plough moved in, just in time for a late crop if the season is kind. We relaxed – saved, as we discovered, by the magic words 'Green Belt'. For at this end of the great twelve-mile-long stretch of Stoke and its neighbours, containment of a kind is being attempted.

Of a kind: on the other side of the road from our house the land is no longer 'green' but 'white'. That is to say, granted that the rules of the 'ordinary planning machinery' are followed, it can be used for haphazard overspill whenever a local council can buy land cheaply or a spec-builder spots a likely opportunity. The result is obvious: sporadic outcrops and ribbons of pre-war houses, which have never belonged to any recognizable place are coalescing by the now familiar process known by another magic name – 'infill' – and still no place is created. The Green

Belt with its handful of precarious-looking fields (one has just been taken over for an as yet mysterious industrial venture) 'contains' the city, so far as its literally contiguous housing is concerned; the new houses must jump into the white area, so that, while the solidly built-up urban-cum-suburban block is now restricted, the suburban hinterland is much larger than it would otherwise have been, particularly since the illusion of 'living in the country' seems to impose on builders, councils and house-owners an ideal of 'spaciousness' greater even than that of pre-war suburbs. Of all the depressing aspects of post-war subtopia, the spread-out look–wide, treeless, any natural influence denied, the houses treated as so many isolated social units– is the most obviously wasteful and destructive, a waste not only of critically precious land but of the opportunity to create any decent sort of human environment. This kind of environment will never mature.

Yet this is the almost direct outcome of good, if hazy, intentions. The idea of a green belt, though negative in itself (for it simply says, 'no building here') implies a positive attitude to towns and villages as visually coherent entities standing in a visually satisfactory relationship to one another and to the country around them. And the planning machinery that we have, obviously inadequate though it is, is certainly better than no planning or a total free-for-all. Often, however, a free-for-all is just what, on close inspection of practice rather than theory, we appear still to have. The great importance of such books as Lionel Brett's[1] lies first of all in its mercilessly honest reporting of the facts of the case. By taking a small part of the country and covering the ground really closely, he and his survey team have been able to present graphically the detailed effect of the hit-and-miss application of a half-baked set of planning laws–the details which the *South-East Study* was too grand to look at but which together settle for good or ill the whole appearance of the countryside and a large part of the social life of old and new inhabitants. No one should have any illusions, for example, after looking at the illustrations of Goring or Stadhampton or Chalgrove that infilling is automatically an improvement on ribbon development. The idea or the word is readily invoked as the answer to the wickedness of pre-war sprawl: it means building tight, within recognizable boundaries, preserving and intensifying the visual and social shape of the village. So goes the theory, and the spell is as readily succumbed to locally as called out nationally. What Mr Brett demonstrates beyond possibility of question is that what it means in practice is a snatch at any field or allotments that happen to lie within an arbitrarily drawn ring, and a consequent scatter of infra-low-density housing. Instead of thin tentacles of ribbon development, villages now have a thick layer round what remains of the old core and frequently breaking into it with alien buildings and needlessly wide roads. (A dramatic example, in a different context, of the blanket application of this same fashionable principle is soon to be displayed at Stoke. The city has since the war built on its urban fringes housing estates as dreary and inconvenient as any in England. Now, however, infilling is the thing. So instead of tackling the problem of thousands of decrepit and frequently derelict houses in the old town centres where many people enjoy living, the city has discovered a farm still working only ten minutes' walk from the centre of Hanley and five from that of Stoke. If only one shabby industrial yard were cleared and replanted, this farm could be joined by a still miraculously surviving wedge of country to the open hills to the east. Everyone could walk out into the country–something now barely possible in any large English city. But no: this is a splendid opportunity for infilling; and the farmlands will soon be covered with housing.)

The symptoms of this national disease have been described before. The special advantage of Mr Brett's approach is in the closeness of observation of the cumulative effect of many small items, all of which are there by permission or encouragement of planning authorities and planning regulations. The picture is a shameful one, but no one will suppose that it is exaggerated or that South Oxfordshire is any worse than average. At the end of the book, Mr Brett offers cures which have in the main a disappointingly familiar ring–disappointing because they *are* familiar and have so obviously not worked, or rather have rarely been applied. Nor is it clear that there is a substantially better chance of their being applied now than at any time during the last twenty years. So Mr Brett chastens his own profession with a well-earned jibe at architects' ability perennially to create new clichés; so too he exhorts builders to do better. . . . One proposal is that all villages should have plans prepared by competent architect-planners showing how much and how best they can be enlarged. Mr Brett has himself drawn a first-rate map of how Chalgrove might have been made into a really attractive and richly varied village instead of the squalid mess it is now degenerating into, thanks to piecemeal permissiveness on the part of an understaffed planning department. But, as Mr Brett points out, it is twenty years since Thomas Sharp provided the general technique for this work, in a book which is still in print but which no one ever reads, and in the design of several new villages which were actually half-built before the short-sighted miserliness of the Forestry Commission aborted them. To the sympathetic reader it may seem unthinkable that Oxfordshire at least will not take note of Mr Brett's catalogue of pathetically obvious failures and begin to put its own house into what order remains possible to it. And it is very much to be desired that architects and other activists throughout the country will emulate the work done here. But to those who have ever tried to talk a local authority into a change of heart, the whole effort may seem like once more whistling to the air.

Thus, Mr Brett proposes that planning committees should co-opt people who really understand the landscape and have real skills to bring to the work of planning it. Of course they should; but how often the idea has been suggested before, and how often rejected or ignored! 'What matters is that a county planning committee should be a group of men and women prepared to make a life study, whether as professionals or as amateurs, of the English landscape and townscape as a historical and evolving work of art and science,' (p. 157). The thought is dizzying–to the sceptical probably simply laughable. The reason why the situation is *not* to be laughed at is obvious to anyone with eyes; but the justification for the sceptic's doubt is that, even if such dedicated and sympathetic people could be found in large enough numbers for the job, their solutions would not work, their thoughts would not be properly applied, so long as they had to be imposed on a majority whose habits of life are fundamentally alien to the conception of the landscape presented here. The fact is that most people do not want the country except on terms which, when brought to bear on the scale we must anticipate, are bound to destroy it.

There is a pressing sense of urgency about Mr Brett's book, of the need not to make grandiose plans for the future but to do now what we can with what we have. He looks gloriously into the future to an age when decisions are made rationally and with full sympathy and understanding by rationally constituted local authorities; until then, he sees it as his and our job to hold the fort: military metaphors freely occur in his book. But—not to put too fine a point upon it—'we' shall not beat the Philistines; we must persuade them to join us. Until that blessed time books like Mr Brett's are bound to read like a desperate plea for holding the *status quo*—something in itself quite foreign to traditions by which the rich and diverse English landscape has evolved. For example, he rightly sees the High Street of Thame as 'the top conservation priority' in his area, which 'in present circumstances can probably only be handled by a blanket preservation order over the whole street, to be relaxed only where the old building is exceptionally bad and the new one exceptionally good' (p. 118). So conservation becomes preservation; and certainly such a street is too valuable to be risked as things are— no one can be trusted not to spoil it.[2] Yet its loveliness, as that of so many English towns, is not the product of a single overall design but of steady growth through many centuries. The ugly paradox is that the only way we know of keeping what beauty remains is by a process which is the exact opposite of the way in which it was created: namely by freezing it—and that at a time when houses are needed, *and will be built* at a faster rate than ever before in our history.

2

The great success of Mr Brett's book is to bring home really vividly what an abject mess we are making *now* and, unless things greatly and quickly change, are committed to go on making. Its principal limitation is that it does not go on from spotting the symptoms to diagnosing the disease, and consequently is largely concerned with a holding operation. But to hold the flood for the time being would merely keep off the final disaster for a few years, unless we can probe deeper now. Even within his self-imposed limitations, there is one point which it is disappointing to find Mr Brett surrendering so easily: it is no

LANDSCAPE AND SOCIETY

use, he concedes, 'crying over the spilt milk ... of all the land wasted by thoughtless planning and house-building' (p. 151). No one can be so sanguine as to expect that recently established housing estates, however dismal, can quickly be scrapped and the land re-used properly. But nor must we allow anyone to think of wasted land as permanently wasted, irrecoverable. There are far too many people ready to shrug off present responsibilities by accepting any and every state of affairs as unalterable: if we cannot make immediate changes we must get it well into our thinking that all these mistakes can and eventually will be remedied–just as we are now slowly eliminating the Victorian slums. Even now, very slowly, derelict industrial land is being reclaimed. Years ago Trystan Edwards called on new towns to be scavengers of sprawl, enabling old towns to pull in their scruffy tentacles and regain a decent shape. Actually, of course, most new towns have been large-scale creators of sprawl. We must not only halt this process; we must reverse it: the pressure of population alone is too great to allow the waste to remain waste.

Though he does not say so directly, it is possible to feel behind Mr Brett's whole demonstration the sense that South Oxfordshire has already as large a population as it can comfortably take. If this is true, it is certainly true of the rest of the area covered by the *South-East Study*, much of which is far more densely populated than Oxfordshire, and essentially true of the whole of England. Yet we know that the population will in fact increase steadily, that all official estimates have been too low, and that the rate of increase is liable to quicken. Is it possible, or desirable, to set an upper limit to our population, and if so where should it be? It seems to me that the galloping increase in the British birthrate is accepted far too complacently, as if it were a fact of nature that we can do nothing about. But we know perfectly well that if we really wanted it, the increase could be stopped now. It is entirely within our control. Is it then not *desirable* to call a halt? It must be admitted that Britain *could* support a population of hundreds of millions in reasonable physical health if it were accepted that the country should be wholly industrialized, and that all our food should be imported.[3] We should have to go without fresh milk and meat and vegetables; but most people apparently cannot tell the difference between fresh and frozen anyway. We should also have to do without the countryside, except perhaps for the economically unusable mountains of Wales, Scotland and the Lakes. Britain would become a gigantic factory, in return for other countries' remaining wholly agricultural (which would mean of course that *their* populations could *not* be allowed to rise).

Even if we could make and guarantee the necessary international agreement without further endangering the world food supplies, I do not believe that any Englishman would consider this proposal tolerable for a moment. Why not? What do we expect of the country, even that majority of us who do not live in it? This is the question whose answer Mr Brett has taken too easily for granted. It is the great question which we must ask and find the right answer to before there is a hope that the national planning of land resources will be more than a shot in the dark. Some phrases of Mr Brett's are here revealing because of what they just fail to say. 'The photographs [of new houses at Watlington] tell the dismal familiar story of our loss of touch' (p. 59). Loss of touch with what? 'The failure of the best to influence the rest and the failure of two elements of the same generation to speak a common language denote a breakdown in communications on a phenomenal scale' (pp. 132–3). What kind of communication? 'Development not organic with the landscape' (p. 79). What is it for development to be organic with the landscape?

Let us be quite clear about what really is irrecoverable. A truly organic relationship between man and the land is beyond hoping for in any industrialized country, except perhaps on a few small farms still not dominated by machine cultivation. For it depends on two factors which have gone for good. The first of these is the intense localism (still to be felt to some extent in much of France), by which a man and all his habits belonged essentially to a quite small area, simply because communications of all sorts were so slow and difficult as barely to be worth attempting. Secondly the organic relationship was essentially an economic one: Cotswold cottages look 'organic with the landscape' largely because they were made of the same stone as the landscape, and that because it was both the cheapest material and the one which generations of local people understood how to use.[4] Similarly the relationship between farm, village and market town was also an economic one, a way of life limited by external conditions which until the nineteenth century men were unable to alter. The way was organic inasmuch as the conditions themselves were organic–the nature of the soil, the climate, the seasons. Men responding to these conditions were themselves rooted in the whole natural scene and created the English landscape that we still have, which is the country that the Olde-Englanders seek but not, unfortunately, on the only terms by which it can be understood. However, hardly anyone now seriously wants the country without much that industrialization has brought–cheap electricity, good hospitals and so forth; and very few want the country without cars or TV. So if Mr Brett is right (he is) that we must re-create a philosophy of conservation of the land and its resources, it is not in the hope of a return to Merrie England.

What then do we want of the country–the real country, not the suburbanized kind? Mr Brett is sure that 'those who drive out into the country want it to be country, and that those who discover a village want it to be a village' (p. 132). So, though the local inhabitant wants his TV, the visitor does not want to see the aerial–less, perhaps because it is ugly in itself than because it destroys an illusion. However this may be, I believe Mr Brett is right that behind this searching after an imaginary rural ideal, there is a profound substantial need:

> We confess ... that we started our survey predisposed for multiple use. We saw our whole area as weekenders' and commuters' country (which indeed it is) superimposed on its productive function, with walking and cycling and cruising and picnicking and field sports superimposed on them.... But we subsumed as matrix for all these activities the great broad bosom of rural England, and it was not until we looked more closely at what is actually there, on the ground, that we realized that the matrix itself was being nibbled from so many different directions by so many kinds of animal that great stretches of it had ceased or were at that very moment ceasing to be a decent setting for any of these activities at all. Then the sun rose and all the fields flooded and overflowed with the great golden harvest of 1964, and in the silence before the combines got to work we realized that the real need of our urban and motorized millions, whether we know it or not, is not for all these busy and harmless activities but for silence itself, for secluded villages in which voices

and laughter can be heard, and for oceans of waving grass and corn that have nothing to hide (p. 151).

It is a pity that the language is rather sentimentally misty, for it conceals both the nature of the need and the extent to which it is unconscious. This extent is alarming: there can be no doubt the most people who come for the first time to *live* in a village want to turn it into a suburb; they do not want a way of life radically different from the one they have left. This, I believe, is the principal reason why those who have come to live in what was a purely rural environment have so easily been persuaded that what they want as a house is something from the jazzy commercial pattern books within which they are taught that they will feel comfortably at home. Mr Brett is very good at catching the tone of a way of life in a few words – 'the Berkshire canasta belt with tennis and pony clubs', Peppard with its 'popular Saturday pubs' – the social tone of the life whose visual aspect his photographs expose. The moral implications are somewhat ambiguous here: canasta sounds distinctly petit-bourgeois, but surely quite *nice* people play tennis? But Mr Brett is not shy of making his dislikes felt even where he claims to be neutral: he writes of 'bijou walls', of 'plastic stone', of 'a really nasty collection of Builder's Allsorts' – and also of 'transistorized Merseybeat'. Now as a matter of fact I share almost all the dislikes that Mr Brett makes plain in his book, and his attraction to a way of life which they – obscurely perhaps – contradict. But obviously most people, so far as they are conscious of what they want, do not. The evidence is everywhere: bijou walls are preferred to hedges, Japanese cherries to chestnuts and birches, transistorized pop to bird-song; in each case something alien and imposed to something of traditional or natural growth. I have just read of the fate of a rare and beautiful wild flower which was carefully left on a Sussex roadside when the verges were cut (why do verges need to be cut so often anyway?), only to be torn up by an angry resident who found the 'weeds' untidy. (The word 'weeds' is significant: it implies that all land must be cultivated, and anything wild is undesirable.) Newcomers to the village where I have spent much of my life (just outside Mr Brett's area) have successfully demanded street lights: there may be good arguments for this, but the impulse, I am sure, comes – as in Sussex – essentially from the fear of a different way of life, whose strangeness is brought home as much by the darkness as by the silence of the true country. Conversely, Mr Brett resents the hedgerow trees being 'chain-sawn' on highly mechanized farms. Just *how* they are cut may seem irrelevant, for the chief point is that they are lost. But this is a little more than the gratuitous use of an emotionally loaded word: it registers an objection to a callousness which is part of the highly mechanized mind.

Who then are Mr Brett and I, aware enough of the young families 'entirely happy in their spick and span new houses', to try to cast doubt on the foundation of this happiness? What, that can be saved and is worth saving, is endangered by bijou walls or slovenly planning? On what ground do we air *our* likes and dislikes? Certainly I get a pleasure even from our not-really-rural field that is entirely different from any that can come from something man-made: pleasure from seeing the corn grow and change colour, from relating its growth to the movement of the seasons and the weather, pleasure from watching the wind rippling through it, from the old field pond on which, the cattle having gone, a moorhen has reared a brood of chicks this year, pleasure even from the little birds which the corn attracts, though the farmer must take a different view and though most of them are only sparrows. Most people are not particularly interested in wild flowers or birds or even the growing corn except as potential porridge or cattle food. Why should they be? Only – and here, I think, the case must rest – because these represent a life in which man is not wholly the master, which brings in things outside and indifferent to him. The need of which Mr Brett writes in the paragraph quoted above is not just for silence and for getting away from it all: for that, lonely mountain scenery is better. It is a need to be able to meet a life lived in the daily awareness and acceptance of man's ultimate dependence on things outside man. Street-lights and transistors and insistently tidy roadside verges are a way of shutting out such an awareness – because of course it can be frightening. To try to shut it out for good is not only to miss the delight of the infinite variety which custom does not stale; it is to perpetuate a lie, one consequence of which is the savage way we turn on one another.

NOTES

[1] *Landscape in Distress* by Lionel Brett (Architectural Press).

[2] A crucial eighteenth-century building has just been demolished. The site will be redeveloped from London.

[3] I have just read a statement by the editor of the *Baker's Review* that it is a waste of land to grow English wheat: neither the millers nor the bakers like it, and Canadian is much preferred.

[4] Cf. An episode from bridge-building in Cumberland: 'I had picked up a lump of granite that would have fitted a gap in the wall perfectly except for a kind of snout projecting from one end. I raised the hammer, smacked it against the snout, struck again and again without result. Will said "Nay", took the lump from me, eyed its texture thoughtfully, and hit the end opposite the snout. At once the projection dropped off and the lump snuggled into position as if moulded for the purpose.' (Dudley Hoys, in *Country Life*, 5 August 1965, p 335.). Such 'expertise' implies a closeness to the land that is much more than merely quaint.

Index

Abel-Smith, B., 149
Adams, H., 96
Ali, T., 175, 182
Alvarez, A., 64-6
Amis, K., 27
Anna Karenina, 15
Anthropology, 14, 145-6, 147, 157, 159, 237
Arden, J., 56-9
Arnold, M., 122, 164, 228
Auchinloss, L., 122
Avineri, S., 173

Baldwin, J., 114, 118, 119-20, 122, 123
Banks, L. R., 36-8
Barstow, S., 31-2
Barth, J., 113, 114
Bates, H. E., 16
Bauman Z., 161
Beckett, S., 51-3, 56
Bellow, S., 92-100, 102, 104, 105, 109, 111, 114, 118, 122
Berlin, I., 173
Bernstein, B., 165
Betjeman, J., 69
Bhagwati, J., 69
Blackburn, R., 175
Blake, W., 128
Blechman, B., 123
Bolt, R., 42, 44-5
Booth, C., 147
Bottomore, T. B., 173
Bourjailly, V., 121, 122
Braine, J., 31-2
Brecht, B., 43
Brett, L., 243-51
Britten, B., 233
Brooks, G., 115, 121
Browning, R., 79
Bunyan, J., 128
Burns, J. H., 121
Burns, T., 165
Burroughs, W., 113, 121, 122
By Love Possessed, 24, 39, 122
Byron, Lord, 128

Campion, T., 87
Carr, E. H., 176
Cary, J., 24-6, 30
Caute, D., 173

Caves, R. E., 193
Cheever, J., 122
Chekhov, 41, 42, 43, 51
Chomsky, N., 164, 219-21, 225, 238
Cleaver, E., 122
Cobbett, S., 212
Cohn-Bendit, D., 175
Coleridge, S. T., 122, 164
Comte, A., 151, 152
Conrad, J., 92, 109, 216
Cooper, F., 110
Crane, S., 101, 110
Crankshaw, E., 177
Culture, definitions of, conditions for, study of 13, 61 ff, 92 ff, 141 ff, 159 ff, 211 ff, 234 ff
Cunningham, J. V., 80-1

Debray R., 182
de George, R., 177
Deutscher, I., 177
Dickens, C., 128, 131
Donleavy, J. P., 113, 121, 123
Donnison, D., 149
Dorn, E., 83, 85-7, 123, 234-7
dos Passos, J., 65, 101, 122
Dostoievsky, 116
Douglas, M., 147
Drama, 41-59
Dreiser, T., 94, 95, 99, 102, 110, 116
Duncan, R., 87
Durkheim, E., 146, 151, 164

Eagleton, T., 175
Economics, 14
 as science, 184-93
 as engineering, 193-200
 as social criticism, 200-209
Eliot, G., 15, 122, 131
Eliot, T. S., 51, 68, 69, 70, 71, 74, 77, 84, 116, 122, 150
Elkin, S., 123
Ellison, R., 114, 119, 122
Empson, W., 75
Engels, F., 145

Esslin, M., 50

Fanon, F., 180
Faulkner, W., 116, 117
Faust, I., 123
Feinstein, E., 87
Ferguson, A., 146
Fitzgerald, F. S., 94, 95, 99, 102, 103, 110
Fleming, I., 15
Frazer, J., 146
Freud, S., 158, 164, 225
Fromm, E., 173

Galbraith, J. K., 208
Gass, W., 123
Gelber, J., 123
Glass, D. V., 148
Gold, H., 121, 122
Goldmann, L., 159, 174
Goldsmith, O., 75
Goodman, P., 122
Grebenick, E., 148
Green, H., 22-4
Grossman, A., 123
Guevara, E., 180

Haddon, A., 146
Halsey, A. H., 148
Hardy, T., 76, 131, 164
Harris, N., 165
Hartley, L. P., 26
Hawkes, J., 121, 123
Hawthorne, N., 110, 111, 112
Heaney, S., 79-80
Hecht, A., 87
Hegel, 158
Heisenberg, L., 230
Heller, J., 113, 121, 123
Hemingway, E., 100, 101, 102, 110, 117
Hersey, J., 122
Hill, G., 85
Hobhouse, L. T., 146
Hoggart R., 16, 134, 228
Hopkins, G. M., 83
Huberman, L., 182
Hudson, G., 82
Hughes, T., 79-80
Hume, D., 146

Ibsen, H., 41, 49, 51

Ionesco, E., 50
James, H., 26, 92, 110
Jennings, E., 78
Jevons, 191
Jewkes, J., 190, 205
Johnson, H. G., 191
Johnson, S., 76
Jonson, B., 76
Joyce, J., 94, 106, 116
Jung, 158

Kafka, 116
Keats, J., 73, 75, 220
Kerouac, J., 121, 122
Kesey, K., 113, 121, 123
Kettle, A., 25, 29, 38
Keynes, J. M., 164, 186, 194
Klein, M., 233
Klugman, 174, 175
Kolakowski, 176

Larkin, P., 67–9, 74
Leach, E., 66, 147
Leavis, F. R., 122, 212, 226–30, 233
Le Corbusier, 233
Lefebvre, H., 174
Levertov, D., 87
Levi-Strauss, C., 164
Lewis, O., 128
Lewis, S., 122
Lichtheim, G., 173
Lipsey, R. G., 188
Lipton, M., 198, 199
Listener, The, 63
Liu, Shao-Chi, 178
Livings, H., 50
Lockwood, D., 165
Lowell, R., 65, 88
Lukacs, G., 161, 174
Lupton, T., 146

Macbeth, G., 64
MacDiarmid, H., 88
MacIntyre, A., 62, 165, 215–6, 231
Mailer, N., 99, 100–5, 109, 112, 113, 114, 122
Malamud, B., 110–2, 122
Malewski, A., 161
Malinowski, 146
Mannheim, K., 143, 144, 159, 161
Mao Tse-Tung, 175, 177–80
Marcuse, H., 175
Marshall, T. H., 148
Martin, D., 165

Marx, K., 46, 143, 144, 151, 158, 164, 171–83, 201–2, 204, 205, 207–8
Matthews, H., 181
McCarthy, M., 122
McCullers, C., 122
McLuhan, H. M., 66
Meade, J. E., 204, 208
Melville, H., 82, 94, 97, 110, 116
Mill, J. S., 164
Miller, A., 48–50
Milton, J., 128, 164
Mishan, E. J., 199
Moliere, 42
Moore, B., 156
Moore, H., 233
Montaigne, 128
Montesquieu, 146
Morris, W., 122, 164, 212
Mumford, L., 238
Murdoch, I., 27–30
Myrdal, G., 200

Nabokov, V., 105–9, 113, 122
Negroes, 114–20, 122, 180
New Statesman, 81
Nemerov, H., 122
Norris, F., 122
Novels, 15–40, 93–124

O'Brien, E., 38, 42
O'Connor, F., 121, 122
O'Hara, J., 122
Olson, C., 72, 86
O'Malley, R., 27
Orwell, G., 21–2, 122, 212
Osborne, J., 47–8, 51
Ossowski, S., 161

Parsons, T., 152, 158, 164
Past and Present, 164, 224
Pen, J., 194
Percy, W., 102, 121, 122
Pevsner, N., 76
Platts, S., 65, 87
Piaget, J., 164
Pinter, H., 53–5
Place, F., 221
Plato, 143, 151
Poetry, 61–92
Politics, relevance to literature, study of, place in modern world, 13, 14, 102 ff, 107 ff, 120 ff, 125 ff, 148 ff, 170–83, 211–39
Pope, A., 76
Pound, E., 69, 72, 74, 79

Prince, F. T., 77–9
Prynne, J. H., 87
Purdy, J., 121, 122
Pushkin, 43
Pyncheon, T., 121, 123

Radcliffe-Brown, 146, 164
Rattigan, T., 42
Reading Lists, 39–40, 60, 90–1, Chap. 4, 136–40, 168–9, 183–4, 209–10
Rechy, J., 113, 121, 123
Rex, J., 165
Robinson, E. A., 69, 73–4
Robinson J., 179, 187
Roethke, T., 88
Roth, P., 121, 122
Rostow, W., 154
Rousseau, J. J., 146
Rowntrees, The, 145, 147
Ruiz, R., 181
Ruskin, J., 122, 128, 164, 212

Salinger, J. D., 121, 122
Samuelson, P. A., 188
Scrutiny, 164
Schaff, A., 176
Schram, S., 179
Segal, S., 180, 216
Selby, H., 113, 121, 123
Senghor, 180
Shaeffer, P., 42
Shakespeare, 41, 48, 51, 74, 75, 76, 128, 156
Sharp, T., 245
Shaw, I., 122
Shaw, G. B., 41, 56
Shute, N., 16
Sillitoe, A., 32–3
Simey, T. S., 148, 149
Simpson, N. F., 55–6
Smith, A., 194, 206
Snow, C. P., 17, 31
Snyder, G., 87
Sociology, 14, 141 ff, in Britain, 142–50, as total system, 150–8
Sontag, S., 123
South East Study, 243, 247
Southern, T., 121, 123
Spark, M., 39
Spencer, H., 152
Spengler, 151, 158
Stafford, W., 88
Steinbeck, J, 122
Stephens, A., 83
Stevens, W., 69–72, 84, 87
Stone, R., 196
Storey, D., 33–6

INDEX

Styron, W., 121, 122
Swift, A., 146
Swift, J., 128, 164
Taylor, J. R., 57
Tawney, R. H., 213–6
Teachers, 15, 41, 43–4, 48, 50, 127–31, 133–6, 162–5, 238–9
Tennyson, A., 73
Thomas, E., 76
Thomas, R. S., 85
Thompson, E. P., 164
Time, 102
Titmuss, R., 148, 149
TLS, 64, 178
Togliatti, P., 174
Tomlinson, C., 68, 83, 84–5, 87
Toynbee, A., 151
Trotsky, L., 143, 144, 160, 233
True Pornography, 102
Twain, M., 94, 102, 110, 116

Ulam, A., 177

United Kingdom, 13, 61, 62, 64, 86, 89, 128–30, 133–6, 142–50, 155, 157, 159 ff, 211 ff, 242 ff
Universities, Colleges, Schools, 14, 69, 124, 125 ff, 150, 163 ff, 170–1, 188, 222 ff
Updike, J., 121, 122
USA, 13, 61, 62, 69, 80, 89, 92 ff, 150, 152, 155, 157, 187, 189, 218, 220

Vries, P. de, 122
Vonnegut, K., 123

Wallant, E., 121
Wain, J., 27, 78
Warren, R. P., 39, 122
Waugh, E., 18–9
Webbs, the, 147
Weber, M., 151, 164, 223, 230–2
Wesker, A., 43, 45–7, 50, 51
Whitman, W., 86, 94

Williams, B., 222
Williams, J., 83, 121
Williams, R., 63, 122, 130–2, 164
Williams, W. C., 69, 72–3, 84, 86, 87
Wilson, B., 165
Winters, Y., 80, 81–3, 87
Wittgenstein, L., 158, 170, 233
Woman's Own, 212
Wordsworth, 66, 76, 122, 128
Worsley, P., 147
Wright, Mills, C., 177
Wright, R., 122

X, Malcolm, 180

Yates, R., 121, 122
Yeats, W. B., 53, 59, 69, 71, 72, 84
Young, M., 149

Zeman, 176
Zukovsky, L., 72